Taunton's COMPLETE ILLUSTRATED *Guide to*

Working with Wood

ANDY RAE

The Taunton Press

The Taunton Press
Inspiration for hands-on living®

The Taunton Press, Inc., 63 South Main Street, PO Box 5506, Newtown, CT 06470-5506
e-mail: tp@taunton.com

EDITOR: Paul Anthony
DESIGN: Lori Wendin
LAYOUT: Cathy Cassidy
ILLUSTRATOR: Mario Ferro, except where noted
PHOTOGRAPHER: Andy Rae, except photos on p. 189 (bottom right), p. 190, and p. 191
by Tom Begnal, courtesy *Fine Woodworking*, © The Taunton Press, Inc.; photos on p. 193
and p. 196 by Matthew Teague, courtesy *Fine Woodworking*, © The Taunton Press, Inc.

LIBRARY OF CONGRESS CATALOGING-IN-PUBLICATION DATA:
Rae, Andy.
  Taunton's complete illustrated guide to working with wood / Andy Rae.
    p. cm.
  ISBN 1-56158-683-8
  1. Woodwork. 2. Wood. I. Taunton Press. II. Title.
  TT180.R34 2005
  684'.08--dc22
                              2004019362

Printed in Italy
10 9 8 7 6 5 4 3 2 1

The following manufacturers/names appearing in *Taunton's Complete Illustrated Guide to Working with Wood* are trademarks:
Shade-Dri™, Biesemeyer®, Waterlox®

About Your Safety: Working with wood is inherently dangerous. Using hand or power tools improperly or ignoring safety practices can lead to permanent injury or even death. Don't try to perform operations you learn about here (or elsewhere) unless you're certain they are safe for you. If something about an operation doesn't feel right, don't do it. Look for another way. We want you to enjoy the craft, so please keep safety foremost in your mind whenever you're in the shop.

Acknowledgments

It takes many people to help one become familiar with the intricacies of wood. In truth, my greatest knowledge of woodworking comes from our woodworking forebears, who deserve thanks from all of us. However, I also wish to thank all the woodworkers I've known in my career who helped me understand the material a little better by letting me into their shops to see how they work it. Their names are many, but they know who they are. Their lessons and friendships are priceless.

Special mention goes to my editor, Paul Anthony, who helped as usual to keep my feet firmly planted on the ground. Not only is Paul an ace editor, but he is a woodworker and published writer in his own right. What author could ask for a more qualified collaborator? Also, thanks to my in-house editor, Jennifer Renjilian Morris, editorial assistant Jenny Peters, and executive editor Helen Albert, who all pulled tight when the rigging got slack.

Once again, I am in debt to my family for their support and love. Thanks to them, the home fires burn warm and bright.

Contents

PART TWO Finding and Storing Wood · 24

PART FIVE Bending Wood · 182

PART SIX Smoothing, Gluing, and Finishing · 212

PART ONE

Understanding Wood

THIS BOOK IS ABOUT WOOD, the stuff woodworkers work. To thoroughly understand the material, we need to start at the source: trees. Understanding trees and their nature can help us become much more intimate with our material and can provide a broader understanding of how to work it. This first part of the book aims to give you a basic grounding in the properties of wood, from its botanical structure and classification to its identifying characteristics as milled lumber. Becoming familiar with these basic aspects of wood will provide you with essential building blocks for creating a solid foundation for all your future woodworking.

The Properties of Wood

THE STRUCTURE AND LIVING SYSTEM of a tree provide clues as to the nature of its wood and whether it is a softwood or hardwood. They also help us understand why wood moves after it has been dried, which is a perennial problem for woodworkers embarking on the quest to make fine furniture. Understanding these key properties of wood can minimize the guesswork encountered by beginning and experienced woodworkers alike.

Wood's Structure

Understanding the cellular structure of wood provides a firm foundation for dealing with its appearance, behavior, and often idiosyncratic working characteristics.

Trees gain their sustenance from the roots. Water and nutrients rise from the ground to the branches and leaves, producing sap for new cell growth. All this action surrounds the heartwood in the core of the tree, which is composed of cells that no longer play a direct part in sap production (see the left drawing on facing page).

As an organism, wood is composed of a variety of cell types that perform a range of tasks, including transporting water, providing mechanical strength, and helping the tree withstand natural stresses during its life span. Wood's structure is determined by the type, size, shape, and arrangement of these cells. Of importance to us as woodworkers is that most of these cells are arranged longitudinally in the tree (see the right drawing on facing page).

This longitudinal orientation gives rise to what woodworkers refer to as grain direction, or the direction in which the predominant fibers of wood are arrayed. However, due to the variation in cell type and orientation, a tree's internal structure is anything but homogeneous. This lack of uniformity explains why the characteristics of wood vary between species—and quite often within the same species. For example, it's common for two boards from the same section of a log to have drastically different qualities, and for wood in general to behave in unexpected ways. Learning more

ANATOMY OF A TREE

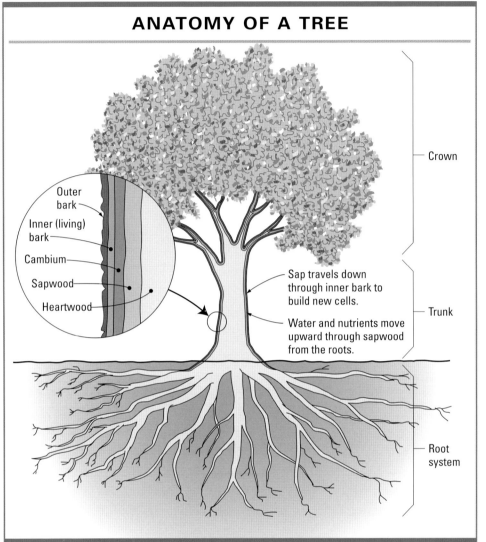

Crown

Outer bark

Inner (living) bark

Cambium

Sapwood

Heartwood

Sap travels down through inner bark to build new cells.

Water and nutrients move upward through sapwood from the roots.

Trunk

Root system

CELL FORMATION IN WOOD

This section from an angiosperm (hardwood) shows a variety of cell types found in a tree.

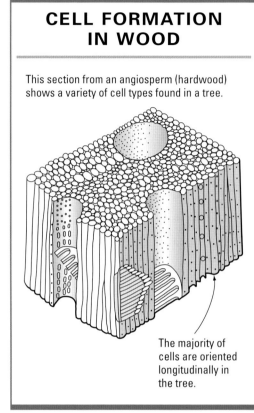

The majority of cells are oriented longitudinally in the tree.

about trees and the way we cut them will better prepare us for those unpredictable moments.

When a piece of wood is cut from a tree, there are three "faces," or planes, that present themselves to us (see the drawing on p. 6). Knowing which way a board was oriented in the tree and the difference between each face allows us to describe the grain in a given board. This provides a big advantage when we're choosing boards.

The cross-sectional face of a board consists of the cut ends of longitudinal cells. This face is essentially end grain and is the hardest surface on a board. Thanks to its toughness, it makes an excellent surface for chopping blocks or other high-wear areas (see the photo on p. 6).

A radial surface displays a series of straight growth rings, or lines.

► See *"Growth Rings"* on p. 15.

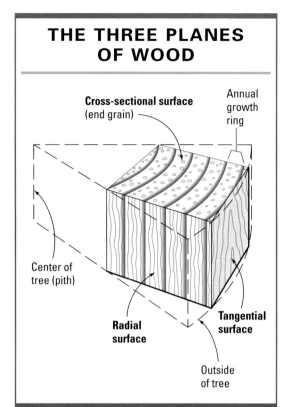

THE THREE PLANES OF WOOD

Cross-sectional surface (end grain)

Annual growth ring

Center of tree (pith)

Radial surface

Tangential surface

Outside of tree

The author arranged the grain direction on his miniature hickory chopping block so the hard end grain faces up to resist sharp knives.

This uniform pattern makes the radial face an excellent candidate for splitting into straight sections, such as when you're making splints or other straight-grained parts, since the split fibers will follow the grain lines. The straight lines can also be used as a visual element when you want a uniform look in your work.

The tangential face typically has more widely spaced rings arranged in an uneven pattern and usually reveals a wilder and more asymmetrical grain pattern, compared to the radial surface. Like the straight lines on a radial face, the irregular grain pattern on a tangential surface can be used as a visual design feature but with a less organized and more organic effect.

Softwoods and Hardwoods

The terms "softwood" and "hardwood" are used to denote the taxonomic division that separates species. Surprisingly, the two terms have little to do with the actual hardness of the wood. By definition, hardwood trees have broad leaves and are deciduous, meaning they lose their leaves at the end of the growing season (see the left photo on facing page). Hardwoods are angiosperms, producing seeds from pollinated flowers. Oaks, maples, birches, and fruit trees are examples of hardwood trees.

Softwood trees are conifers (evergreens) with scalelike foliage or needles that do not drop after the growing season (see the right photo on facing page). Softwoods are gymnosperms, meaning they reproduce by means of cones rather than flowers. Examples of softwoods include the pines, spruces, firs, and hemlocks.

This white pine exhibits the familiar shape of many soft-wood trees. It has numerous bristlelike needles and pro-duces pinecones on its long, straight branches. An ever-green, it won't drop its foliage, but instead grows new needles continually.

With its broad spread of thick, tapering branches sporting large leaves, this mature oak is typical of many hardwood trees. At the end of the growing sea-son, all the leaves drop to the ground.

For furniture, hardwoods reign over the softwoods. The range of hardwood species is greater, giving us a wider variety of woods to choose from. Overall, their characteristics are better suited to furniture making than those of softwoods. However, please don't overlook the softwoods as viable furniture woods. As an old friend and master crafts-man once remarked, "Pine is a great wood. Its softness challenges you to make tight, crisp joints."

Understanding Wood Movement

To make furniture successfully, it's important to understand two simple but essential facts. The first is that wood moves. This means that it takes in and releases moisture in its cells and swells or shrinks accordingly. This swelling and shrinking may be barely notice-able or it may be quite substantial, depend-ing on the type of wood and the amount of humidity in the air.

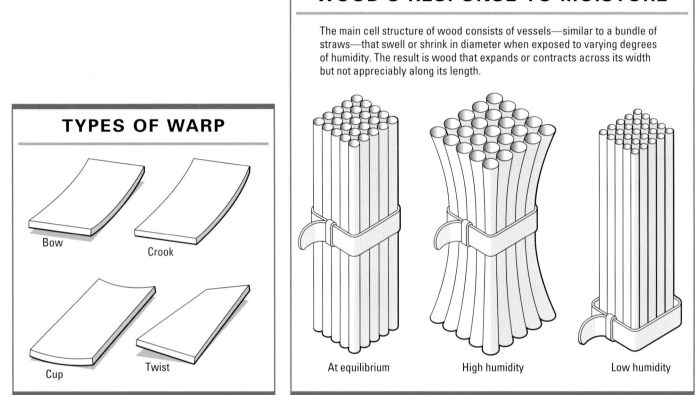

TYPES OF WARP

Bow

Crook

Cup

Twist

WOOD'S RESPONSE TO MOISTURE

The main cell structure of wood consists of vessels—similar to a bundle of straws—that swell or shrink in diameter when exposed to varying degrees of humidity. The result is wood that expands or contracts across its width but not appreciably along its length.

At equilibrium

High humidity

Low humidity

The second fact is that nothing can stop this movement.

Wood swells and shrinks across its width but not appreciably along its length. That's because the basic cell structure of wood consists of a series of fibers packed together in longitudinal fashion, similar to a bundle of straws (see the right drawing above). As they absorb or release moisture, the tubes change in diameter, resulting in expansion or contraction across the total width of the bundle or, in our case, a board.

One of the worst aspects of movement is warp, the result of boards expanding or contracting in uneven patterns, deforming from their original sawn or milled shape (see the

left drawing above). Typically, extreme warping happens during the initial drying stage when the wood is shrinking rapidly. But small degrees of warp continue long after the wood is dry and can be a constant source of grief to a woodworker.

Although you can't stop wood movement, you can limit it to some degree. The way your wood is cut—plainsawn, riftsawn, or quartersawn—has a big impact on movement.

▶ See *"Understanding Grain Orientation"* on p. 23 for information.

Due to its varying grain patterns, a plain-sawn board will undergo unpredictable movement. Quartersawn wood is your best bet when you need the most dimensionally stable material, since any movement occurs more evenly across its annular rings with much less chance of warp.

Another way to control wood movement is to design and build your furniture to allow this movement to take place. For example, you can fit a wide panel to float inside a narrow frame—a typical scenario in frame-and-panel construction. The wider, more movement-prone panel can then expand or contract freely without pushing or pulling on the frame. Gluing or otherwise fixing the panel to the frame will sooner or later result in failure by either breaking the frame joints or splitting the panel, as shown in the drawing at right.

▶ See *"Dealing with Wood Movement"* on p. 78 for information.

To further control wood movement, work with "dry" or "seasoned" wood. This refers to material that's been properly dried from its green, fresh-cut state to a suitable moisture content.

▶ See *"What Is Dry Wood?"* on p. 48.

With material that's been dried to the correct moisture content, you'll minimize the amount of movement and make it more predictable.

Another important consideration is the ambient moisture content of the air surrounding your wood and, ultimately, your furniture. To prevent the various furniture

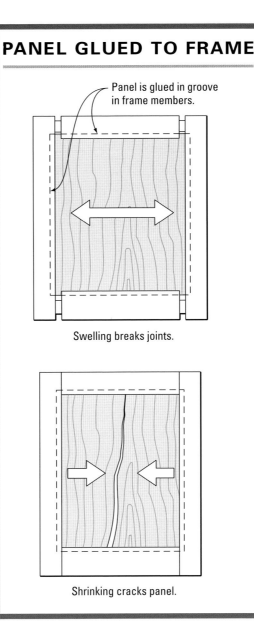

PANEL GLUED TO FRAME

Panel is glued in groove in frame members.

Swelling breaks joints.

Shrinking cracks panel.

parts from expanding or shrinking excessively, it's important to work in a shop environment where the relative humidity (RH) isn't too high or too low.

▶ See *"Controlling Your Shop's Climate"* on p. 78 for information.

The author's shop is a safe haven for wood, with insulated floors, walls, and ceilings, plus windows and doors that seal out the weather. A dehumidifier under the bench draws excess water from the air to keep stock at a stable moisture content.

Finally, a good finish with multiple coats can limit a board's movement. But no finish will stop this movement entirely because the finishes we use in woodworking are not impermeable to moisture transfer. On a microscopic level, the wood still "breathes" and will respond by expanding or contracting as moisture finds its way through the finish and into the cells and pores of the wood. However, following a proven finishing regimen will help greatly in controlling the amount of wood movement in your furniture.

▶ See *"Finishing Wood"* on p. 255.

Reaction Wood

All wood retains a certain amount of internal stress, but certain woods have it in abundance. You'll sometimes encounter these overly stressed woods when ripping a plank on the table saw, as the separated wood starts to either close in on the saw blade or curve away from it, pinching the blade in the process.

Reaction wood can be found in all species and results from abnormal stress in a tree due to its growing conditions. Storms, high winds, growth on the side of a hill, or competition for sunlight can all contribute to reaction wood in a tree. The best examples are trees growing on a severe slope where gravity forces a curve in their trunks, or oceanside trees on which prevailing winds help to form grotesquely shaped trunks and branches. A noticeable bow in the trunk indicates reaction wood in the area of the curve (see the photo below).

Your best bet is to learn to identify reaction wood and avoid using it. Telltale signs include abnormally curved or spiraling logs or boards, an off-center pith in the trunk, or a furry or woolly surface on a board. This type of wood is in compression or tension and will always move in unpredictable ways, making it difficult to machine, sand, or finish.

Constant winds bearing against oceanside trees result in gnarled and twisted trunks and branches—all wood that's full of internal stress.

Identifying Wood

WOODWORKERS should know as much as possible about wood. It's very valuable to know how to spot different species of living trees, how our wood is cut from the tree, the various working characteristics of different woods, and some of the techniques for identifying specific types of wood. All this information aids in selecting the right wood for projects.

Precise wood identification relies in large part on the characteristics of wood cells revealed under a microscope, making this work better left for qualified professionals with the right tools and years of training. Thankfully, most woodworkers can learn to identify species quite successfully by familiarizing themselves with some of the more common characteristics of wood.

Identifying Species

Learning to identify a particular species of living tree can be helpful if you've ever con-sidered logging your own wood. There are many good books on the subject that pro-vide detailed information on specific species. (See Sources, p. 272.) But fair warning: The job is part science and part art. Even sea-soned arborists and loggers are fooled now and then by certain trees. However, there are some basic techniques you can use to spot a species in the wild.

One approach is to study how trees look when bare, typically in the dead of winter or in early spring when the buds are beginning to form (see the drawing on p. 12). Once you begin learning the shapes of trees, you'll find that your eye quickly becomes trained to detect signature characteristics of each species.

Try taking a walk in the woods in winter when the leaves are down. Not only will individual trees be easier to spot, but the entire forest opens up to the eye, offering clues as to the variety of trees that live there.

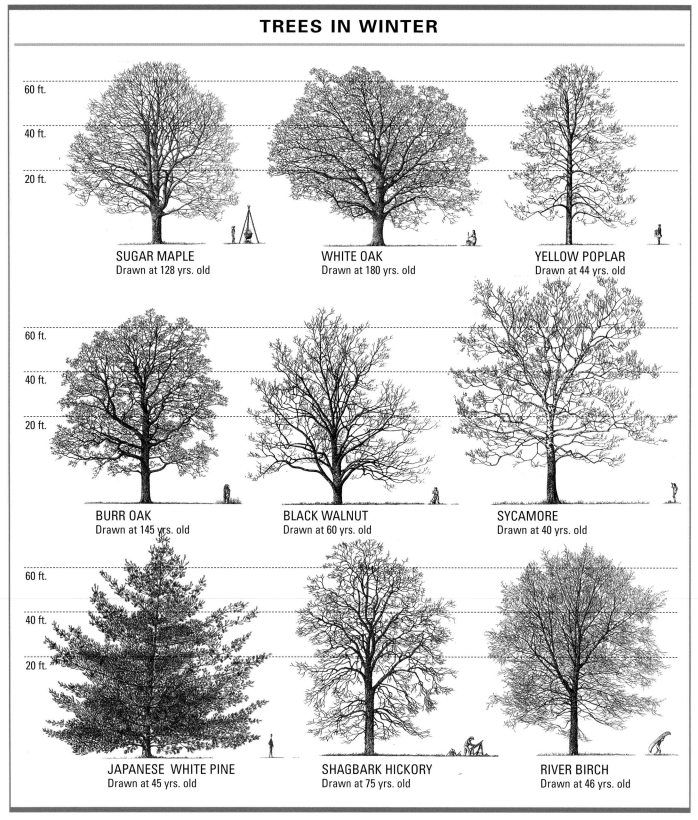

TREES IN WINTER

SUGAR MAPLE
Drawn at 128 yrs. old

WHITE OAK
Drawn at 180 yrs. old

YELLOW POPLAR
Drawn at 44 yrs. old

BURR OAK
Drawn at 145 yrs. old

BLACK WALNUT
Drawn at 60 yrs. old

SYCAMORE
Drawn at 40 yrs. old

JAPANESE WHITE PINE
Drawn at 45 yrs. old

SHAGBARK HICKORY
Drawn at 75 yrs. old

RIVER BIRCH
Drawn at 46 yrs. old

Tree drawings by Anthony Tyznick, courtesy of the Morton Aboretum

When trees are bare, you can spot several species in the woods by observing distinguishing characteristics normally not visible in the growing season.

Important characteristics to look for include the direction and shape of branches, the texture and color of a tree's bark, and the overall shape of the tree (see photos above and at right).

During the growing season, leaves provide a good way to identify various species (see the top photo on p. 14). However, it takes a trained eye and years of study to become familiar with a great variety of species.

A tree's flower, bud, or fruit is also a good indicator of its species. In the spring, you can easily look up to see buds forming on

The multiple branches that sweep upward and outward on this ancient oak tree are easily seen when the tree is bare of leaves.

The smooth, skinlike bark marks this as a eucalyptus tree.

Deep fissures in the trunk of this cedar are distinctive to the species.

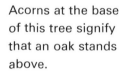

The classic shape and pointed ends of these leaves identify the tree as a red oak.

Acorns at the base of this tree signify that an oak stands above.

branches. Later in the year, look to the ground under a tree for fallen nuts (see the photo below).

Distinctive Wood Properties

Once you become familiar with trees, looking at the boards that come from them will reveal a seemingly endless variety of qualities. All woods have specific characteristics that can help us choose one particular species over another. The more familiar you become with these defining properties, the better your chances for selecting the best wood for your projects. Many of these characteristics are visual, such as a board's color or figure. As you gain a deeper appreciation of these characteristics, you'll be able to confidently add new woods to your inventory, seeking out those that appeal to you.

Sapwood versus Heartwood

Generally, woodworkers prefer to use heartwood over sapwood. Heartwood is found in the heart, or center, of the tree and usually has a darker and more interesting color than the surrounding sapwood, which is found on the tree's perimeter (see the top left photo on facing page). Sapwood is typically white or creamy-yellow in color. Using sapwood in a piece of furniture is often distracting when uniformity is the goal, although many woodworkers intentionally leave the sapwood band as a strong visual statement. For outdoor work, it's best to avoid sapwood since this area of the tree is more prone to fungi, insect attack, and rot.

➤ See *"Decay Resistance"* on p. 20.

See "Decay Resistance" on p. 20.

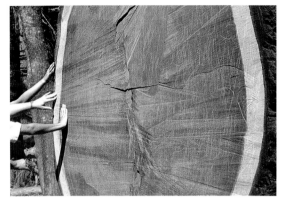

Sapwood is quite distinctive in some species, such as in the striking creamy-white band at the rim of this downed redwood.

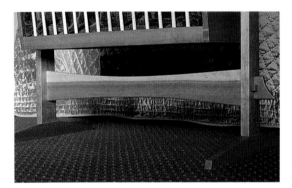

The lower stretcher on furniture maker Robbie Staples's cherry crib sports a bright band of sapwood—a nice design detail that complements the lighter ash spindles above.

Growth Rings

The circular rings on the end of a log reflect a tree's history (see the top right photo). Each ring is the result of one year's growth and is termed a growth ring or annular ring. Pay attention to growth rings as you look at the ends of individual boards. They'll tell you a lot about how and in what conditions the tree grew and what to expect from the boards as you transform them into furniture parts.

Each year of the tree's growth is displayed as a single ring in this cross section of ash.

Rings that are thick and spaced far apart are a sign that the tree grew quickly. Tighter, more closely spaced rings are found on slow-growth wood. Generally, slower-grown wood is more appealing to woodworkers because the tighter ring arrangement provides more strength and stability than lumber from fast-grown trees. However, there are exceptions; the fast-grown wood of certain pines and other woods is denser than the slower growth from the same species, and thus harder and more suited to specific tasks where strength is important.

Part of the growing cycle of a tree includes the faster-grown earlywood, which forms in the spring when most growth takes place. Later, the process slows down and the tree forms a band of latewood, which completes the growing cycle (see the drawing below).

In many woods, especially the softwoods, the difference between earlywood and latewood is quite distinct. Typically, you'll notice a marked difference in density, with the latewood being much harder than the earlywood. Southern yellow pine or redwood are good examples, where the more abundant earlywood is softer and wears away more quickly. You can sometimes feel this with your hand on the surface of a board. You'll certainly notice it if you sand a board carelessly, because the abrasive cuts into the softer earlywood faster than the latewood, creating an undulating surface instead of a smooth, flat area. The trick here is to learn how to sand correctly.

► See *"Smoothing and Preparing Wood"* on p. 214.

Another characteristic of these differing densities is that each area absorbs stains and other finishes at a different rate. The softer earlywood soaks up much more finish than the latewood, which can result in blotching. This is why it's usually a good idea to use a wood conditioner on most softwoods before applying a finish.

Pores and Texture

Pores are the result of cuts made through the ends or transverse sections of cell vessels. Occurring only in hardwoods, pores may be large and distinct, such as those in red oak (see the photo on facing page), or they may be barely visible under magnification, such as those in hard maple. Hardwoods are classified as ring-porous, diffuse-porous, or semi-ring-porous.

Ring-porous woods, like oak, ash, and elm have large pores concentrated in the earlywood area of the growth ring. This arrangement creates uneven grain and a tendency to split more easily along these weaker areas. These woods are said to be coarse-textured, and you can usually discern the rough surface by eye or with the palm of your hand. Ring-porous wood is often desirable when pieces need to be split, or riven, along the grain to make strong chair spindles, for example. On the other hand, the large pores can create finish problems. If you desire a smooth finish on a ring-porous wood, you'll have to fill the pores before topcoating. There is also a tendency for bleed-back due to the larger open pores, because pools of finish can gather in them, spreading out onto the finished surface before drying.

EARLYWOOD AND LATEWOOD

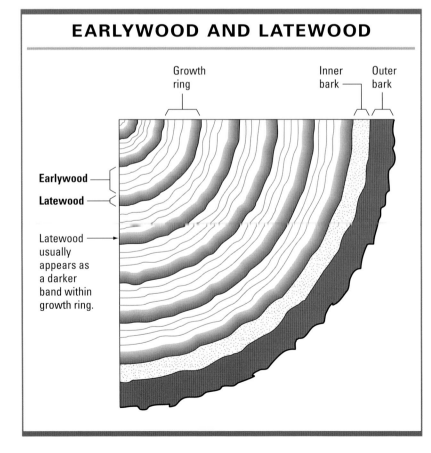

Growth ring

Inner bark

Outer bark

Earlywood

Latewood

Latewood usually appears as a darker band within growth ring.

Ring-porous woods display distinctive grain patterns, such as the elongated pores on the tangential surface of this piece of red oak.

Diffuse-porous woods tend to have smaller pores that are more evenly distributed throughout the early and late growth areas. These fine-textured woods, which include maple, poplar, and cherry, have a uniform appearance with a surface that's compact and dense. This allows you to apply stains and other finishes more evenly. However, some diffuse-porous woods such as mahogany and birch have relatively large pores, although in the same uniform arrangement. These types of diffuse-porous woods accept stains evenly, but you'll need to fill the pores during finishing to achieve a glass-smooth surface.

Semi-ring-porous woods (also known as semi-diffuse-porous) fall in a class somewhere between the previous two types. Overall, these woods contain large pores distributed evenly throughout the growth ring, although they sometimes get smaller toward the latewood. They are semi-coarse in texture, with black walnut and its slightly coarser cousin butternut being two good examples. Like ring-porous woods, these woods need pore-filling before finishing, and their overall uniformity makes them poor candidates for riven parts.

Grain

"Grain" is one of those woodworking terms used to describe just about anything that has to do with the fibers in a piece of wood. For our purposes, it's important to know that grain refers to the arrangement of wood fibers in a board, which includes the direction in which the predominant fibers run and their overall surface pattern.

➤ See *"Understanding Grain Orientation"* on p. 23 for information.

Color

The specific colors of different woods are helpful in wood identification—and vital for choosing the right palette of colors for your furniture.

➤ See *"Wood Species"* on p. 273.

Certain woods stand out more than others, such as Brazilian rosewood, prized for its rich pinkish-purple hues, contrasted by splashes of bright orange demarcated by fine black lines. Pink ivory is a startling pink color, while purpleheart (amaranth) is a rich, royal purple. Gabon ebony is jet black. The colors are endless.

Although specific woods can be characterized by color, this is by no means a uniform rule. For example, the heartwood of poplar is generally a medium-green color with a band of creamy-white sapwood, but sometimes you'll come across boards with swaths of deep purples, browns, and blacks. Keep in mind that oxidation and exposure to light will alter the color of any wood, typically changing it from a light shade to a darker hue. However, some woods hold their color longer than others. For example, pau amarillo is a vibrant canary yellow that can retain its color for years. In contrast, padauk—an almost blood-red wood—usually turns a dull red or brown within days of milling.

Figured Wood

The vast world of figure in wood provides one of the great joys of working our material. Instead of perfunctorily turning off-the-rack boards into furniture parts, you have the option of composing parts from premium boards that display fantastic figure. Studying figure in woods and then using it selectively in your work can really pump up the look and feel of your furniture.

In general terms, figure refers to the characteristic grain markings on the surface of wood. But the term figured wood has a more definitive meaning. It describes wood with very distinctive patterns, usually resulting from the arrangement of its grain. There are numerous types of figured wood and veneers that are beautiful to behold and offer a way to add great distinction to our furniture. Some come from the normal growth struc-

ture of certain species, while others result from abnormal growth and extractives in the wood. For example, the dark streaks and thin lines in spalted wood are the result of the initial stages of decay—a process that is then halted through kiln drying or heat.

Most figured wood can be exploited by judicious sawing of the log. Generally, the best figuring results from quartersawing, in which the growth rings are oriented at 90 degrees to the board's face.

➤ See *"Understanding Grain Orientation"* on p. 23.

However, some figure displays best on the plainsawn face, and other types of figure appear no matter which way the wood is cut, such as in burled wood. Although figure generally occurs in specific woods, almost any wood can display some of these unusual grain patterns on occasion. The terms used to describe specific types of figure and the woods most commonly associated with them are listed in the chart shown on the facing page.

Resin

Resin canals, also called pitch pockets, are found only in softwoods, most typically in the pines. These are tubular passages that exude "pitch," a sticky resin. Resin canals most often occur in or near the latewood zone of the growth rings and show up on milled surfaces as long gashes that seep a gooey mess. Knots are another area where resin sometimes accumulates. While resin is used commercially for such products as turpentine and rosin, it's a pain for woodworkers because it can ooze out of a board

Figured Woods

	TERM	COMMONLY SEEN IN	OCCASIONALLY SEEN IN
	Swirl	Walnut, mahogany, cherry, maple	Rosewood, olive
	Curly	Maple, makore, anigre	Cherry, mahogany, sycamore, walnut, oak, teak
	Fiddleback	Maple, makore, anigre	Sycamore, cherry, mahogany
	Bird's-eye	Maple	Cherry, white pine
	Quilted	Maple, mahogany, sapele	Myrtle, maobi
	Crotch	Mahogany, walnut	Cherry, maple, oak
	Peanut Shell	Tamo ash	Bubinga
	Ribbon stripe	Mahogany, bubinga	
	Bee's wing	Satinwood	Amboyna, mahogany eucalyptus
	Ray fleck	Oak, lacewood	Sycamore, beech
	Burl	Redwood, elm, amboyna, camphor, walnut, madrone	Oak, imbuya, ash
	Pommele	Sapele, bubinga, makore	
	Spalted	Maple, sycamore, beech	Cherry, poplar

Applying one or two coats of shellac is an excellent way to seal in resin and prevent it from bleeding out of knots.

long after a finish is applied. It also has a nasty habit of showing up under paint or other film finishes. Kiln-drying wood usually "fixes" the resin so it doesn't leak onto the surface, and a few coats of shellac will suffice to seal any existing pitch areas in your work (see the photo above). Usually the most realistic approach is to cut around this defect when possible.

Odor

Most woods have a unique odor, and a few are distinctive enough that you can spot them easily with a sniff. All woods smell strongest when green or freshly cut. But many have a strong bouquet even after the wood has been dried. The aroma of dry wood is emitted particularly during sawing. The spicy scent of Spanish cedar, a traditional wood for lining humidors, is unmistakable, as is the odor of yellow cedar. Oak and walnut both have their own characteristic and quite pungent aromas, which are strong enough to cause some woodworkers

to turn up their noses at these woods. On the other hand, sassafras has a sweet, tangy scent that invites hand-planing of the wood just to catch a whiff of its perfume.

Density and Hardness

Density is the measure of a wood's relative weight, while hardness describes the compressive strength of its surface. These two qualities are interrelated, and we typically refer to both physical properties when describing the strength of a particular wood. In general terms, the heavier a piece of wood, the stronger its compressive strength, or its ability to withstand force on its surface. This makes very hard woods great for flooring and other high-impact areas, whereas softer, less-dense woods are a better choice when lighter weight is paramount and strength is less important, such as for ceiling trim or other parts that won't suffer abuse.

Decay Resistance

When wood is left outdoors exposed to the elements, it eventually rots. The leading cause of decay in wood is fungi, which makes its home in material that is exposed to moisture. However, some woods are less susceptible to decay. This makes choosing durable woods for outdoor projects a necessity. While most woods will rot quickly—some in less than a year—there are several hardy species that can last generations, even without a protective finish. The chart on the facing page lists a selection of highly rot-resistant woods suitable for outdoor work, along with their relative strengths and weaknesses.

Outdoor Woods

Black locust	Very rot-resistant; wide boards rare; typically used for posts in fences and buildings; predrill for fasteners
Osage orange	Very rot-resistant; wide boards rare; extremely dense and hard; predrill for fasteners
Teak	Expensive, heavy; turns silver over time; extremely durable, stable, and strong; holds fasteners well; retains smooth surface
Mahogany (genuine)	Expensive; moderately heavy; silvers over time; retains smooth surface (Avoid "Philippine mahogany," a type of lauan)
Jarah	Relatively expensive; very hard, but surprisingly easy to work; glues well; deep reddish color with striking black lines; fades to gray if left unfinished
White oak	Relatively expensive; moderately hard; stained by iron hardware outdoors; weathers coarsely and ray flecks on quartersawn lumber can separate over time
Bald cypress	Limited availability; lightweight, but strong; glues well; blackens with striking tan highlights over time; prebore for fasteners to prevent splitting
Redwood	Soft and lightweight; works well but requires beefed-up joinery for strong connections; turns silver over time
Yellow cedar	Extremely durable; soft, but somewhat stronger than redwood; sweet, spicy scent, traditionally used by native Americans for totem poles and other outdoor carvings

Tricks for Identifying Wood

Once lumber has been cut and dried, identifying its specific species can be a challenge. Scientific investigations with a microscope are usually out of the realm of the average woodworker, but there are several seat-of-the-pants methods for identifying particular woods.

Many of the woods we come across have aged in dusty old barns or have been sitting on shelves, oxidizing for years. Consequently, they're dark and often dirty. To find out if the wood in question is a treasure, give it a good wiping with a stiff brush to remove debris and then scrape or slice the surface with a pocketknife until you expose fresh wood. The color below is almost always lighter and brighter and often indicative of the species.

Cutting just below the surface of this dirty old board reveals the lovely pink hue of cherry.

The relative softness of two similar woods can be tested by indenting them with a fingernail. Butternut (below) accepts an impression while the harder walnut (above) resists marking.

Wetting a piece of wood will boost its aroma so your nose can detect its signature smell.

To differentiate between the oaks, have some fun blowing through a split sample of the wood. Bubbles indicate red oak, which lacks the pore-blocking tyloses found in white oak.

One trick is to test the wood for hardness with your fingernail. You can easily tell the difference between hard and soft maple with this test. Or you can check whether you're dealing with walnut or its much softer look-alike, butternut—two woods that fool even seasoned woodworkers (see the top photo at left).

The odor of certain woods is quite distinctive, so it pays to familiarize yourself with the various scents, which are particularly detectable if the suspect wood is green or moistened. To enhance the scent of dry wood, I usually wet it with a dash of water before sniffing.

Another method for identifying certain species is to check for tyloses, a natural material unique to some hardwoods. This stuff blocks the pores of certain woods, such as chestnut and ash, and is most prominent in white oak and black locust. Determining the presence of tyloses is one way to discern white oak from red oak. Try blowing into the end grain of a split, or riven, sample held in a bowl of water. If you can blow bubbles, the sample is likely to be red oak. If you can't, the pores are blocked, and you're probably holding white oak (see the bottom photo at left).

If you're really stumped, try sending a sample to a lab. That's right; you can mail a sample of the wood in question to one of several identification services, usually for a small fee. In the case of the USDA Forest Service, the testing is free. (See Sources, p. 272.) Most services require only a small sample that you can pop in an envelope. Be sure to include as much information as possible about the wood, such as its area of origin and any common names connected to it.

GRAIN ORIENTATION IN BOARDS

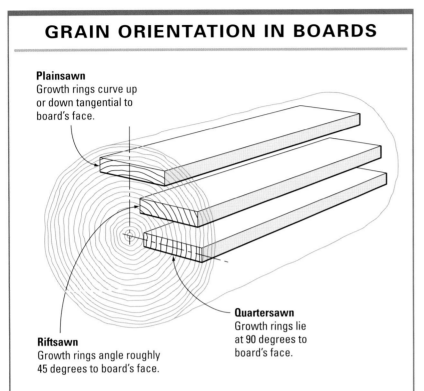

Plainsawn
Growth rings curve up or down tangential to board's face.

Riftsawn
Growth rings angle roughly 45 degrees to board's face.

Quartersawn
Growth rings lie at 90 degrees to board's face.

From left to right: plainsawn, riftsawn, and quartersawn oak boards, each displaying its distinctive grain pattern on the tangential face of the board.

Understanding Grain Orientation

The way a board is sawn from a log determines its grain orientation. There are three types of grain orientation you'll encounter in a sawn board: plainsawn (also called flatsawn), riftsawn (also called riftcut), and quartersawn. Each term denotes how the annular growth rings are oriented in a board. Knowing the grain orientation of a specific board is important because it will help you predict how the wood will behave during cutting, how it will react to moisture and finishes, and how it will look in a piece of furniture. The easiest way to determine the grain orientation is to look at a board's end grain, as shown in the drawing above.

In terms of wood movement, a quartersawn board is the most stable because expansion and contraction occur in a relatively even manner over the width of the material. Riftsawn wood runs a close second in terms of stability, while plainsawn boards will often cup or twist wildly due to changes in the direction of the grain.

So why not use quartered wood all the time? Well, first of all, it's more expensive because quartersawing a log produces less yield, so mills charge more per board foot. Secondly, the tangential face of a quartered or rift-cut board will display straight grain lines as opposed to the cathedral grain pattern found on plainsawn boards, as shown in the photo above. The choice of straight versus cathedral grain is solely a matter of personal style. Most woodworkers combine all three types in their work.

Cutting Your Own Wood,
Page 26

Drying Lumber, Page 48

Buying Lumber, Page 58

Storing Lumber, Page 65

PART TWO

Finding and Storing Wood

T HE QUEST FOR WOOD can be fun, exciting, and at times frustrating. As woodworkers, we want—and should expect—the very best for our money. It's worth taking the time to find good sources for wood, and you may even want to fell and mill your own timber. When you're buying wood, it's a good idea to become familiar with lumberyard parlance to avoid some of the pitfalls common in purchasing milled stock. Once you've acquired lumber, you'll want to keep it in good condition by monitoring its moisture content and storing it in a manner that ensures its quality for years to come. In this part of the book, we'll look at all these aspects of acquiring and storing material so you'll never run short of the best stuff.

Cutting Your Own Wood

Harvesting Trees

➤ Felling a Tree (p. 35)

➤ Cutting Trunks into Logs (p. 37)

➤ Planting a Tree (p. 39)

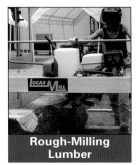

Rough-Milling Lumber

➤ Shaping a Log by Hand (p. 40)

➤ Milling with a Chainsaw Mill (p. 42)

➤ Milling with a Circular Sawmill (p. 44)

➤ Milling with a Band Mill (p. 46)

NOTHING BEATS the pleasure of harvesting and milling your own wood. The money you save is a big benefit, and if you have a woodlot on your property you have the opportunity to manage it in a responsible manner—something the big timber companies often overlook. You're also in direct control of your wood, from choosing the best cuts and matching sequential boards to becoming intimately acquainted with your material through the sweat of your own labor. But the biggest thrill is to turn a log into a piece of furniture. You only get this satisfaction if you mill your own wood.

It's easy to get a bit cavalier about the environment when you're harvesting your own wood, especially after you've gained some experience. Part of responsible harvesting includes replacing what you take by replenishing the forest or your own small lot with saplings for future generations.

➤ See *"Show Your Support of Trees"* on p. 28.

Also, don't forget that felling trees and milling your own logs are inherently dangerous. Please keep safety uppermost in your mind when tackling this kind of work.

Sizing Up a Tree

How tall is that tree? If you're thinking about milling your own wood, this can be valuable information for estimating how many boards a particular tree might hold. Or you might simply want to get better acquainted with trees and their various heights. Thankfully, there's a low-tech way to gauge the rough height of a tree. The only tools you'll need are your thumb—and a partner to serve as a gauge.

If possible, stand in a clearing 100 yards to 200 yards from the tree in question, and have your pal stand at the very base of the tree. Here, my friend Lindsay Carroll wears a light-colored shirt to increase her visibility (see the bottom left photo). Raise your thumb up to eye level, as woodworker Hans Doellgast does here, and move your hand in or away from your body until your thumb just blocks the view of your cohort from head to toe. At this point, the width of your thumb equals the height of the person standing at the tree.

Without moving the relative position of your hand to your body, "walk" your thumb up the tree. Move it in successive steps to the top of the tree without overlapping, and count the number of moves it takes to reach the top. To calculate the height of the tree, simply multiply the height of your partner by the number of thumb moves you made.

Raise your thumb to eye level, and move it in or away from you until its width blocks the view of your helper.

Stand a couple of hundred yards from the tree, with your helper standing at the base of the trunk.

"Walk" your thumb up the tree until you reach the top, counting the number of moves you make.

Sawyer Mike Peters inspects a pile of logs that are ready for sawing into planks.

Harvesting Wood

Taking a tree from the forest is a big job and an even bigger responsibility. The act of felling a tree poses serious, life-threatening dangers due to the immense weight involved. Furthermore, moving and handling one of these behemoths after it hits the ground involves some special techniques and equipment. Equally significant is the fact that you're taking a tree's life. I feel it's important to give the deed due respect. A reverent attitude makes you careful and cautious and ensures that you don't approach the task lightly. In the end, the boards you reap will have much more impact on your furniture making than store-bought boards.

To fell a tree, you'll need either a chainsaw or a hefty ax and a good felling saw. While chainsaws are fast and efficient, the hand-tool approach is safer and quieter. And with practice, it can be just as quick. Either way, it's essential that your tools are sharp for good cuts.

▶ See *"Keep It Sharp"* on p. 30.

TREE CUTS

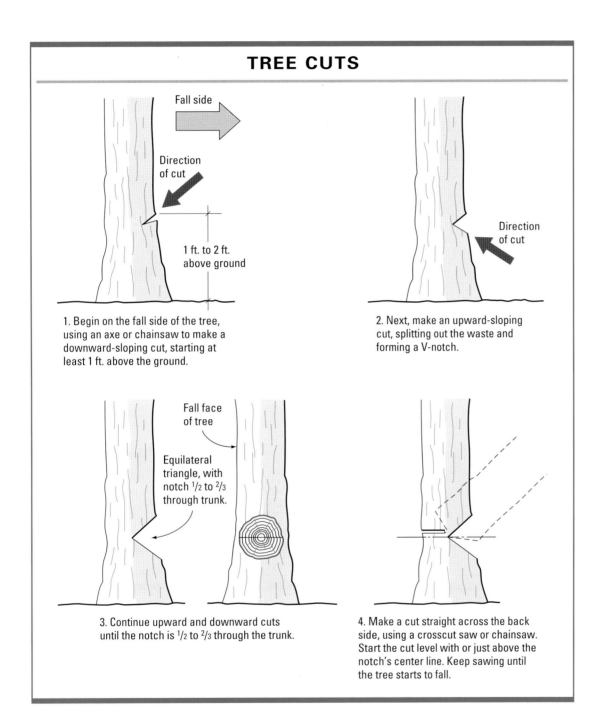

Fall side

Direction of cut

1 ft. to 2 ft. above ground

1. Begin on the fall side of the tree, using an axe or chainsaw to make a downward-sloping cut, starting at least 1 ft. above the ground.

Direction of cut

2. Next, make an upward-sloping cut, splitting out the waste and forming a V-notch.

Fall face of tree

Equilateral triangle, with notch $1/2$ to $2/3$ through trunk.

3. Continue upward and downward cuts until the notch is $1/2$ to $2/3$ through the trunk.

4. Make a cut straight across the back side, using a crosscut saw or chainsaw. Start the cut level with or just above the notch's center line. Keep sawing until the tree starts to fall.

Before you jump into the job of felling a tree, take a few moments to understand the sequence of cuts (see the drawing above). Countless people have lost their lives due to a lack of knowledge or a careless approach; please don't become another statistic. Take your time, and consider gaining some experience by helping an expert before tackling your own felling project.

► KEEP IT SHARP

Saw blades, axes, and other edge tools should be kept sharp for tree work. The coarse material of a tree, especially its dirt-laden bark, will dull tools quickly. The best sharpening regimen is to stop and sharpen when you sense the tool is cutting with difficulty, or if you have to use more force. Use a file on saw blades, stroking all the teeth with the same number of passes, and following the profile of the teeth.

To touch up an ax edge, you can use the same file. Hold the tool firmly against your body and stroke one side by moving the file away from the cutting edge. Then flip the tool over and stroke in the opposite direction until the edge is sharp.

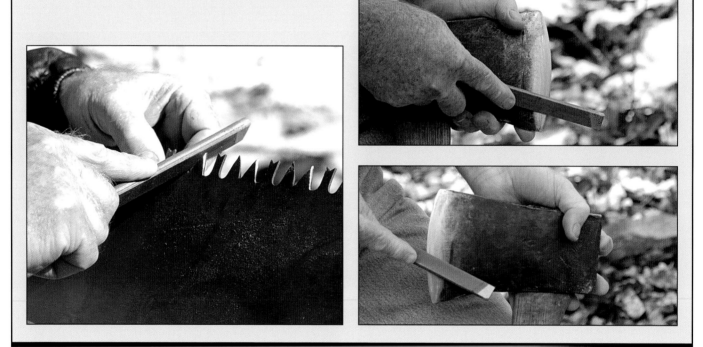

Cutting Logs

Whether you buy your logs or harvest them yourself, sawing them into boards is a crucial step on the road to making furniture. There are three methods for cutting, and each approach has a big impact on the type of board you'll get (see the drawing on facing page).

For boards with a minimum of defects, sawyers like to *grade saw*, which involves turning the log during the sawing sequence so the best face is always the next cut, minimizing defects such as knots, checks, discolorations, and other natural flaws. This is the standard approach in the timber business because it yields the highest-grade boards, and big wood manufacturers want clear,

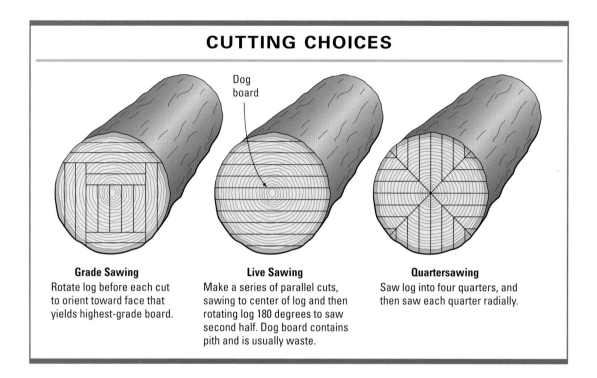

CUTTING CHOICES

Grade Sawing
Rotate log before each cut to orient toward face that yields highest-grade board.

Live Sawing
Make a series of parallel cuts, sawing to center of log and then rotating log 180 degrees to saw second half. Dog board contains pith and is usually waste.

Quartersawing
Saw log into four quarters, and then saw each quarter radially.

Dog board

---

defect-free stock. However, it produces relatively narrow stock and doesn't necessarily give furniture makers the best wood.

Live sawing, also called "through and through" sawing, is something that the big mills tend to avoid. This approach yields wide boards (not particularly desirable to big furniture companies) that are full of natural defects. But for small-shop woodworkers, live-sawn boards can be real gems. You get matched boards (if you keep them in sequence as they come off the log), and the planks are as wide as the tree is round. With sequenced wood, you can match color and incorporate interesting grain patterns in your work. Another boon is the huge size of the boards. Working with wide planks lets you build solid-panel tables and cabinets, which many furniture-makers consider more beautiful and appealing than glued-up panels from narrower boards. Yes, there are imperfections to be dealt with, such as the "dog

board" in the center of the log, which contains the pith and must be cut away. But taking the time to work with and around these so-called defects can make your furniture more distinctive than the run-of-the-mill stuff cranked out in the factories.

► See *"Working Difficult Wood"* on p. 162.

The last approach, *quartersawing*, is the most wasteful of the three sawing methods in terms of yield, since it results in a lot of scrap and several narrow boards too small for use in furniture. It's difficult to find anyone in the industry sawing in this manner today. However, it's worth finding a small mill operator in your area who's willing to take the time to cut wood this way, since you get all the benefits of quartersawn wood.

► See *"Understanding Grain Orientation"* on p. 23.

What Type of Mill Should You Buy?

Sawing your own logs into lumber is a great way to get wood at a fraction of the cost you'd pay a sawyer or lumber dealer. The job can be done with axes and adzes, but a small lumber mill is a more expedient choice. Today's mills can go right to where the tree has been downed, saving you the complexity of transporting whole logs, as opposed to lumber. Of the three basic mills available to the small-shop woodworker—the chainsaw mill, the circular sawmill, and the bandsaw

A chainsaw mill is easy to set up and use and lets you tackle really big logs.

mill—only the chainsaw mill is truly portable. The other two types are mobile, meaning you can move them to the site, but it will involve trailering the unit with a vehicle. It may also require a helper or two.

The least expensive setup is a chainsaw mill, and it's a good option for the beginner. A chainsaw mill employs one or two chainsaws and a simple metal carriage that guides the saw along the log. A key feature is a chain that's designed for rip-cutting rather than crosscutting. Some models can be used quite effectively by one person. Cuts are predictable but slow, and the saw kerf made by a chainsaw is the widest made by any of the small lumber mills, creating the most waste. However, a big advantage is the ability to cut big logs, since you can equip the mill with a long bar for ripping really wide boards. This is a nice system that works well, sets up easily, and gives you a good feel for cutting your own wood without a heavy investment.

A second choice is the circular sawmill, which costs more and requires trailering to the site. The particular mill shown in the top photo on the facing page is lightweight and can be set up and operated by one person. Cuts are relatively fast and produce slightly less waste than a chainsaw. The downside is that these mills tend to be limited in terms of cutting width, making them best suited for milling dimensioned lumber (2x4s, etc.) and not furniture-grade wood.

The third option is to go with a bandsaw mill. This is the most expensive system of the three for small-scale milling and, like the circular mill, must be towed behind a vehicle for on-site work. Its sheer size and weight also means you'll need a helper. However,

A circular sawmill cuts a lot of relatively narrow wood in a hurry and can be operated by one person.

A bandsaw mill like the one shown above can be transported to the job site. Set up under cover (right), this band mill can saw wood all day at great speed.

Cutting Your Own Wood | 33

A handheld metal detector is a good investment if you're thinking about milling your own wood.

The bane of sawyers, big steel nails will knock off teeth and destroy blades.

Iron left in green wood will cause deep staining, such as the dark streaks on this walnut plank.

the band mill cuts very fast, leaves little waste, and can be equipped with a hydraulic dog system that lets you reposition and hold a log automatically during cutting. Fancier versions have on-board computers that you can use to dial in the cuts instead of using a tape measure or ruler.

One sneaky item to watch for when you're milling wood is metal buried in a log. Foreign objects like spikes and steel pins are quite common in some trees, such as shade trees growing around a house or marker trees in a farmer's field. Both might have seen duty as fence posts or other convenient nailing spots. Steel or iron will destroy a chain or blade, and the iron itself will stain wood. To find iron deep within a log, it pays to invest in a metal detector so you can locate and pry out foreign objects before milling.

Felling a Tree

Before felling a tree, it's important to assess the weight of its upper branches and the lean of the tree to judge where it is likely to fall **(A)**. Then gather your tools to begin cutting. Here, wood-wright Roy Underhill uses an ax and handsaw for felling, but the same basic sequence can be applied when you're using a faster-cutting (but louder and dirtier) chainsaw.

> ⚠️ **WARNING** Before making any cuts, clear an escape path 45 degrees away from the fall of the tree in case of an emergency.

Start by making a downward cut on the fall side of the tree, about 1 ft. to 2 ft. above the ground **(B)**. Then make an upward cut that meets the first to form a V-notch **(C)**. Alternate between upward and downward cuts to deepen and widen the notch. Good ax work involves splitting wood, which is much easier on the arms and faster than severing the fibers. With the right technique, you should see large chunks fly from the cut **(D)**. Aim to make a notch an equilateral triangle that's about as wide as it is deep. When the notch reaches one-half to two-thirds back into the tree, you're ready for the back cut **(E)**.

(Continued on p. 36.)

Begin the back cut with a crosscut saw or chainsaw, sawing straight across the face directly opposite the notch cut, and level with or slightly above the middle of the notch **(F)**. As you saw deeper into the trunk, keep your ears tuned to any creaking sounds from the tree, and remember to eyeball the treetop every few strokes to note any sway. These are signs that the tree is ready to fall. Once the tree starts to go, pull the saw from the cut **(G)**. Then run from the tree at roughly a 45-degree angle from its fall line. Above all, never run directly behind the tree, as the butt end may kick back swiftly and without warning **(H)**. If you've made the right sequence of cuts, the stump should show a narrow "hinge" of wood between the notch and back cuts, with very few fibers pulled from the stump **(I)**.

Cutting Trunks into Logs

Handling logs is a challenge because of the immense weight involved, especially when the wood is green and full of sap. However, with a few specialized logging tools, a little woodsman savvy, and perhaps a helper, it can be accomplished without too much sweat.

When trees fall, they typically hang up on ground cover or other trees, such as the poplar shown here **(A)**. The first order of business, then, is to reduce the trunk to manageable lengths that can be moved to a safe spot for subsequent sawing into logs. Pick an area where the trunk clears the ground, and use a two-man crosscut saw to make a saw cut from below, about one-quarter of the way through **(B)**. Then cut from the top until the saw passes through **(C)**. The undercut prevents the saw from binding and allows a clean cut without tearing the fibers **(D)**.

[VARIATION] For a one-person approach, try using an old-fashioned "Folding Sawing Machine," as it was called in the 1800s. A hook at one end of the device grabs the trunk, and downward pressure from a spring keeps the saw in the wood while you push and pull the blade via a long lever.

(Continued on p. 38.)

A

B

C

D

VARIATION

Once you've cut the tree into sections, you'll want to move them to level ground for sawing into smaller logs that can be taken from the forest. Plan on cutting your wood into 10-ft. sections or less, which gives you decent lengths without taxing your back or the vehicle you use to transport the logs. To move the logs into position, use a cant hook, which uses a hooked spike and a long handle for leverage **(E)**.

Position the log so the bulk of it lies as much as possible on the ground. By slipping a scrap of wood or bark under the cutline, you can give the trunk more firm support and protect the blade from dirt as you saw through. As before, use a two-man crosscut saw to cut through the log. The lead man steers the blade and makes the cut on the pull stroke. The helper follows the lead, and then pulls the blade back for the return stroke **(F)**. If the blade starts to bind, tap a wedge into the top of the kerf to keep the sawcut open so you can cut all the way through **(G)**.

Planting a Tree

Planting a young sapling can be done swiftly with the right tool. Using a specialized digging spade called a dibble or dibble bar **(A, B)**, an experienced forester can plant as many as 1,000 trees in a single day. Start by digging up a shoot, such as this white ash taken from a garden **(C)**. Be careful not to damage the plant's roots while digging and planting, especially the central taproot **(D)**.

Begin a hole for the sapling by piercing the full length of the dibble straight into the ground, and then wiggling it back and forth **(E)**. When the hole is about 6 in. wide, take hold of the sapling and push its roots into the hole until the upper-most roots are slightly below the ground **(F)**. Now plant the spade full depth a few inches in front of the sapling and lever the tool forward to push the dirt toward the shoot **(G, H)**. Finish up by tamping the loose dirt with a foot **(I)**. There's no need to water unless the area is experiencing drought. Total planting time: about 30 seconds.

Shaping a Log by Hand

Before machines, woodworkers used hand tools exclusively to mill and shape wood. Hewing logs into beams was one of these tasks, and it is still a viable method for producing big timbers today. The method is simpler than you might think.

Begin by positioning a fresh log on a pair of short log sections to raise it off the ground. Cut V-notches into the sections to help stabilize the log. Then clamp the log to each section by using an ax head to pound in a pair of pinch dogs, also called log staples **(A)**.

Using a plumb bob and chalk, strike two parallel lines on one end of the log to mark the desired width of the beam **(B)**. Transfer the marks onto the face of the log with a chalkline by snapping the line onto the bark **(C)**, then remove the bark at each line with a drawknife **(D)**. With the bark gone, use the chalkline again to snap hewing lines onto the more-visible white wood **(E)**.

To remove the bulk of wood on one face, employ a two-step process. Standing atop the trunk, use a felling ax to make a series of V-shaped notches along the log, just shy of your layout lines **(F)**. Then swing the ax along the trunk and between the notches to split off large chunks **(G)**.

Next, use the same ax to make a series of kerfs in the face of the log to the depth of your line **(H)**. Stand astride the work and use a broadax to refine the surface, making slicing cuts by lifting the ax and letting it fall so that its weight does all the work for you **(I)**. Finish one side by rotating the log so the flat surface faces up, and again working on top, use an adze to smooth the face. Swing the tool toward you and between your legs, taking a thin shaving with each pass **(J)**. Repeat the hewing process on the opposite face, then square off those faces to produce a four-sided beam.

> ⚠️ **WARNING** To avoid injury, wear sturdy work boots and always keep the cutting path of the adze between your legs, never to the side.

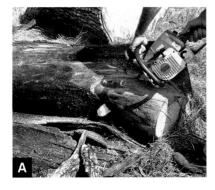

Milling with a Chainsaw Mill

A chainsaw mill provides one of the simplest ways to get acquainted with milling your own wood. The system is very easy to transport and can often be used alone. Keep in mind that the kerf left by the chain is about ½-in. wide, which wastes a fair amount of wood. But with a chain mill, you have the option to saw really wide boards by equipping the mill with a long bar— a big plus.

Since this log is too wide for his mill, chairmaker Don Weber starts by lopping off excess areas with a chainsaw **(A)**. Then he uses a cant hook to position the log so the desired cutting surface faces up. Wedge the log underneath if necessary to keep it stable **(B)**.

Square up the ends of the log as best you can with the chainsaw **(C)**. Then attach an end board at one or both ends with lag screws, using a pair of levels to align the top of each board across the log, and level with the highest point along the log's length **(D)**. Next, use a level to strike a level line across the center of the log through the pith **(E)**. This becomes your reference line for laying out the first cut. Also, if you cut directly into this line later, you'll minimize unstable pith in the boards adjacent to the center.

Lay a homemade beam over the log and onto your end boards **(F)**. The beam must be sturdy and straight, so it's best to make it from 2x material attached to a length of angle iron along each edge. Referencing the line you drew earlier on the end of the log, adjust the mill for the first cut by lowering or raising the mill bars **(G)**. This first cut is a waste, or slabbing, cut to remove sapwood and define a flat surface for the first board, so make sure to adjust the mill with this in mind. Be careful not to make this cut too shallow or you'll cut into the end boards that hold up the beam.

Once you've adjusted the mill, start the saw and push it through the wood to make the initial slabbing cut **(H)**. As you push, concentrate on keeping the mill flat on the surface of the beam. Once you've established the cut, drive a couple of wedges into the kerf to prevent the sawn piece from collapsing onto the bar **(I)**. When the cut is almost complete, drive a few more wedges into the kerf near the end of the log, and then push the mill through to finish the cut **(J)**.

After removing the slab piece, adjust the depth of cut to the desired thickness of the plank you wish to mill **(K)**. Now make your second cut similar to the first, but this time you'll be cutting a plank of even thickness **(L)**. Remove the first plank from the log **(M)**, and continue adjusting the depth of cut and cutting through the log from the top surface down, milling individual planks until you reach the bottom slab section.

> ⚠ **WARNING** Mechanized mills generate a lot of noise and dust. Always protect your eyes and ears with safety eyewear and hearing protectors.

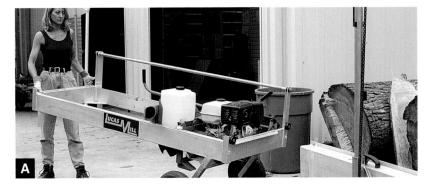

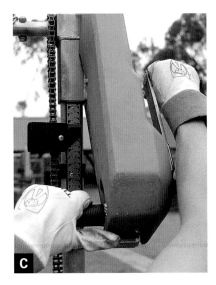

Milling with a Circular Sawmill

A circular sawmill can be set up and operated by one person. Here, woodworking instructor Lisa Pieropan sets up a mill by wheeling the saw carriage inside the beams of the saw's frame, an easy task for one person **(A)**. Working with a log that's already been sawn on one face by a band mill, she squats down and sights the beams parallel to the top of the log **(B)**. The same technique works with an unsawn whole log; you simply sight along its top edge. A crank at each end of the frame lets you adjust the beams up or down as necessary **(C)**.

Before sawing, dial in the desired thickness and width by setting the stops at the front of the saw carriage **(D)**. Make the first cut with the blade parallel with and to one side of the log, pushing the carriage into the work **(E)**. With the carriage at the far end of the log, release the carriage lock, rotate the blade 90 degrees **(F)**, and pull the saw back through the work to complete the first cut **(G)**. This first slabbing cut removes waste from the edge of the log and creates a straight edge for the first board **(H)**.

Rotate the saw back to parallel, and push the carriage into the log to slab, or thickness, the first board **(I)**. Again, rotate the blade to 90 degrees and pull the saw back to complete the cut **(J)**. The finished board has two straight and parallel sides, and the log is ready for the next board-cutting sequence **(K)**.

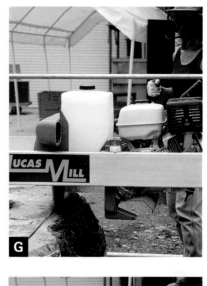

Milling with a Band Mill

This bandsaw mill is set up under cover to keep the wood and sawyers Michael Talbot and Forrest Edens in the shade and out of inclement weather **(A)**. The mill uses a flexible metal blade, or band, that travels around two wheels on the saw carriage. The thin blade has aggressive, hook-shaped teeth that cut through logs very quickly with minimal waste **(B)**.

Here, cherry logs are the milling order of the day. Cutting begins when the sawyers slice a log down its center. With this particular mill, the log is dogged to the platform and remains stationary while the saw carriage moves along the cut **(C)**. After the first cut, the saw operator sets a row of metal dogs to hold the face parallel, or at 90 degrees, to the blade, depending on the desired cut. The sawyer then measures the width of the log in order to raise or lower the blade for maximum yield **(D)**. Once this is set, the operator saws the half-log into two quarter-logs **(E)**.

With a quarter-log in place, board milling begins. The operator adjusts the blade for the thickness of the cut, measuring from the bottom of the log. The saw carriage begins its movement through the log from the near, or operator's, side of the mill **(F)**. At the end of the cut, the blade exits and the log drops down onto the sawn board **(G)**.

A helper shifts the log and pulls the sawn board from the platform **(H)**. Immediately after sawing, it's important to stack the boards onto a stickered pile **(I)**.

➤ See *"Stickering a Pile"* on p. 54.

With a band mill, the sawn surface displays a series of straight sawmarks perpendicular to the edge of the plank **(J)**.

Drying Lumber

Drying Lumber

ALL LIVING TREES contain sap, which is mostly water, or moisture. When we mill a tree into lumber, we have to reduce this moisture content in the wood before turning our boards into furniture. The technique for drying wood is quite an art. It requires drying our material fast enough so it won't mold or rot, yet not so fast that it stresses the wood, which results in checking, splitting, and all sorts of other nasty traits.

In this section, we'll learn about the correct moisture content for our material—and some of the pitfalls of wood that's too wet or too dry. We'll also look at how wood is dried, and how to choose an appropriate method for drying your own boards to ensure that you're always working with premium wood.

What Is Dry Wood?

Drying, or seasoning, wood correctly is the key to using it for furniture construction. The drying process takes place either through air-drying or through a combination of air- and kiln-drying, as I'll explain shortly. The basic approach involves the initial removal of all the *free water* in the green wood, which is liquid and moisture trapped inside the cells. Following that, the wood is further dried by removing a portion of the *bound water*—the moisture that saturates the walls of the cells.

It's important to understand that as the bound water evaporates, the wood starts to shrink. This is why your drying schedule should give the wood enough time to shrink slowly. Otherwise, unequal stresses in the wood will lead to warping and cracking. However, drying too slowly will invite fungal attack on the surface of the wood. Therefore, it's necessary to carefully monitor the moisture content of the wood as it dries.

The moisture content (MC) of wood is defined as the ratio of the weight of water in a given piece of wood to the weight of that piece of wood when it's completely dry (known as oven-dry weight). This ratio is expressed as a percentage.

➤ See *"Reading Moisture in Wood"* on p. 81.

Knowing the MC of your wood is critical because not all wood is dried to the same extent. For furniture making, wood should be in a range between 6 percent and 8 percent MC. In contrast, construction-grade lumber used for building houses is usually kiln-dried to 12 percent to 14 percent MC—too wet for our purposes.

It's important to realize that wood is hygroscopic—that is, it always expands and contracts in relation to the amount of moisture in its environment. Fortunately, this movement isn't arbitrary; wood does eventually reach a state of equilibrium with its environment. This simply means that, at a given level of relative humidity, the wood no longer takes on or releases water. At this point, the amount of water in the wood is referred to as its equilibrium moisture content (EMC). The EMC of wood will be greater when the weather is humid and less in the dry season.

Sealing Fresh Wood

As we've seen, part of the process of drying wood involves slowing down the rate at which water escapes the cells, but not slowing it down so much as to promote fungal attack. And the place to begin is with whole logs right after they're felled. Start by checking the bark. If it's sound, it's okay to leave it on the log. However, be sure to remove any loose bark because it will invite fungi to take up residence and start the decay process.

The next—and probably most important—step is to seal the end grain of the log. Again, do this immediately after felling. Sealing this area is important because the severed ends of the cell cavities release moisture much more quickly than the long-grain fibers, and fast water removal results in checking as the wood dries out too quickly. If you wait or ignore this step altogether,

As soon as you've cut your logs, thoroughly cover them with paint or wax on their ends to retard checking.

your beautiful log will become scrap. You can use ordinary house paint or a product made specifically for the purpose: a wax suspended in a water-based emulsion. Using a paintbrush, make sure to apply a thick coat to both ends of the log.

Stacks of wood dry
in the air under
cover at the
Nakashima work-
shops in New Hope,
Pennsylvania.

Sawyer Mike Peters
uses a shipping
container for a kiln,
operating it 24 hours
a day.

Drying Techniques

The hobbyist and small-shop woodworker
who is drying his or her own wood should
first let it air-dry, even if it will ultimately be
kiln-dried as the final step. Initial air-drying
is more economical and gives the wood time
to relax while losing much of its free water.
Although large commercial kiln operators
will stack freshly cut material in their kilns,
chances are you'd have some serious problems if you tried this approach yourself. It's
likely that checking and interior splits would
turn your prized stock into a firewood pile.
So even if you're thinking of using a kiln for
drying, you should become familiar with the
air-drying process.

First stack all your wood in piles so air
can get around it (see the drawing on facing
page). Once the wood has dried to around
20 percent MC, you have two options: Put it
into a kiln or leave it to dry further. Most of
the commercial wood we use is kiln-dried. If

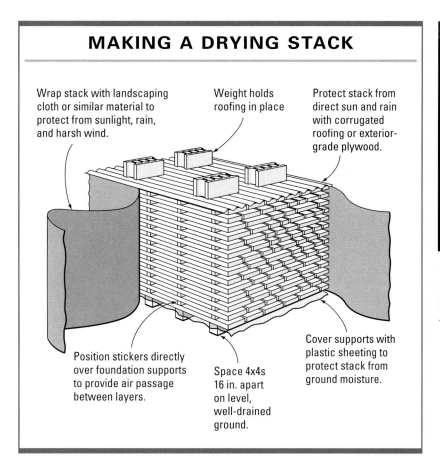

MAKING A DRYING STACK

Wrap stack with landscaping cloth or similar material to protect from sunlight, rain, and harsh wind.

Weight holds roofing in place

Protect stack from direct sun and rain with corrugated roofing or exterior-grade plywood.

Position stickers directly over foundation supports to provide air passage between layers.

Space 4x4s 16 in. apart on level, well-drained ground.

Cover supports with plastic sheeting to protect stack from ground moisture.

Not uncommon with kiln-dried wood, cupping on the inside face of these resawn boards indicates case-hardening, a condition caused by improper drying.

done correctly, the operation yields wonderfully stable, uniform stock in a relatively short time. While kiln-drying has the advantage of speeding up the drying process, air-drying has its own benefits.

Air-Drying

The biggest advantage of air-drying wood is the utter simplicity of the process. With some careful preparation, all you need is a flat area in which to store your stock and a little time. Another plus is that wood dried by air alone is free of some of the stresses that kiln-drying often imparts. One such unpleasant characteristic is case-hardening, in which the outside, or shell, of a board has been dried too quickly, creating stress in

the interior, or core. You can spot a case-hardened board at the mill by looking for small, isolated checks on the face of a board. In the shop, you've got case-hardened wood if you rip a board in half and see cupping across the inside face. Sometimes a board will cup to the outside, a reverse situation of case-hardening. Serious case-hardening can result in honeycombing, where the stresses in the core create small tears, or checks, in the center of the wood, typically in dense, thick woods. You'll want to avoid material with any of these traits.

Another potential benefit of air-drying lumber is the preservation of its color. Woods like walnut have richer, more vibrant hues when left to dry outdoors. However,

Isolated splits deep within wood result from severe case-hardening. Called "honeycombing," the defect is difficult to see without opening up a board.

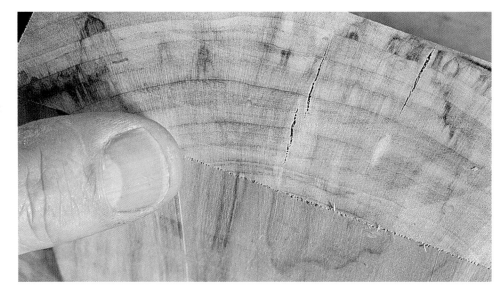

the reverse is sometimes the case, as with pear, which takes on a deeper tone when dried inside a kiln with moisture and heat. It's worth experimenting with drying different woods both ways to see which approach works best for you.

A general rule of thumb for air-drying wood is to wait one year for every inch of thickness. However, this depends on climate and species. Softer, lower-density woods such as pine or poplar generally dry more quickly than denser species such as oak or rosewood. Still, many woodworkers use this rule as a guideline for drying. Therefore, if you have a stack of 8/4 (2-in.-thick) wood, you might have to wait as long as two years before it's dry enough to bring indoors.

Outdoors, wood will typically only dry to about 20 percent MC, depending on the climate and species. Bringing it into an enclosed but unheated building like a barn or shed can lower the moisture to around 12 percent MC. This intermediate step is often a matter of convenience and allows you to store wood that's almost, but not

quite, ready for working, without cluttering up your shop. Eventually, though, you'll have to bring your stickered stash inside an environmentally controlled (heated) building like your home or shop to get it down to 6 percent to 8 percent MC.

Once your wood has dried to within this range, you'll want to continue monitoring it with a moisture meter to see that it remains within the range or has reached equilibrium with its new environment (EMC).

▶ See *"Reading Moisture in Wood"* on p. 81.

In general, it takes about a month for wood to reach this desired state and acclimate to indoor conditions.

Kiln Drying

Overall, drying wood in a kiln is much faster than air-drying and allows you to work the wood much sooner. In general, you should air-dry your stock for six months to a year before putting it into a kiln. When loading the kiln, stack the lumber in much the same

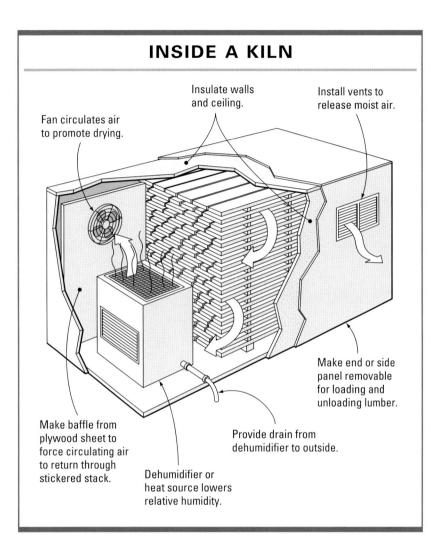

INSIDE A KILN

Fan circulates air to promote drying.

Insulate walls and ceiling.

Install vents to release moist air.

Make baffle from plywood sheet to force circulating air to return through stickered stack.

Dehumidifier or heat source lowers relative humidity.

Provide drain from dehumidifier to outside.

Make end or side panel removable for loading and unloading lumber.

manner that you stacked it outdoors, keeping it stickered so air can flow freely around the boards.

The working components of a kiln are very simple, and many woodworkers make their own from salvaged and otherwise foraged parts. The kiln will need to be insulated on the inside and impervious to the weather. Shipping containers make excellent kiln boxes, or you can construct a container from sheets of plywood insulated with rigid foam. Inside, a fan circulates the moist air while a large dehumidifier—often coupled with a heating unit—pulls moisture from the pile

(see the drawing above). Commercial kilns use an electronic controller that records the moisture content in the kiln, but a handheld moisture meter will suffice and allows you to keep tabs on the condition of sample boards.

Kiln-drying schedules vary, depending on the species and thickness, but one to two months is not uncommon for bringing wood down to around 7 percent MC. After removing lumber from the kiln, remember to store it in the shop for a few weeks before working it so it can attain equilibrium with your shop's ambient humidity.

Stickering a Pile

Proper stacking of freshly cut boards is vital for keeping your wood flat and ensuring that it dries in the correct manner. It's best to pick level ground that's shielded from prevailing winds and direct sunlight. A dry spot under some trees usually does the trick.

Here, sawyer Mike Peters begins laying out a stack by placing a pair of 10-ft.-long 4x4s on the ground. He uses a level and short 4x4s on top of the beams to level them with each other, using shims under the beams where necessary **(A)**. Next, Peters positions a series of short 4x4s across the ground beams, spacing them every 16 in. on center and making a center mark on both ends of each crossbeam **(B, C)**.

When stickering like this, begin stacking the first layer by placing your wood across the crossbeams, with the outermost board flush with the ends of the beams **(D)**. As you stack, butt each board up to its neighbor. Subsequent drying and shrinking ensures that there will be an adequate gap between boards for a good flow of air **(E)**. When you get to the opposite side, measure the width of the stack at each end to ensure that it's even. This is critical to a making a stable stack, especially with the first layer **(F)**.

For the second layer and all subsequent layers, place stickers across the previous layer and directly over the center marks you made earlier **(G)**. Use only fully dried wood for your stickers (kiln-dried is best), making them ¾ in. to 1 in. square, and be sure to choose a mild species such as poplar or maple that won't leach extractives and other stains into your pile and discolor it.

[VARIATION] Instead of using wood stickers, you can buy a commercial plastic variety. The plastic tubes have concave surfaces that reduce contact area with the wood, and the material itself helps eliminate sticker stain.

Build the second layer as you did the first, keeping the boards together with their ends flush **(H)**. It's best to work with the same lengths of boards when possible, but if you have shorts, make sure to place them so they're supported by the stickers and are as even as possible with at least one outside edge. As before, make sure the last board in the layer is even with the edge of the stack **(I)**.

[VARIATION] To speed up making a stack, Peters designed and built an L-shaped metal enclosure that lets him sticker his wood right off the mill. He butts boards into the corner, which ensures that the stack stays even, and then he moves the pile with a forklift to a suitable drying spot.

Continue building layers until you reach an appropriate height. Generally, it's best to keep your stacks under 8 ft. tall so they're stable and easy to access. To protect the pile from rain and sun, you'll need a roof of some sort. Sheet-metal roofing works well as long as it extends past the pile a few inches and is weighed down with concrete blocks or stumps of wood. Peters uses his tractor to lift a prefabricated roof made from sheet metal screwed to an old pallet to cap off a finished stack **(J)**.

VARIATION

H

I

VARIATION

J

Wrapping a Stack

A properly stacked and stickered pile will stand for years. And with a roof on top it will dry without taking on or releasing excessive moisture. But in really humid or dry climates, adding fabric around the pile will minimize the effect of the sun, rain, and wind, ensuring that your wood dries more evenly.

One option is to use regular landscaping cloth, which lasts a couple of seasons before breaking down. Starting at one corner of the stack, screw one end of the cloth to the top of the pile under the roof, either into one of your boards or into the roof structure **(A)**. Then walk the cloth around the sides of the pile, securing it at every corner with more screws. To avoid damaging the fabric, make sure the cloth doesn't rub against the boards **(B)**. When you're done, the material should be well secured at the corners and hang loosely at each side **(C)**.

[VARIATION] For the best protection of your stacks, you can use a material called Shade-Dri™, one of several products made expressly for this purpose. This special material shields the sides of your pile from sunlight, rain, and strong winds, while its open-weave construction allows air to pass through for good ventilation. Although more expensive than landscaping cloth, the material is designed to withstand years of weather.

UPS for small boards, or common carrier for larger stock, and orders are often filled the same day. Many companies do not require a particular minimum order, and some will even walk you through the selection process over the phone, offering advice on cut and figure and hand-picking boards for you.

Thankfully, dealers who are in the business of mailing wood are for the most part reputable people providing a quality product, and you can rest assured that you'll receive wood that's good enough for fine furniture. This is often a great way to get spectacular boards for that special project.

A good hardwood supplier stocks a variety of species and often will surface your wood for an extra fee.

A

B

C

D

Picking Lumberyard Wood

Going in person to the lumberyard has some real advantages over ordering by phone. Most yards let you hand-pick through their stacks (as long as you restack the pile the way you found it), which gives you the opportunity to get some really great wood—and steer clear of the bad stuff. Like woodworker Gabe Aucott here, you'd be wise to wear heavy work gloves when shopping for wood, since roughsawn stock is notorious for its splinters **(A)**.

Getting to know the quality of wood at a particular supplier is important. It usually takes several visits to become familiar with what it stocks. And to avoid the pitfalls that lead to buying "bad" lumber on your next lumberyard visit, it's a good idea to bring a few supplies that will help you in your board selection.

Bring a moisture meter for reading the wood's moisture content to ensure that it has been dried properly **(B)**.

▶ See *"Reading Moisture in Wood"* on p. 81.

Carry a tape rule as well as your project's cutting list, if possible. Use the rule to check widths and lengths, and then mark the parts off your list **(C)**. Whether you're buying lumber for particular projects or just stocking up the shop, carry a calculator so you can tally the amount of wood in board feet **(D)**.

Before pulling anything from the racks, check the ends of boards to note their end-grain orientation. This will tell you whether you've got plainsawn, riftsawn, or quartersawn wood. Have a small plane handy so you can take a few swipes to remove paint or rough saw marks, allowing you a better view of the grain pattern **(E)**. You might get lucky and find two or more sequential boards that were sawn adjacent to each other in the tree, which would allow you to bookmatch grain patterns and colors. Look for complementary grain lines or similar saw marks on the end grain as clues, and then inspect the faces of the boards to see if they are indeed a match.

As you start pulling boards from the rack, inspect each one systematically. First, sight down a board's length to check for warp, such as twist, bow, or cup **(F)**. Then look for obvious defects such as sticker stain, knots, and end checks **(G)**. If you haven't rejected the board at this point, inspect it closely for signs of improper drying.

(Continued on p. 64.)

Avoid any boards with a series of tiny surface cracks, which can indicate an overly accelerated drying schedule **(H)**. Also look for small, individual splits surrounded by good wood, a sign of case-hardening **(I)**.

If a board checks out so far, try smoothing a small area on the face with a block plane (always ask first!) to inspect the color and figure **(J)**. Over time, as you gain experience shopping for lumberyard wood, you start to see all these tell-tale signs of good wood with your eyes alone, and it won't be necessary to bring along all the accessories.

Once you've selected your boards, it's time to load up. Remember that most yards stock boards up to 16 ft. long. As a precaution, carry a small crosscut saw with you, just in case the yard can't (or won't) crosscut wood and the board you've got is too long for your vehicle to carry safely **(K)**. When you load your stash, abide by the rule of thirds: Make sure two-thirds of the wood is supported by your vehicle (tailgates up, please), and don't forget to tie the cargo as a unit securely to the vehicle **(L)**. Otherwise, you'll risk losing the load down the road. Finally, make sure any overhanging lumber is properly flagged to warn following motorists. If you ask, most lumberyards will provide a square of red plastic to make your load more visible **(M)**.

Storing Lumber

Handling Sheet Goods

➤ Lifting and Carrying Plywood (p. 71)

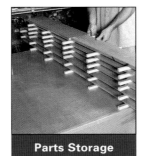

Parts Storage

➤ Stickering Parts (p. 73)

➤ Weighting a Stack (p. 74)

➤ Protecting with Shrink Wrap (p. 75)

Stocking up on wood is one thing, but it's important to store it in a manner that keeps it in good condition. Luckily, there are several proven methods shown in this section for storing your stock, from stashing it in outdoor sheds and barns to storing it in a variety of indoor areas that will keep it in prime condition. Handling and storing plywood is also an issue for those of us who work this bulky and heavy sheet material. I'll show you how to move it without breaking your back, and how to store it properly so it—and you—stay in good shape for years to come.

As woodworkers, we typically work our wood in stints from day to day. But leaving parts of a project lying around at the end of a day invites disaster in the form of warp. I'll discuss how best to store your parts in process while you take a break, so you can come back to the same great stuff you started with.

Storing in Sheds and Barns

Many woodworkers like to store a large part of their wood supply in an enclosed but unheated area, such as a barn, keeping the more valuable real estate of the shop free from unnecessary clutter. Keep in mind that wood stored in an unheated space will have a high moisture content and must be allowed to acclimate to indoor conditions for a few weeks or so before being worked.

Rafter storage and a cement floor allow you to keep your stock outdoors, but out of the weather.

Woodworker Sam Maloof's vented storage box, made from plywood and covered with a plastic tarp, keeps hundreds of board feet of lumber dry without the investment in a dedicated building.

➤ See *"Drying Lumber"* on p. 48.

There are a few precautions to take when storing wood in an unheated space. Material must be kept from the rain and sun, so a good roof and walls are in order. Stack your wood in an orderly fashion, and make sure to keep it off the bare earth to prevent ground moisture from finding its way into the pile and ruining your treasure. Most sheds and barns provide a desirable flow of air while offering important protection from direct wind. Avoid areas that get too hot or dry, such as an unvented attic. Your wood will become too dry and possibly cup, twist, and split.

Open sheds make great storage areas, as long as the stock doesn't sit on dirt. One simple solution is to build a storage box from exterior-grade plywood. Incorporate vents in the side to promote good airflow, and a tarp for a roof.

Many woodworkers build a dedicated wood-storage building for housing their material. A concrete pad keeps out moisture, and large doors provide easy access. Inside, it pays to have good lighting from either standard light fixtures or, better yet, from large windows and skylights that provide natural daylight. If you lay your wood flat, make sure to raise stacks off the floor by using dry 4x4s or other suitable spacers. Consider standing long boards on end to conserve space, which also allows you to leaf through the boards like the pages of a book.

A large woodshed with a cement floor and wide-opening doors is a stockpiler's dream come true for storing lots of wood.

Keep your stacks off the floor by resting them up on large wood supports.

High ceilings and good light in the form of skylights help you stock and select the boards you need.

Woodworker Mira Nakashima inspects a plank stored vertically without having to hoist its heavy weight.

Stocking Material in the Shop

The benefits of storing wood in the shop are compelling. Your material is always at hand, and after it's been in the shop for a few weeks, it will be in equilibrium with your shop's environment, meaning it is stable and ready to work when you are. But, it is important to keep any wood in the shop organized and accessible.

You basically have two options for storing raw material in the shop: You can store it horizontally or vertically. The first approach usually requires less space, while the second method makes picking and sorting through your stash a little easier.

Where possible, I like to store my wood vertically against a wall so I can more easily inspect its condition, figure, and color. Keep in mind that this approach eats up valuable wall space and requires high ceilings for long lumber, as well as some means of keeping planks from tipping over. The simplest approach is to strap a board to the wall. For bigger collections, you can bolt standard

Woodworker Sam Maloof stands by a prized board. A stout strap hooked to the wall ensures that the panel remains upright.

Furniture maker Lon Schleining's shop-made rack houses short or long stock and keeps it organized in sectioned bays.

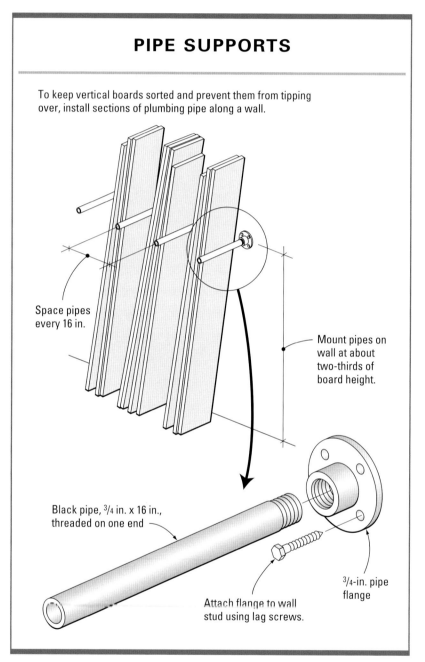

PIPE SUPPORTS

To keep vertical boards sorted and prevent them from tipping over, install sections of plumbing pipe along a wall.

Space pipes every 16 in.

Mount pipes on wall at about two-thirds of board height.

Black pipe, 3/4 in. x 16 in., threaded on one end

3/4-in. pipe flange

Attach flange to wall stud using lag screws.

plumbing pipe to a wall to keep boards better organized (see the drawing above). Another scheme is to construct a wooden rack from scrap wood and plywood and separate your stock with wooden sticks every foot or so. For the ultimate in organization, consider building dedicated racks for individual species.

Storing wood horizontally lets you stack a lot of material in a relatively small area. One approach is to build a freestanding rack, which can be accessible from both sides and includes a center section for storing sheet goods. For walls, you can buy a commercial rack made from tubular steel

If you have the space, consider building individual racks for specific species or types of wood, such as the stands shown here that store figured maple boards.

Woodworker Paul Anthony's free-standing rack is a wonder of organization in a relatively small space. Depending on the rack placement, stock can be accessed from all sides.

This commercial metal rack features stout steel arms that can be adjusted to the shelf height you need.

with adjustable supports, making it versatile and plenty strong.

Don't overlook plywood storage. These large 4-ft.-by-8-ft. sheets can consume a lot of shop space if you don't figure out a viable means of keeping them organized and accessible. Storing your sheets flat will keep them that way, but most of us can't give up the floor space this entails. A vertical rack is a better option and can be made from sheets of plywood and other leftover stock lying around in the shop. If you separate sheets with plywood dividers and keep the rack

The plywood rack in cabinetmaker Frank Klausz's shop stores numerous panels in a vertical position, taking up a minimum of precious floor space.

Stickering wood on a flat bench and placing a few heavy I-beams on top will keep stock straight and flat and ready to go when you return to work on it.

Wrapping parts in plastic prevents them from falling prey to wild swings in ambient moisture levels, keeping them flat and stable.

full, you'll avoid sagging or bowing of individual sheets.

As you work your wood, you'll need to stash it between sessions. When you do, it's vital to store all solid wood in the correct manner, because fluctuating moisture levels can wreak havoc on milled parts. At this point, you've invested a lot of time and effort to get your parts dimensioned straight, flat, and square. Left carelessly on a bench, they'll invariably warp.

There are a few shop strategies you can adopt for keeping your wood in good condition as you're working it into furniture. Whenever possible, stack milled parts horizontally on a known flat surface such as your bench. Use stickers between them and place weight on top to keep the stack flat.

If you don't have the space for stacking parts horizontally or if your work is irregular in shape, try wrapping it in plastic to ward off fluctuating humidity levels. This simple approach keeps your stock stable until you can work it again.

Lifting and Carrying Plywood

Moving large sheets of plywood alone can challenge the best of us, and storing them in a well-supported and accessible manner is a must. To place a sheet in a vertical plywood rack, cabinetmaker Klaus Hilgers tilts it on one corner **(A)** and then eases the leading corner between two other sheets in the rack **(B)**. Then he simply pushes the sheet home **(C)**.

One of the hardest parts of pulling a sheet from the rack is getting it started. To help, you can make a simple wooden lever **(D)** and place it under the bottom corner of a sheet **(E)**. By stepping repeatedly on the stick **(F)**, you'll ease the

(Continued on p. 72.)

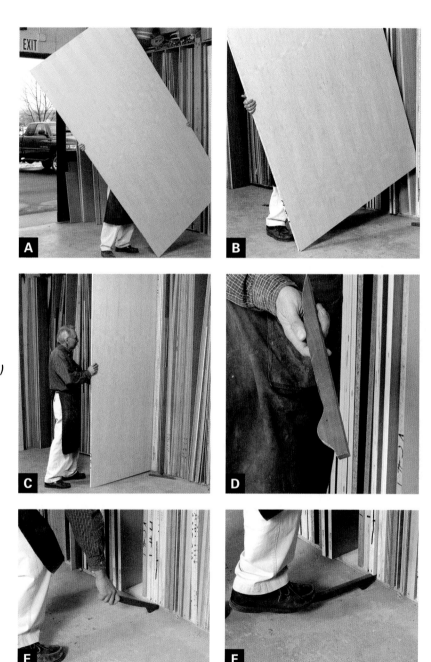

first few inches of the panel out of the rack so your hands can get a grip **(G)**. Then it's a simple matter of pulling the rest of the sheet from the rack **(H)**.

Never use your back to lift a sheet; instead, use your legs. With the sheet standing upright, grip the edges with your legs bent **(I)**. Then straighten your legs to lift the sheet **(J)**. Now, without changing your hand position, pivot it horizontally and let the side of your body and shoulder carry the weight as you take it to the saw or out the door **(K)**.

Stickering Parts

Stacking parts in process is very similar to stickering wood outdoors, except you're usually working with precisely machined pieces that you've spent a lot of time flattening. To keep them that way when they're not being worked, start by laying out a series of identically thicknessed stickers every foot or so on a dead-flat surface, such as a bench **(A)**.

Start stacking by placing your longest, heaviest board on top of the stickers. It's okay if your boards are longer than your stacking surface, but make sure your bottom board is thick enough to resist sagging on its unsupported ends **(B)**. Next, place another series of stickers on top of the board, aligning them over the stickers below **(C)**.

Continue building the stack in layers, placing boards over each new series of stickers until you've stacked all of the pieces. Put your smallest boards on top. If you have multiple boards in one layer, make sure they're the same thickness and butt their ends together over the same sticker for good support **(D)**.

Weighting a Stack

Weighting a stacked pile of parts helps keep it flat. Start by placing pairs of sticks on top of the work and in line with the stickers below **(A)**. Then grab whatever is handy and heavy and place each weight over each pair of sticks. I keep a collection of iron parts and bricks on hand for this very task **(B)**.

[VARIATION] Many of us have weights lying around the shop in the form of heavy cast-iron planes. These work well for weighting down your work, especially big jointer planes.

Don't forget to weight down any lone areas that aren't supported by boards above **(C)**. The finished stack should have weight evenly distributed over the length of the pile so your wood stays flat until you're ready to work it again **(D)**.

Protecting with Shrink Wrap

One way to ensure stability of parts in process or to safely store veneer is to wrap it in plastic. Shrink wrap—a thin sheet plastic that sticks to itself—is perfect for protecting parts from drastic changes in ambient humidity **(A)**. To cover a batch of parts, unroll a section of the plastic on the bench and lay the parts on top **(B)**. Pull the leading edge over the work and "stick" it to the trailing sheet, pulling tight to keep parts snug **(C)**. Now start wrapping around the work, orienting the roll so it unrolls to the outside of the work **(D)**. Wrap several times to tighten the bundle, flipping the work over until four of the six faces are well sealed **(E)**.

Twist the roll a couple of times to create an "X" **(F)** and then wrap the remaining two faces **(G)**. Cross the plastic again to use it much like rope so it pulls the pile tight **(H)**. Finish up by punching through the thin film to tear it from the roll while pressing it flat to stick it to the bundle **(I)**.

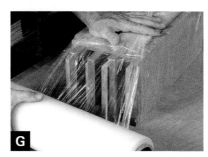

Dealing with Wood Movement, Page 78

Choosing Joints, Page 104

Selecting Your Material, Page 123

from your home's heating system to cool the shop down a bit until it reaches the desired relative humidity. Last, try running a humidifier. These devices are relatively inexpensive and offer a quick way to add more moisture to the air.

During summer months, it's common for the shop's air to become overly moist. This is especially true with basement or other below-grade shops. If your shop becomes excessively wet during a humid spell, you can use a dehumidifier to pull moisture from the air. And don't overlook air-conditioning. If you have it in the house, it may be possible to direct it into the shop. Air-conditioning is even more effective for drying out the air, but keep a watchful eye on your hygrometer to avoid creating an overly dry atmosphere.

Reading Moisture in Wood

Knowing the precise moisture content of your wood will help you keep your stock at optimum moisture levels. First, you'll need to know whether the wood you're about to work has stabilized to shop conditions. You can check this by monitoring its moisture content over the course of a few weeks. When your weekly readings stop changing, the wood has acclimated to the shop's environment and is ready to work. In addition, you'll want to keep track of the moisture content in specific pieces of wood during the course of regular woodworking. You'll also want to check moisture content when acquiring wood from an unfamiliar supplier.

The easiest way to check your stock is to use a moisture meter. While a moisture meter can mean an investment of $200 or more, it pays off as a proven tool for accurately monitoring the moisture content

During high humidity, a centrally placed dehumidifier can help dry the air. This unit—located under the bench for easy access—collects water in a removable container.

of your wood. A modern handheld moisture meter will serve most small shops well. There are two principal types of meters: pin and pinless.

Pin-type meters use metal pins that you drive or press into the wood to measure the electrical resistance of the water in the wood, which is then expressed in a percentage of moisture content. For accuracy, the pins should be driven in to at least one-fifth of the board's thickness to avoid reading the

The pin-style moisture meter at left includes a remote probe with long pins for reaching the center of thick stock. The short pins on the center meter are simply pushed into the stock. The pinless meter at right won't mar your boards.

drier wood at the surface. Some pin-style meters include a remote probe that can be hammered deep into thick boards for an accurate reading of the core. The shorter pins on some pin-style meters are meant to be pressed into the surface by hand. However, dense woods such as oak or hard maple may resist full insertion of the pins, impeding an accurate reading.

Pinless meters are generally more expensive, but will not leave holes in your wood—a distinct advantage, especially if you're taking readings on finished work. A pinless meter relies on radio frequencies to read moisture below the surface and requires only contact with the face of a board. It will take a reading well below the board's surface to arrive at an accurate average moisture content.

Regardless of the style of meter you buy, shop for one that reads at least as low as 6 percent MC, in order to accurately read stock that has been seasoned enough to use for furniture.

Predicting Wood's Movement

Once you're working with stable stock of a known moisture content, you still have to contend with wood movement. Part of this involves being able to predict how much a given board will move over its width and how evenly. To find out what our stock is likely to do, we must first recognize two important forms of wood movement that concern us as woodworkers: tangential movement and radial movement.

Shrinkage Percentage from Green to Oven-Dry

Wood Type	Radial	Tangential	R/T Ratio	Wood Type	Radial	Tangential	R/T Ratio
Alder, red	4.4	7.3	1.7	Lauan, red	4.6	7.2	1.6
Ash, black	5.0	7.8	1.6	Locust	4.6	7.2	1.6
Ash, white	4.9	7.8	1.6	Madrone, Pacific	5.6	12.4	2.2
Aspen, white	3.5	6.7	1.9	Mahogany, African	2.5	4.5	1.8
Balsa	3.0	7.6	2.5	Mahogany, American	3.0	4.1	1.3
Basswood	6.6	9.3	1.4	Maple, bigleaf	3.7	7.1	1.9
Beech American	5.5	11.9	2.2	Maple, red	4.0	8.6	2.1
Birch, yellow	7.3	9.5	1.3	Maple, sugar	4.8	9.9	2.1
Bubinga	5.8	8.4	1.4	Oak, northern red	4.0	8.6	2.1
Butternut	3.4	6.4	1.9	Oak, white	5.6	10.5	1.9
Catalupa	2.5	4.9	2.0	Pine, eastern white	2.1	6.1	2.9
Cedar, Spanish	4.1	6.3	1.5	Pine, sugar	2.9	5.6	1.9
Cedar, western red	2.4	5.0	2.1	Pine, western white	4.1	7.4	1.8
Cedar, yellow	2.8	6.0	2.1	Poplar, yellow	4.6	8.2	1.8
Cherry, black	3.7	7.1	1.9	Purpleheart	3.2	6.1	1.9
Chestnut	3.4	6.7	2.0	Redwood (old growth)	2.6	4.4	1.7
Cocobolo	2.7	4.3	1.6	Redwood (young growth)	2.2	4.9	2.2
Cottonwood, eastern	3.9	9.2	2.4	Rosewood, Brazilian	2.9	4.6	1.6
Cypress, bald	3.8	6.2	1.6	Rosewood, Indian	2.7	5.8	2.1
Ebony, Gabon	9.2	10.8	1.2	Sapele	4.6	7.4	1.6
Ebony, Maccassar	5.4	8.8	1.6	Sassafras	4.0	6.2	1.6
Elm, American	4.2	9.5	2.3	Spruce, Sitka	4.3	7.5	1.7
Fir, douglas	4.1	7.6	9.1	Sweetgum	5.3	10.2	1.9
Hickory, shagbark	7.0	10.5	1.4	Sycamore	5.0	8.4	1.7
Holly, American	4.8	9.9	2.1	Teak	2.2	4.0	1.8
Hornbeam, American	5.7	11.4	2.0	Walnut, black	5.5	7.8	1.4
Imbuya	2.7	6.0	2.2	Willow, black	3.3	8.7	2.6
Ipe	6.6	8.0	1.2				
Jarrah	7.7	11.0	1.4				

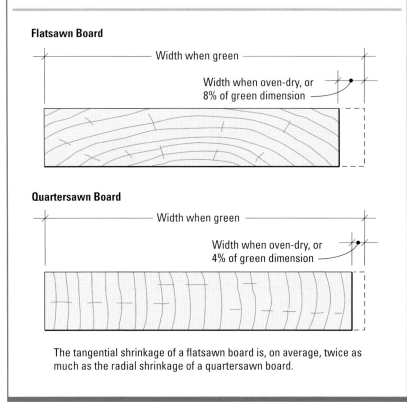

TANGENTIAL VERSUS RADIAL SHRINKAGE

Flatsawn Board

Width when green

Width when oven-dry, or 8% of green dimension

Quartersawn Board

Width when green

Width when oven-dry, or 4% of green dimension

The tangential shrinkage of a flatsawn board is, on average, twice as much as the radial shrinkage of a quartersawn board.

As wood initially dries from its green condition to a suitable moisture content, the amount of shrinkage it experiences differs, depending on its grain orientation. This is best exemplified by comparing two different cuts of wood dried from their green to oven-dry state, where no moisture is left in the pores (see the drawing above). As the drawing shows, tangential shrinkage, which takes place parallel to the growth rings, is about twice as great as the radial shrinkage that occurs perpendicular to the growth rings. (Keep in mind that movement along the grain is negligible.)

From these facts we can deduce the general principle that suitably dried flatsawn wood will shrink and expand across its width about twice as much as quartersawn stock. We could save ourselves a ton of trouble by simply working with quartersawn stock all the time, but this isn't really practical. The reality is that the cut of most boards is a mix of plainsawn and riftsawn wood. Fewer boards include true quartersawn wood.

Now let's add to this the fact that different species of wood move at different rates. For any species, the difference between its tangential shrinkage and its radial shrinkage can be expressed as a ratio (see the chart on p. 83). In general, the lower the ratio, the less prone the wood is to wild dimensional changes and warp. The most stable woods are those with a relatively low shrinkage percentage and a low tangential-to-radial shrinkage ratio, such as mahogany or teak. Conversely, woods with a higher shrinkage percentage and tangential/radial ratio, such as beech and some of the oaks, are prone to wilder swings in movement.

While few of us work with green stock, and no one uses oven-dry wood, these percentages provide a good idea of the range of wood movement you can expect from various species.

Designing for Movement

Good furniture design must accommodate wood movement to ensure that our joints and other constructions will survive us. Remember that the moisture content of wood constantly changes in response to its environment. Ideally, you would construct and assemble your wood parts at the mid-range

ACCOMMODATING WOOD MOVEMENT

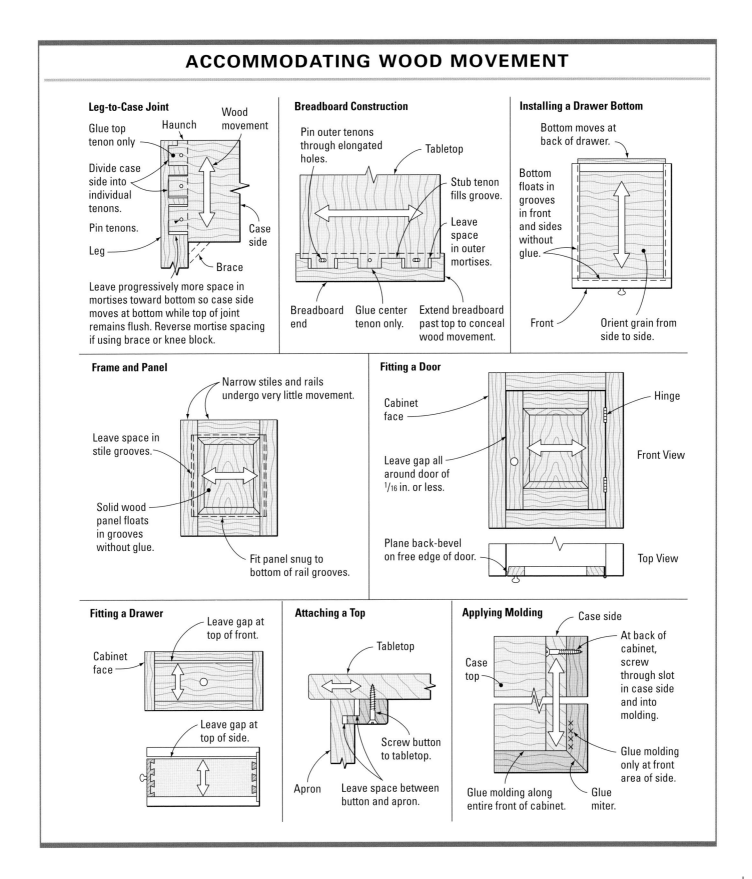

Leg-to-Case Joint

Glue top tenon only

Haunch

Wood movement

Divide case side into individual tenons.

Pin tenons.

Leg

Brace

Case side

Leave progressively more space in mortises toward bottom so case side moves at bottom while top of joint remains flush. Reverse mortise spacing if using brace or knee block.

Breadboard Construction

Pin outer tenons through elongated holes.

Tabletop

Stub tenon fills groove.

Leave space in outer mortises.

Breadboard end

Glue center tenon only.

Extend breadboard past top to conceal wood movement.

Installing a Drawer Bottom

Bottom moves at back of drawer.

Bottom floats in grooves in front and sides without glue.

Front

Orient grain from side to side.

Frame and Panel

Narrow stiles and rails undergo very little movement.

Leave space in stile grooves.

Solid wood panel floats in grooves without glue.

Fit panel snug to bottom of rail grooves.

Fitting a Door

Cabinet face

Hinge

Leave gap all around door of 1/16 in. or less.

Front View

Plane back-bevel on free edge of door.

Top View

Fitting a Drawer

Leave gap at top of front.

Cabinet face

Leave gap at top of side.

Attaching a Top

Tabletop

Screw button to tabletop.

Apron

Leave space between button and apron.

Applying Molding

Case side

At back of cabinet, screw through slot in case side and into molding.

Case top

Glue molding only at front area of side.

Glue molding along entire front of cabinet.

Glue miter.

of expected MC. This way, dimensional changes would occur on either side of this median. However, this goal isn't very practical unless you have total control over the humidity in your shop.

To avoid trouble, it's best to use wood with a moisture content between 6 percent and 8 percent. But there's a wrinkle: Our completed projects will be subjected to greater swings in MC, anywhere from 4 percent MC to 14 percent MC. This depends, of course, on where your furniture resides and the specific atmospheric conditions surrounding it.

Dry Climates

Now let's add another twist: You might be building in a relatively dry part of the country, but your furniture may someday live in a much wetter climate. Therefore, rather than building to our specific geographic conditions, it's safer and ultimately more successful to build our furniture to accommodate the greatest possible extremes of dimensional change.

But where to start? How can we accurately calculate swelling and shrinking of our furniture parts?

The best approach is to become familiar with seasonal relative humidity levels in your shop. If you're building during the middle of summer, your stock is likely to be at its highest moisture content, and you should allow for parts to shrink when the dry winter weather rolls around. For example, when fitting tongue-and-groove backboards into a cabinet during the humid season, you should butt the boards tightly against each

other. As the air dries, the joints between the boards will open a little. Conversely, in winter you need to fit parts a little loosely so they have room to swell when the humid summer returns.

How much room do you allow for movement? Start by assuming most kiln- and air-dried woods will change dimensions by as much as $1/4$ in. for every 12 in. of width, if you're working with flatsawn stock. Due to the many types of woods and their individual idiosyncrasies, this is only an approximation, but it's close enough to encompass most situations. The best teacher is the experience gained from tracking the dimensional changes of a specific wood as you work with it.

Once you understand wood's seasonal expansion and contraction, building furniture to accommodate wood movement isn't difficult. The trick is to understand the different types of constructions and joinery that allow wood movement to take place. The drawing on p. 85 shows some of the more common approaches to dealing with wood movement.

Using a Moisture Meter

Using a pinless-style meter is very simple. Because the device reads below the surface, you can place the meter right on the wood to get an accurate reading at its core. Keep in mind that some less expensive meters only measure to a depth of ⅝ in. or so and may not provide an exact reading of the MC at the core of thick boards. As with all meters, be sure to read 6 in. or so in from the end of a board to avoid this drier area, and stay away from knots **(A)**.

Using a pin-style meter can be more complicated. For a rough estimate of moisture, work on the face and in from the end of the board, making sure that the pins have good contact with the wood **(B)**.

For a more accurate reading, first crosscut 6 in. to 12 in. off the end of a board **(C)**. Then press the pins as deeply as possible into the center of the stock and take your reading **(D)**.

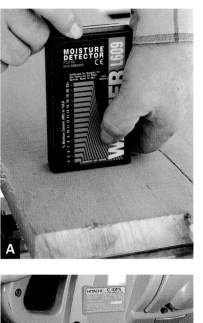

A

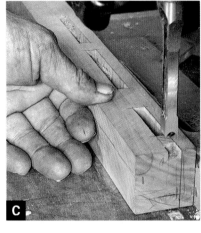

C

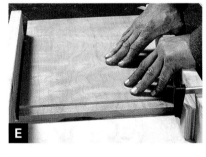

E

G

B

D

F

Cutting a Leg-to-Case Joint

In a leg-to-case joint, where a wide rail connects to a leg with a mortise-and-tenon joint, the tenons on the rail should be divided to allow room for the side to move. The first step is to lay out the joint on both the rail and leg, leaving room at the bottom of the joint for the rail to swell or shrink while the top of the joint remains flush. (Or you can reverse the order, allowing the upper part of the joint to move. This works best for pieces with fixed knee blocks below the rail, such as a lowboy. An overhanging top conceals the movement at the top.) Divide the rail into multiple tenons, each less than 4 in. wide, perhaps with a haunch at the top to prevent twist. Then lay out the mortises, leaving progressively more space on either side of the tenons as you move down the leg (**A**).

Cut the mortises first. You can cut them using either a plunge router and a jig or a benchtop hollow mortiser, as shown here. Make your first cuts at each end of the mortise, and then finish up by wasting the middle section (**B**). Reset the chisel depth and cut the groove for the haunch at the top of each leg (**C**).

After cutting the mortises, make the tenons to fit them. Saw the cheeks first, using a dado blade and a crosscut sled. Place the stock flat on the sled and cut the first side using a stop block clamped to the sled's fence to define the shoulder (**D**). Then flip the stock over and cut the opposing cheek (**E**).

Next, cut the haunched tenon by standing the rail on its edge and raising the blade height. Keep the same stop-block setting you used for the shoulders. Make the first pass by holding the stock firmly against the fence and away from the block (**F**). Now add a spacer stick equal to the desired haunch length against the stop block and hold the stock against the stick to cut the haunch to the correct length (**G**).

After cutting the haunch, reset the blade height and cut the opposite short shoulder by using the same stop-block setting, but without the spacer **(H)**. This shoulder doesn't include a haunch.

Lay out the tenons once again, this time on the cheeks. Then reset the blade height, stand the rail vertically, and plow out the waste to create the separate tenons **(I)**. Test the fit of your tenons in their mortises by dry-assembling the joint by hand, using no clamps. If the tenons are too tight, trim the cheeks with fine cuts from a shoulder plane **(J)**.

The upper tenon gets fixed in place, while the two lower tenons are permitted to move with seasonal changes. Pegging the tenons will strengthen the joint, but correct peg-hole layout is the key to accommodating this movement. First, dry-assemble the joint and use a drill bit or a hollow-chisel mortiser to cut through both the leg and the rail at once, making sure the holes are centered on the width of the tenons. Then disassemble the joint and elongate the two lower tenon peg holes, using a piercing saw to first lengthen the peg-hole shoulders **(K)**. Follow up by squaring the ends of the holes with a mortise chisel **(L)**.

To assemble the joint, apply glue to the upper tenon only and its mortise **(M)**. Clamp square across the joint, drop a dab of glue into the peg holes, and drive the pegs into the leg and through the tenons **(N)**. The finished joint has nice, tight shoulders with functional and decorative pegs standing slightly proud of the surface **(O)**.

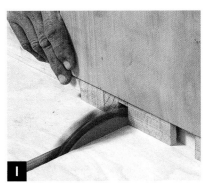

A

B

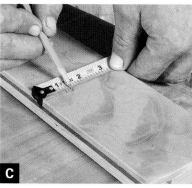

C

D

E

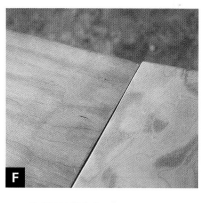

F

G

H

Constructing a Breadboard End

Adding a breadboard end to a wide solid-wood slab such as a tabletop helps prevent the slab from warping or cupping, without restricting wood movement. The joint is made in the same way as a leg-to-case joint, except that you fix a central tenon so the slab will expand and contract evenly outward from the center, and you include a stub tenon between each tenon to further stiffen the joint.

Here, furniture maker Jan Derr demonstrates the process. Start by laying out and cutting the mortises in the breadboard ends, then rout or saw a shallow groove along the length of each board. Cut the tenons on the ends of the tabletop to fit the mortises, leaving stub tenons to fill the grooves. As with a leg-to-case joint, make the two outer mortises wider than their mating tenons. For strength, make the central tenon slightly wider than its neighbors **(A)**.

Dry-assemble the joint and use a square to mark the centerline of each tenon on the breadboard end to help with laying out for pegs **(B)**. Then mark the distance of the peg holes from the inner edge of the board **(C)**. Now use a drill or a hollow-chisel mortiser to cut the peg holes through the breadboard end while the joint is assembled **(D)**.

Before going any further, disassemble the joint and lightly chamfer the edges of the breadboard end and the shoulders of the tabletop using a small plane **(E)**. This results in a nice shadow line when the joint is assembled **(F)**.

Next, use a file or a piercing saw to elongate the peg holes in the outer tenons **(G)**, and then square the ends of the holes with a chisel **(H)**.

To add visual detail, use a fine, tapered file to lightly chamfer the edges of the peg holes **(I)**. Cut pegs to fit the holes and chamfer their ends by rubbing them over a piece of sandpaper **(J)**. The chamfer on one end of a peg makes it stand out visually when the table is assembled, while the chamfer on the opposite end eases insertion.

To attach the breadboard end, apply glue to the center mortise only and its mating tenon **(K)**. Tap the joint together, then place a spot of glue in each peg hole and drive in all the pegs. No clamps are necessary, since the pegs hold the joint while the glue dries **(L)**. By carefully tapping the pegs flush with the surface of the breadboard end, you'll create beautiful shadow lines around each peg **(M)**.

[VARIATION] Instead of leaving exposed grooves at the ends of your breadboard ends, you can add a contrasting spline for a more finished look. Rout a groove in the tabletop to match the groove in the breadboard end, and glue the spline in only the breadboard end so the tabletop is free to expand and contract with seasonal changes.

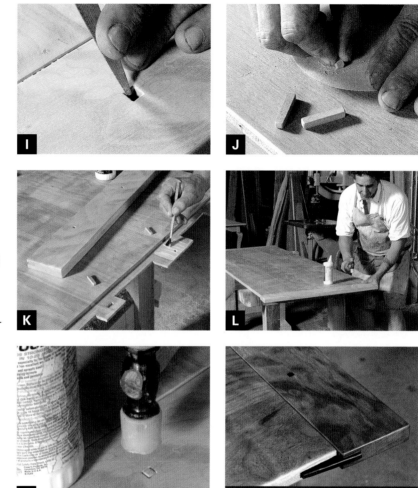

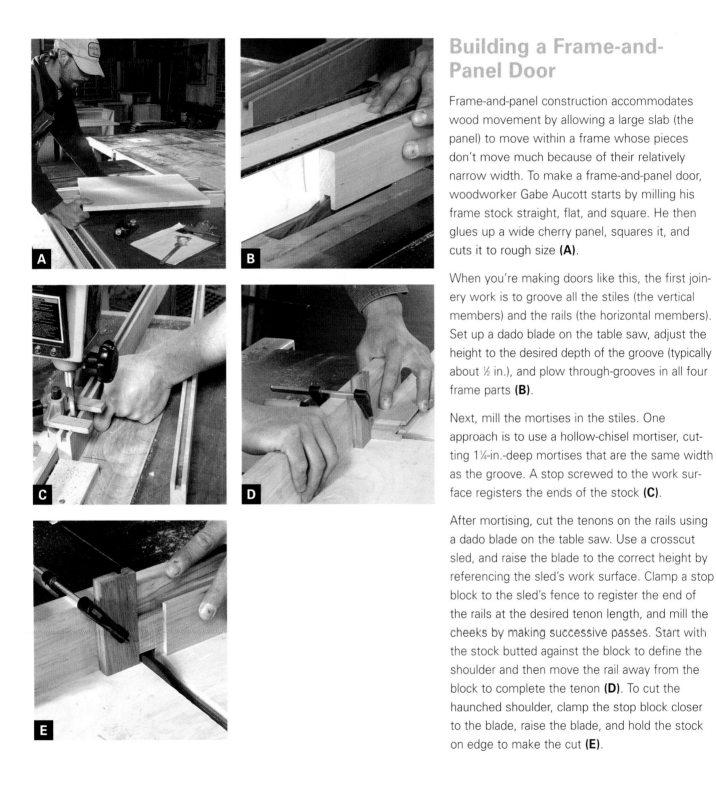

Building a Frame-and-Panel Door

Frame-and-panel construction accommodates wood movement by allowing a large slab (the panel) to move within a frame whose pieces don't move much because of their relatively narrow width. To make a frame-and-panel door, woodworker Gabe Aucott starts by milling his frame stock straight, flat, and square. He then glues up a wide cherry panel, squares it, and cuts it to rough size **(A)**.

When you're making doors like this, the first joinery work is to groove all the stiles (the vertical members) and the rails (the horizontal members). Set up a dado blade on the table saw, adjust the height to the desired depth of the groove (typically about ½ in.), and plow through-grooves in all four frame parts **(B)**.

Next, mill the mortises in the stiles. One approach is to use a hollow-chisel mortiser, cutting 1¼-in.-deep mortises that are the same width as the groove. A stop screwed to the work surface registers the ends of the stock **(C)**.

After mortising, cut the tenons on the rails using a dado blade on the table saw. Use a crosscut sled, and raise the blade to the correct height by referencing the sled's work surface. Clamp a stop block to the sled's fence to register the end of the rails at the desired tenon length, and mill the cheeks by making successive passes. Start with the stock butted against the block to define the shoulder and then move the rail away from the block to complete the tenon **(D)**. To cut the haunched shoulder, clamp the stop block closer to the blade, raise the blade, and hold the stock on edge to make the cut **(E)**.

With the joinery complete, dry-clamp the frame and measure its opening in both directions. At this point, cut the panel to the size of the frame opening plus the combined depth of two grooves. You'll trim the panel for a proper fit later.

Use the router table and a panel-raising bit to raise the panel, beveling its edges and milling a tongue to fit into the frame grooves. Use a featherboard clamped to the fence to keep the stock firmly on the table, and take successively deeper cuts by raising the bit about ⅛ in. after each pass. Make the first cut across the end grain, orienting the panel facedown on the table and pushing the stock at an even speed to avoid burning **(F)**. Make the second cut by rotating the panel 90 degrees and routing the long-grain edge. This cutting sequence removes any tearout from the previous cut **(G)**. Continue in this manner until all four edges are raised and the tongue slides easily by hand into the grooves in the frame pieces.

> ⚠ **WARNING** Use a router that's qualified to spin large, panel-raising bits, and take a succession of relatively light cuts, raising the bit after each pass. Make the last pass a very light cut for the smoothest finish.

To allow for seasonal expansion of the panel within the frame grooves, remove the appropriate amount from the long-grain edges on the jointer **(H)**. In the case of the relatively wide panel shown here, removing about 3⁄16 in. from each edge allows enough room for the panel to swell in the frame without bottoming out in the side grooves. Don't joint the end-grain edges as the

(Continued on p. 94.)

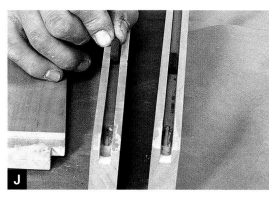

panel won't swell appreciably along the grain. Jointing off material in this manner after sizing the panel to the depth of the grooves ensures that the mitered bevels meet precisely in the corners of the frame. To glue up the door, use a small brush to spread glue in the mortises and on the tenons only. Be careful not to get any glue in the grooves or on the panel so it can float freely after assembly **(I)**. To keep the panel centered in its grooves and to prevent rattling, place a couple of rubber spacers in the grooves in the stiles **(J)**. These commercially available spacers will compress when the panel expands, and then swell again when the panel shrinks, holding it in place without damaging the joints.

Place the work on a flat surface, and clamp across the joints, making sure to align the clamps square to the work and centered over the tenons **(K)**. Before leaving the panel to dry, check diagonal corner measurements to ensure that the frame is square.

Fitting a Door

To fit a frame-and-panel door to its opening, begin by sizing the door to completely fill its opening in the cabinet. After assembly, square the door, just in case things got a little out of whack during glue-up. To do this, place the assembled door on a crosscut sled and trim about ¹⁄₃₂ in. off one end **(A)**. Then place the sawn end against the rip fence and trim another ¹⁄₃₂ in. from the opposite end, producing a panel that's square to its sides **(B)**.

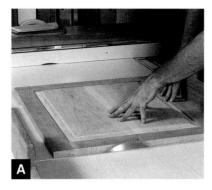

Once you've squared the door, check its fit to the case. Position a couple of shims on the bottom of the cabinet opening, equal in thickness to the desired door gap (about ¹⁄₁₆ in.), and place the door atop the shims. Temporarily tape the door to hold it in place **(C)**. Now check the gap along one stile. Chances are you'll notice a taper, which tells you the door opening did not come together perfectly square **(D)**.

Note the amount of taper, and take the door to the bench for planing. Clamp the panel securely in a vise, and use a bench plane to remove the same amount of taper, but from the appropriate edge of one end of the door—not its side **(E)**. As you plane, keep test-fitting the door in the opening as before. When the side gap is straight, crosscut about ¹⁄₃₂ in. off the opposite end of the door using the rip fence on the table saw **(F)**. Of course, this approach assumes the top and bottom case rails are perfectly parallel. If they're not, you'll need to plane, rather than crosscut, the opposite end to suit the amount of taper.

(Continued on p. 96.)

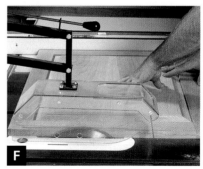

Test-fit the door again. This time, hold the hinge stile tight against the opening and inspect the gap at the top of the door, checking that it's straight, consistent along its length, and equal to the gap at the bottom **(G)**. If it isn't, make any corrections now on the top edge with the plane.

Now it's time to install the hinges. At this point, the door should be too wide to fit the opening, so you'll need to first remove some material from one edge to allow clearance for the hinges. You can do this on the table saw by ripping about 1/16 in. from the hinge stile. Alternatively, you can handplane the stile, taking relatively aggressive cuts **(H)**.

Once you've installed the hinges, check the fit again, this time sighting the gap along the free-swinging stile. The gap will probably be too small for clearance at this point and may still taper along its length **(I)**. To provide clearance, remove the door from the case and plane a slight back-bevel on the edge of the stile **(J, K)**.

Once again, hang the door on its hinges and check your gaps **(L)**. The finished door should have a consistent gap of 1/16 in. or less all the way around the cabinet opening **(M)**.

Installing a Drawer Bottom

When you're installing a solid-wood drawer bottom, it should never be glued in place, and the grain should be oriented side-to-side. That way, the bottom is free to expand towards the rear of the drawer where it passes under the drawer back. If the grain runs front-to-back, the bottom will expand against the sides of the drawer, causing an ill fit and possibly breaking the drawer joints apart. A plywood bottom can be fitted in any direction and glued into the grooves, since it won't swell or shrink as a solid panel will.

Crosscut the bottom to length using a crosscut sled on the table saw **(A)**. The length should equal the side-to-side drawer-box opening plus the combined depth of the opposing grooves milled in the drawer sides.

Next, mark lines on the stock as an aid to beveling its edges so it will fit the grooves in the drawer box. First, use a marking gauge to scribe lines around the edges of the bottom equal to the width of the drawer grooves **(B)**. Then mark pencil lines on the underside of the stock on the sides and front, roughly equal to the width of the desired bevel. Use a finger as a fence to guide the pencil **(C)**.

Use a small plane to begin planing a bevel on the three edges, or stand the work vertically against the rip fence and use the table saw to make this cut. Start with the end-grain edges first **(D)** and stop when you reach the gauge line **(E)**.

(Continued on p. 98.)

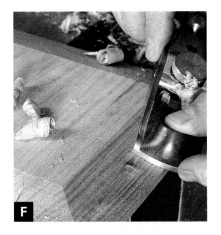

Finish with the long-grain edge to remove any tearout on the corners from the previous end-grain cuts. On the last few passes, set the iron for a very light cut to leave a smooth surface with very little tearout **(F)**.

Go back to the table saw and, standing the stock vertically in the crosscut sled, notch the back of the panel for a screw **(G)**. Then slide the panel into the grooves in the drawer box and drive a screw through the notch and into the underside of the drawer back **(H)**. You can leave the drawer bottom proud of the back, which allows the panel to shrink if necessary, without showing a gap in the drawer **(I)**.

The finished drawer bottom will swell or shrink towards the back of the drawer, where it won't affect the joinery of the drawer box **(J)**.

Fitting a Drawer

There are two significant areas of wood movement in a drawer: the drawer front and the drawer sides. These areas require clearance to allow the stock to swell across its width without jamming in the cabinet opening. Building a drawer so it operates smoothly involves a few careful steps.

To determine the correct width of the drawer stock, offer it up to the drawer opening and mark it to the exact height of the opening **(A)**. Rip the sides and front to this width. Now cut one end of the drawer-front stock square, and use the same approach to gauge the length of the drawer front by marking the precise length of the opening on the stock **(B)**. Once the parts are cut to width and length, you can assemble the drawer box. Don't install a knob or pull at this point.

If you build your drawer in the manner described above, it shouldn't quite fit its opening. To get the right fit, start by planing the sides of the drawer with a plane set for a very fine cut. Clamp a stout board across your bench, and, with the drawer bottom removed, support the drawer on the board as you plane the sides. To avoid tearout at the corners, first plane inward from one end of the drawer **(C)**, and then from the opposite end **(D)**. Keep shaving the sides in this manner until the box just fits into the opening from side to side. But be careful; taking two or three extra shavings can result in a loose-fitting drawer that racks as it slides in and out of the opening, causing it to stick.

To help with checking the fit, install a screw in the drawer front as a dummy handle for pulling the drawer out of the opening **(E)**.

(Continued on p. 100.)

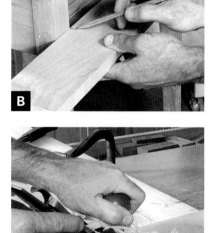

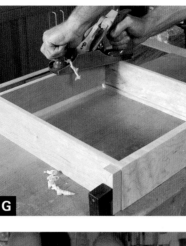

Next, reduce the height of the drawer by clamping it to the bench and using the same plane to level the top and bottom edges **(F)**. To keep the edges square, rotate the plane around the corners so its sole is supported throughout the cut **(G)**. Make sure to plane both the top and bottom of the drawer, and use a flat surface such as your bench to check that the box is flat. Keep working the height of the drawer down until you have an appropriate gap. For example, a 3-in.-high drawer should have a clearance of around $\frac{1}{16}$ in., while a 12-in.-high drawer might require as much as $\frac{1}{4}$ in., depending on the wood species and whether you're fitting in dry or wet weather.

The correct side-to-side fit leaves almost no gap between the drawer sides and the opening. The thickness of a dollar bill is about right **(H)**. With the drawer fully installed, you should have a small, consistent gap above the drawer front **(I)**. For symmetry, you can plane a small bevel on the bottom edge to create a matching gap at the bottom of the drawer. The last step is to check that the front is flush with the frame. If the drawer needs a stop, install it now. If the front isn't flush when the drawer is pushed all the way in, remove the screw and plane the face until everything looks good. Then install the drawer bottom, mount a knob or handle, and you're done.

Attaching a Tabletop

L-shaped wood "buttons" are a great way to attach a tabletop to its base while allowing the top to expand and contract during seasonal changes. Make buttons by starting with a long strip of wood. Use a crosscut sled and a ½-in.-wide dado blade to mill a series of evenly spaced, ½-in.-wide notches along the strip. A stick of wood nailed to the sled's base registers each previous notch, making cutting multiple notches a snap **(A)**.

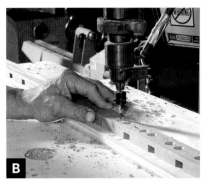

Next, use the drill press and a drill/countersink bit to drill two countersunk clearance holes in each button for a pair of screws. Register the work-piece against a low fence **(B)**. Crosscut individual buttons from the strip with a miter saw, aligning the blade with the shoulder of each notch. This technique leaves a tongue about ⅜ in. long **(C)**. Use a stationary belt sander or the bandsaw to miter the ends of the tongues to accommodate the curvature of the slots you'll cut.

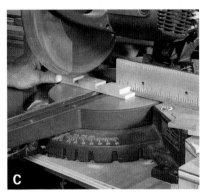

Next, cut the slots in the table apron to accept the tongues of the buttons. This can be done using a slotting cutter in a router, but I prefer to use a biscuit joiner. I set the cutter on the biscuit joiner to cut just below the thickness of what will be the upper face of the tongue. An easy way to do this is to hold a button up to the machine, project the blade, and adjust the fence height by eye **(D)**. This technique ensures that the buttons place sufficient pressure against the top when they're installed.

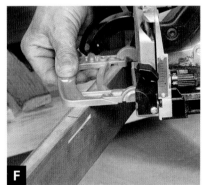

Set the joiner's cutting depth to "20," and plunge a series of slots in the table apron. Make the first series of cuts at the first fence setting **(E)** to produce a notch at the correct depth from the top of the apron **(F)**.

(Continued on p. 102.)

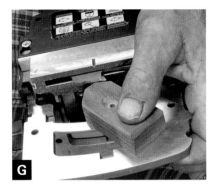

Then reset the fence, using a button tongue as before, but this time measuring from its lower face **(G)**. Now repeat all the slotting cuts around the frame to widen the slots for the buttons **(H)**.

To attach the top, place all the buttons that are oriented parallel to the tabletop grain tight against the aprons (typically the end aprons on a table) **(I)**. The buttons that get oriented perpendicular to the grain (usually along the long aprons) are spaced to leave a gap that allows the top to swell without bowing the apron outward **(J)**. Ten buttons will suffice to hold a reasonably large top to a base. Placing pairs of buttons close to the legs in each corner not only holds the top tight but helps to strengthen these corner joints **(K)**.

Applying Case Molding

To attach moldings across the side of a wide case, you must allow for the swelling and shrinking of the case. The first step is to cut and miter the front molding, and then glue it full length to the front of the cabinet. Next, install a dovetail bit in the router table and plow a dovetail socket into the back of each side molding **(A)**. Then miter and fit the side moldings to the front molding and flush with the back, but don't install them yet.

Rout a set of dovetail blocks to fit the sockets in the side moldings, using the same bit. The easiest approach is to mill a piece of wood that's slightly thicker than the width of the dovetail bit and oversize in length and width. Without changing the bit height, make the first pass to shape half the dovetail, routing both edges so you make two tail blanks from one piece of stock. If you set up the fence correctly, the bit should remove just a hair of wood along the side of the stock at the widest part of the tail **(B)**. Turn the stock around and rout the second pass on each edge to create the full dovetail **(C)**. Then rip the tail sections from the blank and crosscut them into individual dovetail blocks about 3 in. long.

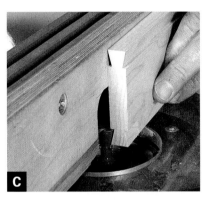
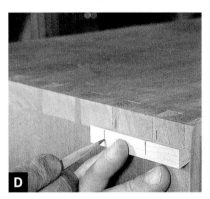

If you're attaching molding over case joinery such as for through dovetails, where end grain is exposed, be sure to drill the screw holes into face-grain sections **(D)**. Then attach the dovetail blocks to each case side with screws, spacing them equally across the sides of the case **(E)**.

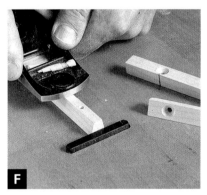

Test the fit of the tails in the socket by sliding the molding over the blocks and onto the case from the back. If the molding isn't tight to the sides of the case, you can easily tweak the fit. Simply unscrew the blocks and plane a little wood off the back of each **(F)**. Once the molding fits snugly, apply glue to the miters and the front 3 in. or so of each case side, and slide each side molding onto the case from the back **(G)**.

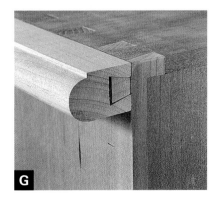

Choosing Joints

A T THE HEART of your furniture is the joinery holding it all together. While this book doesn't go into the specifics of constructing joints (see *The Complete Illustrated Guide to Joinery* by Gary Rogowski, The Taunton Press), it's important to understand when to use the appropriate joints for your work and how to design them so they're strong and durable. You need to size your components correctly, considering the thickness of a mortise cheek wall, the length of a tenon, or the slope of a dovetail. Not to be forgotten is the all-important fit of a joint. Too loose, and a joint can fall apart; too tight, and you'll have problems during assembly. And of course, wood movement must be taken into account for your joints to last. This section takes a look at these joinery issues so you can be confident that your constructions will get years of enjoyable use.

Designing a Joint

The success of a particular joint depends on your choosing the right material, sizing the joint correctly, milling and cutting it accurately, and assembling it in the proper order. It's vital to remember that wood has its physical limits, beyond which you risk joint failure. Also, it's important to understand that glued end-grain surfaces offer little strength. This is why effective joints are designed to provide long-grain-to-long-grain contact, such as on the mating surface between tenon cheeks and mortise walls in a mortise-and-tenon joint. Bear in mind that many long-grain joints actually consist of two or more long-grain parts running cross-grain to each other. With this type of joint, such as for a mortise and tenon, you'll need

A long tenon with smooth cheeks makes a good connection. Clean up rough surfaces with a plane or shoulder plane, and chamfer the end of the tenon with a chisel to ease assembly.

Mortises should be deep with relatively clean cheeks. (A rough bottom is okay.) To test the strength of the outside walls, squeeze them with your fingers.

to keep parts relatively narrow to minimize the amount of movement each part undergoes as it expands or contracts across its mating part.

▶ See *"Understanding Wood Movement"* on p. 7.

For mechanical strength as well as gluing strength, joints must be carefully dimensioned so the parts work in unison. In a mortise-and-tenon joint, for example, the tenon should be long and stout. Short tenons don't have sufficient penetration to hold in a mortise, and thin tenons risk breaking under stress. Mortises must be deep enough to house a tenon, and the cheek walls should be thick enough so they won't crack or give way under stress, as shown in the photo above. Intersecting parts—the tenon cheeks and the walls of the mortise—should have smooth faces so they make close contact with each other.

When it comes to sizing tenons, my rule of thumb is to make them as long as the receiving mortise will allow—which is some-

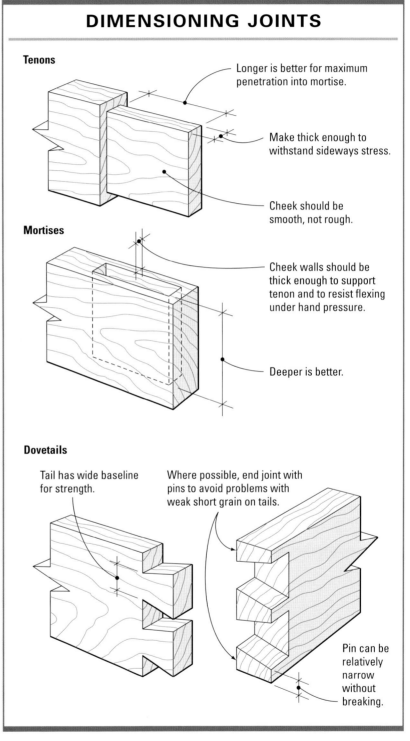

DIMENSIONING JOINTS

Tenons

Longer is better for maximum penetration into mortise.

Make thick enough to withstand sideways stress.

Cheek should be smooth, not rough.

Mortises

Cheek walls should be thick enough to support tenon and to resist flexing under hand pressure.

Deeper is better.

Dovetails

Tail has wide baseline for strength.

Where possible, end joint with pins to avoid problems with weak short grain on tails.

Pin can be relatively narrow without breaking.

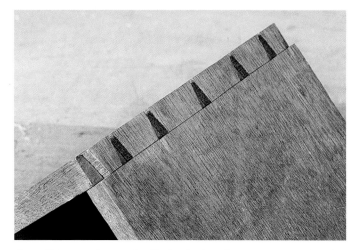

A well-formed set of tails includes the proper angle of slope and a wide baseline to prevent snapping. For strength, the joint should terminate with pins at each end, not tails.

avoid extremely acute angles when laying out dovetails because the tips of the tails and pins become fragile and can break off. Conversely, a shallow angle won't provide the mechanical lock that this joint is known for. Generally, angles of between 7 degrees and 14 degrees are adequate for strength, with more acute angles for softer woods. Widely spaced pins are the norm because they ensure wide tail baselines for strength. And ending on the edge of the work with a pin—not a tail—keeps this area strong thanks to the long-grain orientation of the pin.

If you use tenons, mortises, and dovetails as examples of general design rules, then it's a simple matter of applying the same principles to all your other joinery.

Testing Your Joints

The best way to find out if your joints are up to par is to put them to the test. I routinely assemble sample joints, then pound on 'em or cut 'em apart to check their strength. One unfailing criteria is that if the wood surrounding the joint breaks or fails, then the joint itself is sufficiently strong for your purposes. The simplest way to test this is to glue up an edge joint, and then break it intentionally. If the fibers on either side of the glueline give way, then you can rest assured that the joint is stronger than the wood you're using.

The fit of a joint is always the key to its strength. The goal is to have intimate wood-to-wood contact inside the joint. Glue alone will not hold joints over the long haul. To check the contact, you can saw apart a glued joint to inspect the inside.

In the real world, we typically don't have the time or resources to test all our joints.

times limited by my tooling. A typical tenon destined to fit into $^{3}/_{4}$-in.-thick stock should be at least 1 in. long, but longer is even better. In the same $^{3}/_{4}$-in.-thick stock, the mortise should be $^{1}/_{4}$ in. or $^{5}/_{16}$ in. wide, which makes for a sufficiently thick tenon while providing mortise walls sturdy enough to withstand the strain of daily use. Another way of looking at this is to use the rule of thirds: When sizing a mortise, make its width equal to one-third of the thickness of the stock. This rule won't necessarily apply in all situations, since you can make a thick tenon with relatively narrow shoulders as long as the cheeks in the adjoining mortise are sufficiently thick, such as when when you join a thin rail to a thicker post. And you can size a mortise wider than one-third when the stock is particularly thick. Still, the rule of thirds is a good place to start.

Dovetails provide another good example of how to design and dimension a joint. The slope of the tails and pins, plus their spacing, can make or break the joint. You'll want to

With the joint line slightly overhanging the bench, whack the panel (left) to test the joint. A well-made joint shows torn fibers around the glueline but not along the joint itself (right).

This sawn-apart joint reveals a tight-fitting biscuit that's securely bonded in its slot.

But there's a simple hands-on test that you should do with all your joints. It's the trial fit, which means assembling the joint without glue. For example, when cutting a mortise-and-tenon joint, you should hand-fit the tenon into its mortise. If you can insert the tenon with hand pressure alone, you have a fine-fitting joint. If you have to pound on it with a hammer, you're looking at trouble because the addition of glue will cause

Standard procedure when checking the fit of tenons is to push them into their mortises without glue. A good fit requires hand force alone.

Light taps from a hammer are all that's needed to drive home a well-cut dovetail (left). Look for obvious gaps, and test the fit by wiggling the rail from side to side (right).

Edge-to-edge joints connect long-grain parts. Mating surfaces need to be smooth and straight, and no nails, screws, or biscuits are necessary for a strong bond.

swelling and probable breakage during final assembly. On the other hand, if a tenon drops easily into its mortise with no persuasion, it's too loose, and no amount of glue can compensate for the necessary wood-to-wood contact.

The same approach holds for dovetail joints. A light tap is all that's needed for a perfect fit. Once a joint is assembled, try wiggling it. If you can rack the joint, it's probably too loose, and you'll need to fix the joint or remake your parts for a tighter fit.

Common Joints

The best way to design long-lasting furniture is to understand the joints at your disposal. Once you're familiar with them, you'll need to pay attention to the orientation of the components so joint strength isn't compromised, especially when it comes to wood movement. For a long-lasting connection, some joinery requires the addition of mechanical fasteners such as nails, staples, or screws. The following joints have all proven their worth over time.

Butt Joints

Butt joints are the simplest of all the joints to construct. Edge-to-edge joints are typically used to make wide panels from narrow stock, while end-to-face joints are often used in box construction. When both mating surfaces are long-grain oriented in the same direction, as in an edge joint, no fasteners are necessary as long as the mating surfaces are flat and smooth. To create a smooth surface suitable for gluing, it's best to joint the area, either on the jointer or with a hand plane. Cuts from the table saw are typically

BUTT JOINT

Edge to Edge

Long-grain edges must be straight and smooth for good bond. No fasteners are needed, just glue.

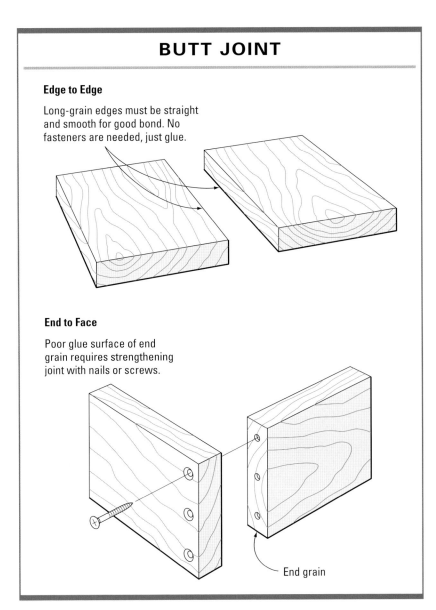

End to Face

Poor glue surface of end grain requires strengthening joint with nails or screws.

End grain

Face frames glued to solid wood or plywood cabinets are long-grain joints and need only sufficient clamping pressure for a lasting joint.

End-grain surfaces, such as in this corner butt joint, must be reinforced with nails or screws.

too rough and scored with saw marks to make a reliable joint that will hold up in use.

▶ See *"Dimensioning Wood"* on p. 142.

When connecting end grain, as in an end-to-face joint, you must reinforce the joint with nails, screws, or other mechanical fasteners because end grain does a poor job of holding glue. Still, it's wise to ensure as good a glue bond as possible by initially sizing the end grain with a preliminary coat of glue lightly thinned with water or simply spread very thinly on the surface. Let this size coat tack up for a few minutes before applying a second coat of fresh glue prior to assembly. This approach lets the thirsty end-grain

Pocket screws driven into the rear face of a centered butt joint help draw the joint tight during assembly and strengthen the end-grain connection.

Corner joints must be reinforced with fasteners, such as these pocket screws driven into the back face of the joint.

RABBETS

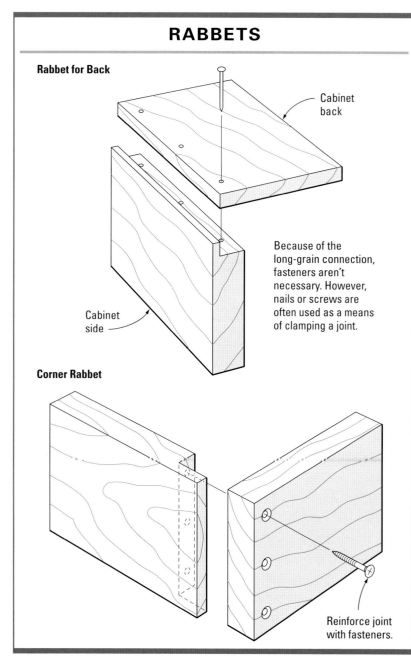

Rabbet for Back

Cabinet back

Because of the long-grain connection, fasteners aren't necessary. However, nails or screws are often used as a means of clamping a joint.

Cabinet side

Corner Rabbet

Reinforce joint with fasteners.

pores fill up with the first coat so the second glue application remains near the surface for a good bond.

Rabbets

A rabbet is an L-shaped notch cut into the edge or end of a piece of wood. In a typical rabbet joint, only one of the members is rabbeted to accept the mating member. A rabbet joint is commonly used in the rear edge of a cabinet side for letting in a cabinet back. A rabbet is also often cut into the ends of drawer parts or cabinet partitions to create a tongue that then fits into a dado or groove. As with butt joints, long-grain-to-long-grain connections can simply be glued, while rabbets with end grain must be reinforced with fasteners.

A standard application for a long-grain rabbet joint is in attaching a case back to a cabinet. The rear edges of the case are rabbeted to accept the case back, hiding the edges of the back while providing a mechanical connection to the case. It's common to

A rabbet milled along the edge of a cabinet side conceals the case back and provides a shoulder to help it withstand racking.

This corner rabbet is a good choice for drawers and other small boxes, but be sure to reinforce the connection with nails or screws.

A double rabbet at a corner provides additional gluing area for increased strength, although fasteners must still be used.

install the case back into its rabbets without glue, for temporary disassembly when you're finishing case parts. You can use screws or other removable fasteners driven through the back and into the case rabbets to make a permanent connection.

End-grain rabbets can be beefed up by machining a double rabbet, so there's increased mechanical advantage that also offers more surface for glue. However, as for all end-grain connections, you must still bolster the joint with nails or screws.

Dadoes

A dado is technically a square-edged slot cut cross-grain into a piece of wood. A groove is of the same shape but runs parallel to the grain. In a dado joint, a dado cut into one of the pieces accepts the end or edge of the mating piece, usually for connecting shelves or partitions. The depth of the dado should be kept relatively shallow to avoid compromising the strength of the dadoed member. For example, when cutting dadoes for join-

ing $\frac{3}{4}$-in.-thick stock, I routinely mill them only $\frac{1}{8}$ in. to $\frac{1}{4}$ in. deep so there's plenty of material below the dado to support the joint or accept fasteners. Even when they are cut to be relatively shallow, the square edges, or walls, of the dado are end grain and have sufficient strength to support the weight of a shelf or another heavy load.

When dadoes are used with solid wood, the grain direction of mating parts should run parallel so they expand and contract in unison. Because the connection of a dado

DADOES

Orient grain in same direction so parts move in unison. Secure with nails, staples, or screws.

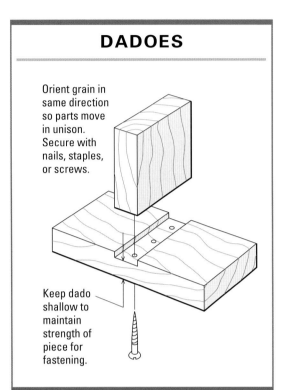

Keep dado shallow to maintain strength of piece for fastening.

A dado is a good joint for connecting small frame parts, but be sure to add nails to strengthen the connection.

A well-cut dado joint has a flat bottom and is relatively shallow, leaving enough thickness to support screws or other fasteners.

joint is end grain to face grain, the joint is often strengthened with nails, staples, or screws. Because of the end-grain-to-face-grain connection, it's also important that the joint be tight, especially in solid wood. When you're joining plywood parts together at right angles, the glued joint is actually stronger than in solid wood because about half a plywood edge typically consists of long grain, and, as we've discussed, long-grain-to-long-grain contact makes the best glued connection.

It's not unusual to use a dado joint to connect plywood to solid wood. For example, you may want to install thick, solid-wood shelves for better weight-bearing strength in a plywood case. In that circumstance, you must leave room for the shelves to expand and contract while the case remains dimensionally stable. You can do this by making the shelves slightly shallower than the depth of the case, and then gluing only the front 4 in. or so of the shelf to the case. Drive a few thin nails through the case and into the ends of the shelf to hold the rest of the joint. The nails will flex slightly while keeping the joint intact as the shelf moves toward the back.

Splines

A spline joint consists of a stick of wood, or spline, that connects two parts that have mating slots milled into their edges, faces, or ends. It's commonly used in box and case construction, or as an effective method for strengthening miters in frame work. Splines can be made from solid wood or thin plywood and glued into place or left dry. When you're using plywood splines, grain direction doesn't matter. Grain orientation in solid-wood splines, however, should be carefully considered. The spline can be either long grain or short grain (running across the width of the spline), depending on the application. In glued frame joints, for example, it's best to orient the grain perpendicular to the joint line for strength. Installing a long-grain spline in a frame joint is inviting disaster, since the spline might split along its length when the joint is stressed.

A long-grain-to-long-grain spline joint can be assembled without glue, allowing adjacent boards room for seasonal movement. If you don't glue a spline into its grooves, orient its grain with the joint line to avoid the risk of snapping the spline during installation.

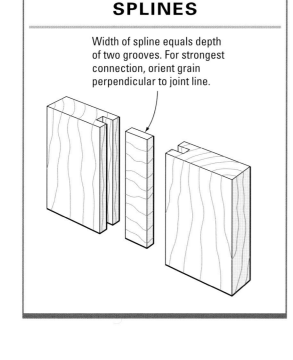

SPLINES

Width of spline equals depth of two grooves. For strongest connection, orient grain perpendicular to joint line.

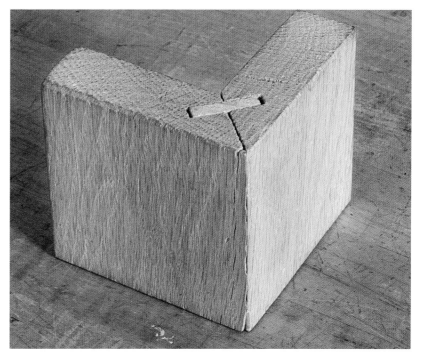

A splined miter helps strengthen this joint and aligns the parts to make assembly easier.

Splines are a good choice for aligning joints, especially when parts are joined at odd angles.

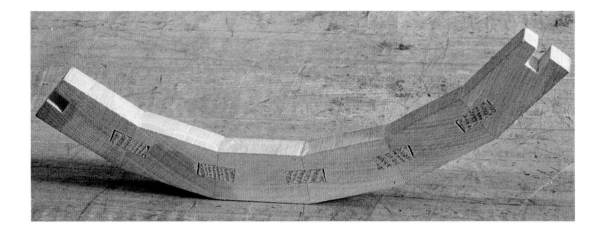

Dry splines are great for aligning parts, such as when you're fitting a series of grooved boards together to form a wider panel. The best example is when you're constructing a solid-wood case back. Here, you'll want to use long-grain splines so the spline itself is strong enough to resist flexing between boards without cracking. Also, when you're making long lengths of splines, it's much more efficient to make long-grain splines, which can be ripped from stock as a single solid length. Cross-grain splines for a long joint would have to be made up from a number of shorter lengths crosscut from wide boards.

Biscuits

Thanks to the simplicity and speed with which it can be cut using a biscuit joiner, the biscuit joint has found its way into many cabinetmakers' shops as a viable substitute for grooves and dadoes. In addition to their use in casework joints, biscuits are great for joining frames. However, the biscuit's relatively shallow penetration does not make this joint a good choice when a lot of strength is required. A deep mortise-and-

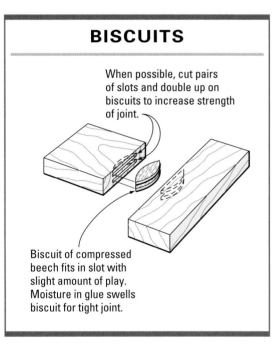

BISCUITS

When possible, cut pairs of slots and double up on biscuits to increase strength of joint.

Biscuit of compressed beech fits in slot with slight amount of play. Moisture in glue swells biscuit for tight joint.

tenon joint is far superior in most applications, although doubling up pairs of biscuits can effectively increase the strength of a joint. Biscuits are particularly useful as alignment aids, such as when edge-joining two boards or gluing lippings to work surfaces.

Made of compressed wood, biscuits are designed to swell when water-based glue is applied, creating a tight joint. However, the relatively large amount of swelling can create

Biscuit joints work well for frame joinery as well as case construction, such as in the corner case joint shown here. When you add water-based glue, the compressed biscuits swell tight in their slots.

problems during and after assembly. With complex assemblies requiring lots of biscuits, I've found that instead of applying glue to each biscuit, it's better to coat the biscuit slots. Installing dry biscuits in the wet slots gives you more time to assemble the joint before the biscuits swell and grab.

After assembling a biscuit joint, be sure to allow enough time for the moisture in the joint to fully evaporate and the wood to stabilize before planing or sanding. On softer woods particularly, the glue moisture can often raise biscuit-sized bumps on the surface of the work. If you level or smooth these areas too soon, you'll be left with football-shaped hollows once the wood dries back to its normal MC. Therefore, let an assembled joint dry at least overnight before working it further.

Dowels

A dowel joint will connect and align parts during assembly and is commonly seen in casework, including drawer boxes and cabinets. You can also use dowels to join frames or chair spindles. To make the joint, you can use a commercial drilling jig to align parts and guide the drill into the stock. However, many woodworkers use their own shopmade alignment jigs for drilling the holes accurately. You can use standard dowel stock for dowels, but spiral-grooved or fluted dowels have superior holding power and are more effective in spreading glue into the joint during assembly.

One inherent problem with a dowel joint stems from its round shape. Dowels and dowel holes must be perfectly round to mate together soundly. This usually isn't a problem during construction and assembly. But over time, the smallest amount of wood movement can deform a dowel or dowel hole into a slight ovoid shape, with the result that only a few areas of the dowel make con-

DOWELS

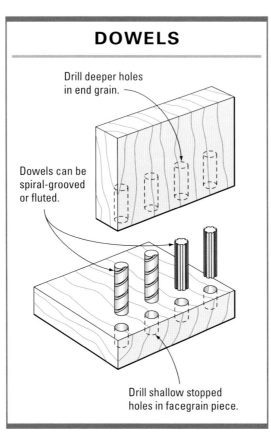

Drill deeper holes in end grain.

Dowels can be spiral-grooved or fluted.

Drill shallow stopped holes in facegrain piece.

Using a series of dowels is an effective method for joining frame pieces or case parts. Dowel holes must line up perfectly, which is possible with the aid of a dowel drilling jig.

tact with the hole. This partial failure at the glueline often precipitates total joint failure. The best way to beat the odds here is to minimize wood movement by using dowels $\frac{1}{2}$ in. or less in diameter.

With today's advances in joinery methods, techniques, and tooling, the common dowel joint has largely been replaced by more efficient joinery methods. But the simplicity of the joint makes it a good candidate for the small shop, especially for the beginner or those of us with limited power tools.

Lap Joints

The lap joint comes in many flavors and is typically used in frame construction to join corners or other intersecting members. The sheer number of variations of this joint and its relative simplicity often make it a good choice for a variety of applications and for woodworkers with limited tooling. Because

LAP JOINT

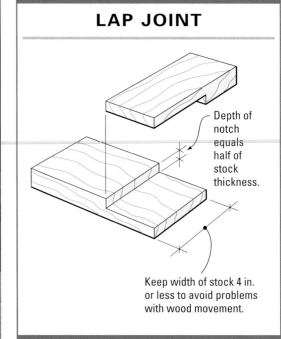

Depth of notch equals half of stock thickness.

Keep width of stock 4 in. or less to avoid problems with wood movement.

it relies on cross-grain connections, the joint should only be used to connect relatively narrow parts. Otherwise, wood movement will eventually break the glue bond. Pieces that are 4 in. wide or less will typically make a strong connection.

To achieve a good glue bond, mating surfaces should be as smooth and flat as possible. Lap joints are easy to make on the table saw using a dado blade and then cleaning up the joint faces afterward with a shoulder plane if necessary. You can cut end laps by carrying the workpiece on end across the blade with a tenoning jig.

When possible, it's a good idea to reinforce the joint with pegs, nails, or other fasteners to help overcome cross-grain wood movement, especially when the joint is subject to great stress, such as in a door frame. Alternatively, you can construct a dovetailed lap to provide mechanical resistance.

An edge lap is similar to a cross lap and is used when joining narrow frames. Here, the stock is turned 90 degrees, and half-notches are cut in the edges instead of the faces.

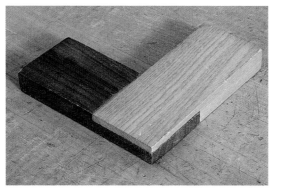

The corner lap is one of the more common types of lap joints and is often used to join simple frames.

The cross-lap joint is useful for connecting parts that intersect at a midpoint, such as in a divided face frame.

A dovetail lap is similar to a basic half lap, with the addition of mechanical resistance in one direction due to the wedging action of the tail.

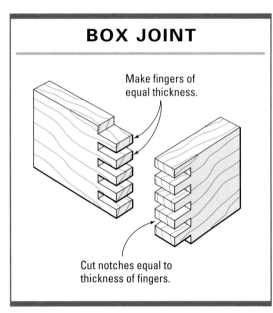

BOX JOINT

Make fingers of equal thickness.

Cut notches equal to thickness of fingers.

The box joint's multiple fingers make it very strong and a good choice for joining the corners on small boxes. Be sure to orient the grain in the same direction around the box to ensure strength and consistent wood movement.

Box Joints

Also known as a finger joint, the box joint consists of identically sized, long-grain "fingers" on the end of one piece that fit into matching sockets cut into the end of the mating piece. As the name implies, the joint is typically used in box making, although it is sometimes found in larger casework.

Wood movement won't be a significant issue as long as you orient the grain around the box. It's a very strong joint because it provides about three times the gluing surface of a butt joint and the mating faces of the fingers are all long grain, not end grain. However, parts intersect across the grain, so fingers should be kept relatively short—say, 1 in. or less—to limit cross-grain wood movement. Luckily, in box making the thickness of the box sides determines the length of each finger, and it's rare that sides are thicker than 1 in., so a well-constructed joint will hold reliably with glue alone.

Mortise-and-Tenon Joints

The mortise and tenon is one of the strongest joints for connecting frames and is found in doors, face frames, table bases, chairs, or wherever you need to join relatively narrow parts cross-grain to each other. I consider it an indispensable joint for furniture making because, when made correctly, it solves the problem of connecting slender parts at right angles to each other in a long-lasting, reliable manner. The key to a successful joint is to proportion the parts correctly, including making the tenon long enough to provide mechanical resistance.

MORTISE-AND-TENON JOINT

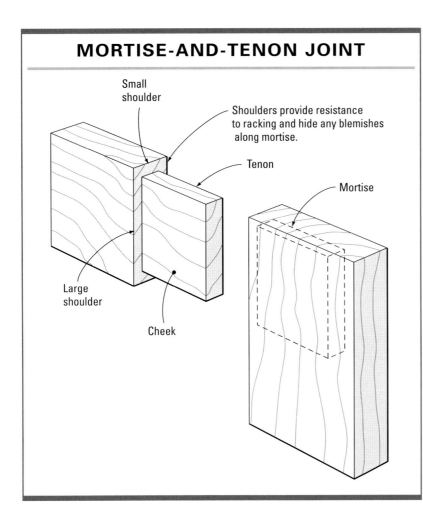

Small shoulder

Shoulders provide resistance to racking and hide any blemishes along mortise.

Tenon

Mortise

Large shoulder

Cheek

The through-tenon joint reveals the end of the tenon and the outside of the mortise. The joint must be cut cleanly for a good look.

Since this is a cross-grain joint, tenon width shouldn't exceed about 4 in., or you risk breaking the glue bond due to seasonal movement. Tenon thickness should be sufficiently stout to resist flexing and breaking. As a rule, I generally machine my tenons to $5/16$ in. thick when joining two pieces of $3/4$-in. stock. When I'm mortising into a thicker mating piece, I'll make the tenon thicker. While laying out the mortise, make sure its outer walls are thick enough to withstand flexing, or they can break under stress. For laying out a mortise in $3/4$-in.-thick stock, a $5/16$-in.-wide mortise centered in the piece will yield outer walls $7/32$ in. thick—just

A wedged through-tenon remains locked in its mortise and adds a touch of decoration.

Sawn apart, this wedged through-tenon joint exposes heavily tapered wedges that spread the tenon to meet the sloped walls of the mortise, creating a mechanical lock.

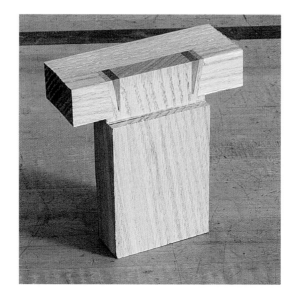

This protruding through-tenon is pinned twice through its cheek to prevent racking, allowing the joint to be assembled without glue.

Another option for through-tenon joints is to allow the tenon to protrude past the adjoining part for visual effect.

shy of ¼ in. and plenty strong in all but the most delicate of woods.

The fit of the tenon in its mortise is of prime importance in this joint, and achieving it can be challenging to novices. The mechanical strength of the joint depends on a "slip fit" of the tenon in its mortise, ensuring that the mating surfaces are in intimate contact with each other before you add glue. Test the fit by dry-assembling the joint. If the parts slide together without pushing, the joint is too loose. On the other hand, if you have to smack it with a hammer, the joint is too tight. The correct fit should require only hand pressure or light hammer taps to bring the joint home.

A plunge router and straight bit guided by a jig is the most economical way for the small-shop woodworker to cut the mortises. The tenons can be cut admirably with a tenoning jig or with a dado blade on the table saw. Regardless of your preferred tooling method, it's best to cut your mortises first, and then fit your tenons to them. That way, if your tenons end up a bit too tight, you can easily reduce their thickness with a few passes from a shoulder plane or some sandpaper wrapped around a flat block of wood. It's much more difficult to adjust the width of a mortise.

Another area to proportion carefully is the length of your tenon respective to the depth of your mortise. It's wise to leave a little space at the bottom of the mortise by cutting your tenons $1/32$ in. or so shorter than your mortise is deep. Since this is an end-grain area with a poor gluing surface anyway, a tight fit here is not critical. More important, this approach ensures that the tenon shoulders tightly abut the mortised piece to provide resistance to racking and a neater overall appearance for the finished joint.

Dovetails

When it comes to connecting slabs and other wide-panel work, the dovetail joint can't be beaten in terms of strength. I consider this joint a staple in my joinery repertoire, like the mortise and tenon, and well worth the effort it takes to make. The joint has a unique visual appeal, and many woodworkers go to great lengths to display it in their work, although traditionally the joint was concealed under moldings or hidden by adjoining parts. Thanks to its wedge-shaped pins and tails, the dovetail joint creates a mechanical connection while still allowing the parts to move uniformly with the seasons. In fact, many dovetail joints don't require any glue for a successful connection. Through and half-blind versions are used for joining drawer boxes and case parts, while

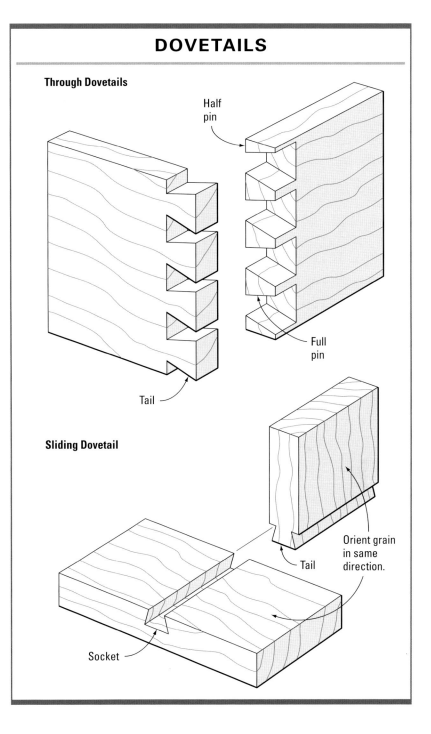

DOVETAILS

Through Dovetails

Half pin

Full pin

Tail

Sliding Dovetail

Orient grain in same direction.

Tail

Socket

Through dovetails are exposed on both faces and form a strong, inter- locking joint.

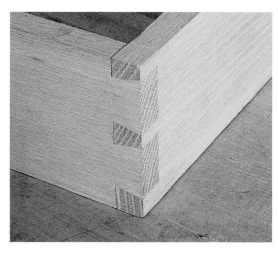

Half-blind dovetails have the same strength as through dovetails but are concealed on one face, making them a good choice for connecting drawer fronts to sides.

Sliding dovetails make sturdy con- nections for shelves and dividers. They can also be assem- bled without glue for telescoping parts, such as table- extension hardware.

sliding dovetails connect shelves, partitions, drawer boxes, or pedestal-style tables.

As with box joints, be sure to orient the grain of adjoining parts in the same direc- tion to prevent cross-grain wood-movement problems. Pin and tail angles between 7 degrees and 14 degrees have sufficient slope to mechanically hold the joint in one direction. To avoid problems with joint deformation and stress failure, limit the use

of steeper angles to denser, stronger woods or to exceptionally long tails.

A router equipped with the appropriate dovetail bit and guided by a commercial or shopmade jig is an excellent choice for cutting this joint. However, hand-cutting this joint can bring tremendous satisfaction. If you've never hand-cut dovetails before, start with some straight-grained pine or other softwood. You won't have to be as fussy with the fit as you would be with hardwood, since the fibers of softer woods will crush together without breaking or splitting. With luck, your pins and tails will fit tight and look great the first time around. With hand-cut through dovetails, there has been a long-standing debate over whether to cut the tails or pins first, since one completed part must be used as a template to mark the adjoining piece. While I am a tails- first kind of guy, it really doesn't matter which methodology you use as long as you're com- fortable with the one you choose.

Selecting Your Material

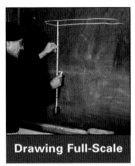

Drawing Full-Scale

➤ Sketching
Dimensions on
the Blackboard
(p. 131)

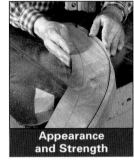

**Appearance
and Strength**

➤ Working Around
Defects (p. 132)

➤ Maximizing Parts
from a Plank (p. 134)

➤ Sawing Out Straight
Grain (p. 136)

➤ Arranging Grain
Between Boards
(p. 137)

➤ Stiffening a Shelf
with Lippings
(p. 138)

➤ Making a Torsion-
Box Shelf (p. 139)

To BUILD STRONG FURNITURE with a
look that says "fine woodworking,"
you'll want to select your material
carefully for the proper strength and visual
attributes. You'll need to ensure that you
don't underbuild a piece, and that parts like
shelves and dividers are stiff and rigid
enough to hold the loads expected of them.

A sketch is often in order to ensure that all
the parts work as a whole and that the proportions are pleasing.

If you want to incorporate curves and
bends in your work, it's worth getting to
know the attributes of working with green,
unseasoned stock. Equally important are
the visual characteristics of your material,
such as its color, tone, and grain markings.
Understanding all these elements and incor-
porating them in your work will help you
select the best material for the best work.

Using Green Wood

"Green woodworking"—the craft of working
with unseasoned stock—is a long-standing
tradition. While most of us want to avoid
green material, it has some distinct qualities
that we can incorporate in our work. For
one, when the wood is fresh and full of
natural moisture, the fibers are in a more
relaxed state that allows us to bend the
wood easily. Another benefit is the relative
softness of green material, which can work
to your advantage when you're carving or
turning. Keep in mind that green wood
will typically warp or crack if not dried in a
controlled manner. Carved or turned bowls
must be stored carefully, often by wrapping
them in plastic or covering them in wet
shavings, so they'll dry slowly.

Green-wood chairmakers often take
advantage of green wood's drastic movement
during drying to make naturally locking
joints. For example, chair legs made of green
wood can be drilled out to accept an over-

Cherry, a notoriously hard wood to bend when dry, is easily pushed into a curve by hand when the wood is fresh and green.

sized tenon on the end of a dry, seasoned chair rung. The oversized tenon is forced into the mortise in the wet, flexible leg without risk of damage. Then, as the leg shrinks, its mortise squeezes onto the dry tenon, deforming into an ovoid shape and locking the parts tightly together.

Using Rived Wood

Rived wood is material that's been cleft, instead of sawn, from a billet of wood. Riving wood produces a workpiece with grain that runs the entire length instead of running out at an edge, which is often the result of sawing wood. Rived material is typically used by chairmakers to produce parts where extra strength is required, such as in spindles and chair rungs.

To rive wood, you begin with a straight log free of knots, branches, or spiraling grain. Use a species that splits well, such as cedar, butternut, or oak. The riving procedure involves laying out a grid on the end of a log and then splitting the log into sections with an ax. You then split each section into individual squares using a froe and a wooden

Turning wood in its green state allows deep, fast cuts that produce less friction, heat, and wear on cutting edges. Long, slurpy shavings are a telltale sign that the wood is wet.

Lay out a grid of squares on the end of a log, and then split the log into sections with an ax by tapping the blade along the lines of each section with a mallet.

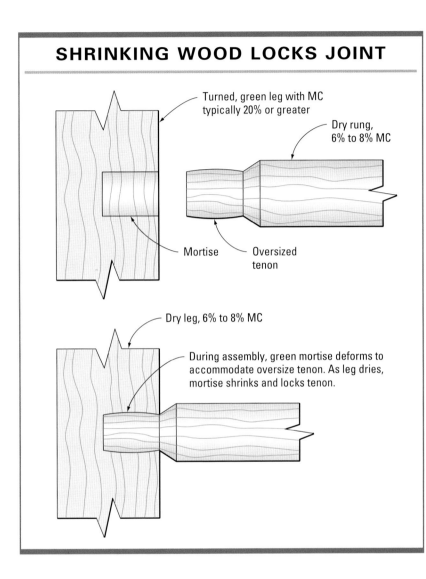

SHRINKING WOOD LOCKS JOINT

Turned, green leg with MC typically 20% or greater

Dry rung, 6% to 8% MC

Mortise

Oversized tenon

Dry leg, 6% to 8% MC

During assembly, green mortise deforms to accommodate oversize tenon. As leg dries, mortise shrinks and locks tenon.

Tap the froe blade into the section to start the split, then lever the tool by hand to separate individual squares.

mallet. This creates pieces of strong stock with true, straight grain. An added benefit of working with such straight-grained material is that it can be easily worked with hand tools due to the negligible grain runout.

Composing Figure, Grain, Color, and Texture

Many of us often overlook the aesthetic attributes of our wood, treating it simply as building material. While it's vital that wood's relative strength, seasonal movement, warp, and natural defects are taken into account, you owe it to yourself to also consider its figure, grain, color, and texture. Careful composition of these characteristics can make your furniture stand out above the crowd. It's important to train your eye to view the aesthetic possibilities that wood provides and to take the time to carefully arrange the grain before cutting your pieces.

As we've seen, wood comes in practically every hue imaginable. The trick is learning how to incorporate these colors in your work without getting carried away and overwhelming a piece. Bold colors such as the

Light, dark, sub-dued, or vibrant—the color range of woods is practically endless. From left to right: yellow poplar, Maccassar ebony, padauk, and crotch walnut.

The colors of this walnut and spalted-maple bench blend harmoniously together, providing visual interest to an otherwise conventional design.

The highly visible, coarse-looking pores of red oak (left) create a different texture and feel compared to the smoother appearance of bigleaf maple (right).

violet shade of purpleheart or the canary-yellow of pau amarillo are typically overpowering if used extensively on a case piece or table. Think small. Brightly colored woods are better left for accents and details like pulls and decorative trim.

▶ See "Wood Species" on p. 273.

Combining two or more woods in the same piece provides an opportunity for dramatic effect. However, it's wise to exercise restraint. Seek a quiet, harmonious blend when choosing your palette. But by all means, experiment and try all sorts of different woods together or alone. For starters, through, try working with more subdued woods to get a feel for the design process. When combining woods, keep the hues similar, using creamy maple, for example, with one of the mild-colored fruitwoods like pear or cherry.

In addition to how you use color, the surface quality of your material also has a big impact on how a piece looks. Oak, ash, and other ring-porous woods with large, open pores reflect light differently than denser diffuse-porous species, such as maple or sycamore, which look more polished. Both types are fine for furniture and can often be combined successfully in one piece. Try to imagine how your chosen wood is going to look in the finished product before you cut any pieces.

Don't forget that certain woods can reflect light in curious ways. Viewed from opposing angles, the same plank can appear darker or lighter, richer or duller, or with the grain patterns more subtle or more prominent. For example, a plank of riftsawn mahogany may display a strong ribbon-stripe pattern when viewed from one direction, while the pattern appears muted when seen from the opposite direction (see the photos on facing page). Whenever possible, arrange boards in a similar direction to minimize any alternating light-and-dark effect. For example, when gluing up a series of boards to create a tabletop, arrange them so that the light plays evenly on all their surfaces.

➤ MARKING YOUR WORK

Before cutting your joints, it pays to make a few marks on your stock to keep things in order and keep track of parts. This is especially true with leg-to-rail joints, where you're typically working with four identical-looking legs. Bundle the four legs together in the order they'll appear in the table, chair, or cabinet, making sure the best-looking faces point to the front, and draw a circle on the top of the bundle, marking the inside faces where the joinery will go. Then number the legs sequentially, which helps keep matching faces in order and aids laying out and cutting the mortises. Later, when you're dealing with a single leg, you'll know right away which face receives joinery and which face is a show side.

Calculating Wood's Strength

One of the greatest mysteries a beginning woodworker faces is understanding the relative strengths of different woods in order to select the best species for a specific application. While the best education derives from working with as many species as possible, a few guidelines can help when you're dealing with unfamiliar woods.

"Strength" can be defined as resistance to any number of stresses placed upon wood, including compression, tension, and shear. But by far the most important factors that contribute to wood's strength are its density and stiffness. Both characteristics give wood the ability to resist bending.

Density is measured as weight per unit volume and is often considered the prime indicator of a wood's strength. For example, a wood that's heavier is generally stronger than a lighter wood. However, in an effort to standardize comparisons of wood species, specific gravity is typically used as a gauge

These photos show the same face of a board under the same lighting conditions, but viewed from opposite ends. At left, the grain is more prominent, but when the board is rotated 180 degrees (right), the lines became more subdued.

instead of density. In the case of wood, specific gravity refers to the ratio of the density of a particular wood compared to the density of water. Stiffness is measured by wood's modulus of elasticity (MOE). The higher the MOE, the stiffer the wood. Knowing the specific gravity and MOE of a particular wood gives you a good idea of its strength.

In addition to density and stiffness, other attributes help determine a wood's strength. Clear, straight-grained wood is stronger than wood with curving grain that runs out at the edge. And the natural grain configuration of a particular species can also add strength, such as in the interlocked grain found in woods like beech and some of the mahoganies. Conversely, knots and other defects can significantly weaken a board, causing splits in localized areas.

Of course, hardwoods are generally the best choice for applications where stiffness is needed. Oak, elm, ash, and hickory are all relatively strong woods that withstand bending stresses. Many hardwoods, however, are

Density and Stiffness of Wood

SPECIES	AVERAGE SPECIFIC GRAVITY (OVEN DRY) RATIO TO WATER	MODULUS OF ELASTICITY (MOE) 106 PSI
Alder	0.41	1.38
Ash	0.49	1.77
Bald cypress	0.46	1.44
Basswood	0.37	1.46
Beech	0.64	1.72
Birch, yellow	0.62	2.01
Butternut	0.38	1.18
Cedar, western	0.32	1.12
Cherry, black	0.50	1.95
Elm	0.50	1.34
Fir, douglas	0.50	1.95
Hemlock, western	0.45	1.49
Hickory, pecan	0.66	1.73
Lignum vitae	1.22	NA
Locust, black	0.69	2.05
Maple, red	0.54	1.64
Maple, sugar	0.63	1.83
Oak, northern red	0.59	1.82
Oak, white	0.68	1.78
Padauk	0.77	NA
Pine, eastern white	0.35	1.24
Pine, sugar	0.3	1.20
Pine, yellow (longleaf)	0.59	1.93
Poplar, yellow	0.42	1.58
Redwood (old growth)	0.40	1.34
Rosewood, indian	1.0	NA
Satinwood, Ceylon	0.9	NA
Spruce, Sitka	0.40	1.57
Sweetgum	0.52	1.64
Sycamore	0.49	1.42
Walnut, black	0.55	1.68

brittle and likely to crack or split under stress. Brittle woods like cherry, holly, some of the rosewoods, and some of the ebonies will chip, split, or crack more readily when subjected to shock or severe stress, such as a fall onto a hard floor.

One of the most common decisions we face when selecting wood for strength is whether a particular shelf will hold up in use without sagging. A fully loaded bookshelf is subject to about 20 lbs. to 25 lbs. per running foot of books, meaning that a 3-ft.-long shelf loaded with books will weigh 60 lbs. to 75 lbs. That's some heavy reading, and your shelves need to be designed to take the weight.

While solid hardwood is the preferred material for strong shelves, plywood and particleboard are also commonly used. When designing shelves, you'll need to consider the type of material used, its thickness, and the distance it has to span. As the chart above shows, solid wood is less susceptible to sagging than particleboard or plywood, and thicker material is stiffer.

Preventing Shelf Sag

We've seen that choosing the appropriate material and dimensions for your shelves will keep them straight and true, but there are a few techniques you can adopt to give you a little more design freedom without sacrificing stiffness.

Sometimes it's possible to keep your shelves relatively thin while minimizing sag by attaching the rear of the shelf to a case back. However, this isn't a viable option for adjustable shelves that need to be repositioned at different heights.

No-Sag Shelving (10-in.-deep shelf, 20 lbs. per linear foot)

MATERIAL	THICKNESS (IN.)	MAXIMUM SPAN (IN.)
Particleboard	¾	26
Hardwood plywood	¾	30
Yellow pine	¾	36
Yellow pine	1	48
Yellow pine	1½	66
Red oak	¾	44
Red oak	1	52
Red oak	1½	78

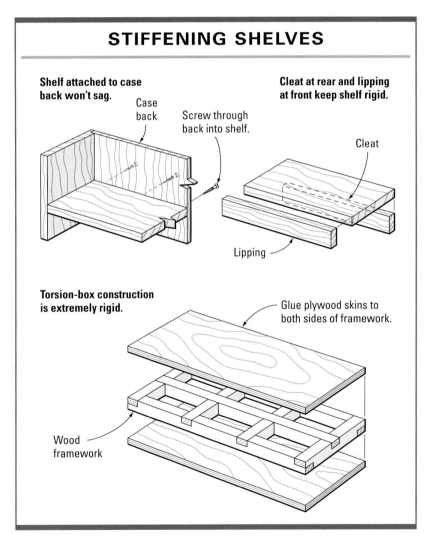

STIFFENING SHELVES

Shelf attached to case back won't sag.
Case back
Screw through back into shelf.

Cleat at rear and lipping at front keep shelf rigid.
Cleat
Lipping

Torsion-box construction is extremely rigid.
Glue plywood skins to both sides of framework.
Wood framework

This ½-in.-thick cherry shelf was hung on shelf pins in a cabinet, then loaded with books. A straightedge held under the shelf indicates a total sag of almost ¼ in.

After a 1-in.-wide mahogany cleat is screwed to the underside of the shelf, there's no measurable sag.

To stiffen a fixed or adjustable shelf, the simplest approach is to add a lipping at the front, and possibly a cleat at the rear. Lipping can be glued to the front edge to help conceal a plywood edge, and cleats can be screwed or nailed to the bottom of a shelf. The wider the lipping, the stiffer the shelf will be. Generally, ³/₄-in.-thick by 1-in.- to 1¹/₂-in.-wide lipping will suffice for most shelves. For really heavy-duty shelves,

you can increase the width of the lipping to increase the overall rigidity.

For extreme rigidity, you can build a shelf with torsion-box construction, which incorporates a framework of thin wood members sandwiched between two plywood skins. Like the wing of an aircraft, a torsion box can span very long distances and support heavy loads without flexing or sagging.

Sketching Dimensions on the Blackboard

Good furniture design involves testing the look of a piece before committing to the real thing. Woodworker and designer Frederic Hanisch finds the blackboard a good place to start. As he shows here, you can easily draw your idea full-scale, refining the design before cutting any wood. A tape measure will help you gauge proportions.

For practice, draw a small table, indicating the top with a few horizontal lines and then laying out the length of a leg and its relationship to the top **(A)**. Mark the leg's width at the bottom where it will meet the floor **(B)**. The great thing about drawing full-size on a blackboard is that you can easily refine your measurements **(C)**. If things don't look right to you, simply erase the chalk and draw a new line.

To get a better sense of proportion, try your hand at a perspective view. Sketch the top first, and don't be concerned about your artistic efforts. A rectangle falling on its side is enough to get a sense of what the top might look like **(D)**. Add legs to one end of the table, remembering that in your full-scale sketch the top overhangs the legs **(E)**. Then draw one back leg, giving the table a planted feel **(F)**.

Once you're happy with the overall design, use the existing full-size sketch to draw a plan view (from above, looking down) to determine specific dimensions, such as for the top overhang and apron-to-leg joinery **(G)**. A sketch such as this is often all you need to do before cutting out parts.

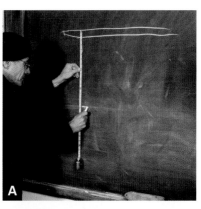

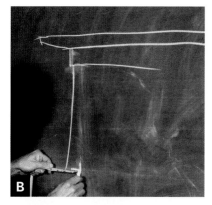

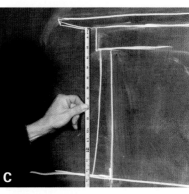

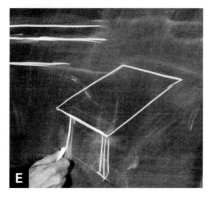

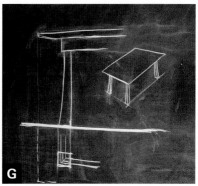

Working Around Defects

If you're careful, you can often get a surprising yield of parts from a board that some might consider scrap. For example, this questionable plank of ash actually contains a full set of table legs (and more), which you can determine by making some basic measurements and marking the potential parts out in chalk **(A)**.

When working with planks like this, begin by marking any defects to avoid, such as checks on the end of a board or any knots along its length **(B)**. Continue down the length of the plank, marking out parts and noting, for example, where two legs might be cut side by side **(C)**.

To conserve wood, sight the plank for warp, and then crosscut the stock where a part ends nearest the most severe section of warp **(D)**. This approach yields straighter pieces that won't require much jointing to flatten. Joint one face **(E)** and one edge **(F)**, and then plane the stock to the desired finished thickness **(G)**.

With the stock now flat, straight, and with one edge squared, lay out the individual blanks for the parts. Use a ruler and chalk or pencil, making sure that the parts fit within the confines of the blank, while allowing for any necessary saw kerfs **(H)**. Start by ripping the board down the middle, referencing the jointed edge against the rip fence **(I)**. If the stock warps after ripping, it may need rejointing. When everything is straight, rip the blanks to final width **(J)**.

Cut the legs to finished length. Here, a stop block clamped to a crosscut sled on the table saw allows accurate multiple cuts **(K)**. Cut from the opposite side of the blade to remove any knots or other defects **(L)**, and then butt the stock against the stop to finish the cuts **(M)**.

With this type of careful layout and precise cutting, you can end up with more defect-free parts than you originally planned on **(N)**.

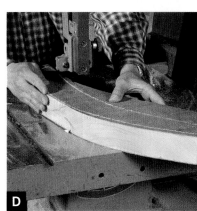

Maximizing Parts from a Plank

A great way to make the most of your wood is to work directly with rough stock, cutting out individual parts before any surfacing begins. With many blanks, the first order of business is to scrub away dirt and debris with a stiff metal brush to avoid dulling your cutting tools **(A)**.

The best approach to laying out is often to use a template made from thin plywood to trace the parts onto your blank **(B)**. Using a template allows you to preview the wood quality and grain direction and facilitates nesting the parts as closely as possible for maximum yield.

The most efficient way to cut out complex or curved shapes is to use the bandsaw. Start by separating the plank into bite-size chunks **(C)** and then into oversized blanks for individual parts **(D)**.

Once you've cut the parts to rough shape, flatten one face of each part on the jointer **(E)**.

This process straightens one side while revealing the full extent of its grain pattern **(F)**. Next, send the parts through the thickness planer **(G)**. Keep planing until the stock is at the desired finished thickness **(H)**.

[**TIP**] **When thickness-planing stock, plane an equal amount from both sides to balance any internal stresses that may otherwise induce warp.**

Use the template again to lay out the final contours of the parts **(I)**. Then go back to the bandsaw and saw as close to the line as you can **(J)**. Finish up by sanding and fairing the contours smooth.

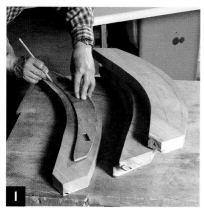

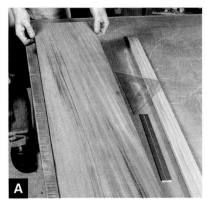

Sawing Out Straight Grain

This is a nice plank of ribbon-stripe mahogany, but the curve of the grain doesn't follow the edges of the board, and parts cut from it will look skewed. Although this reduces the overall width of the board, it's worth cutting the plank to rearrange the grain so that it runs parallel to the edge of the board **(A)**.

Begin by laying a straightedge parallel to the grain as best you can by eye, starting at one corner of the board, and angling the straightedge toward the opposite end, following the grain. To check the width of board that will remain, use a right angle and a ruler to measure from the straight-edge to the opposite edge of the board **(B)**. Following the straightedge, draw a line onto the stock **(C)**.

Cut as close to the line as you can on the band-saw **(D)**. Then joint the sawn edge straight **(E)**. Finally, register the jointed edge against the rip fence and saw the board to width **(F)**.

The finished plank lost about 2 in. of width, but the grain is now aligned with the edges of the board **(G)**.

Arranging Grain Between Boards

When you're making a panel from a series of narrower boards, arranging the grain of adjacent boards can make all the difference in the look of a piece. Here, cabinetmaker Frank Klausz positions three rough-jointed boards in preparation for laying out a tabletop **(A)**. Whenever possible, it's best to orient each board so the side that pointed towards the center of the tree faces up. This "inside face" has a richer, deeper appearance, especially after a finish is applied. You can easily identify the inside face by reading the annular rings on the end of the board, which curve upward at their ends **(B)**.

Arrange the boards edge to edge, and then slide each board back and forth until the grain patterns merge as harmonious patterns. Once the boards are arranged to your liking, mark a V across them so you can reorient them later during glue-up **(C)**. Mark and crosscut the boards, leaving them about 4 in. oversized in length for now **(D)**.

Be sure to check for necessary width **(E)**, and then mark the stock in preparation for removing any sapwood or other blemishes **(F)**. Once all your marks are made, rip the boards to width and joint each mating edge. Then reassemble the boards in order and glue up the top.

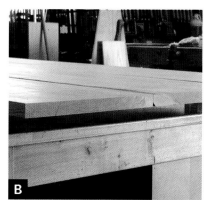

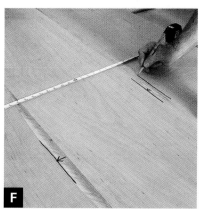

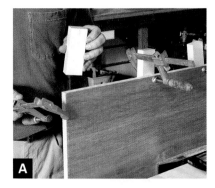

A

B

Stiffening a Shelf with Lippings

Adding a wooden lip to the front of a shelf can substantially increase its stiffness and prevent it from sagging during use. To begin, prepare the shelf by clamping blocks wrapped in clear tape to the top face of the shelf **(A)**. The blocks help align the lipping flush to the shelf; the tape resists glue squeeze-out.

C

D

No special joinery is needed; a good coat of glue spread evenly along the front edge is enough to bond the lipping to the shelf **(B)**. Once you've spread the glue, position the shelf horizontally, place the lipping against the shelf, and use more clamps to draw the lipping against the blocks **(C)**. Use longer clamps to pull the lipping tight against the edge of the shelf. The sign of adequate clamping pressure is a small bead of glue escaping along the entire joint **(D)**.

E

F

Once the glue has dried, remove the clamps and blocks, and smooth the joint by scraping it and then lightly sanding it **(E)**. To dress up the face of the shelf, you can rout a decorative profile on the top and bottom edges of the lipping **(F)**. After routing, crosscut the ends of the lipping flush with the shelf. Thanks to the stout lip, the finished shelf will hold stacks of books or other heavy items without deflecting under load **(G)**.

G

Making a Torsion-Box Shelf

Built like an aircraft wing, a torsion box can withstand incredible loads, spanning long distances without sagging. Furniture maker Lon Schleining starts by making an inner framework, cutting a series of rabbets and dadoes in ¾-in. by ¾-in. pine stock. End rabbets are easily cut on a crosscut sled on the table saw, with a dado blade and a stop block to register the cuts **(A)**. Reposition the stop block to make the dado cuts **(B)**.

With one sheet of ¼-in. plywood under the work, assemble the framework by gluing all the lap joints **(C)**. Once the frame is together, spread glue over its entire face **(D)**, and then lay a second sheet of plywood onto the frame **(E)**. Repeat the gluing procedure to coat the first sheet by flipping the assembly over and spreading glue on its opposite face.

Place a ¾-in.-thick platen made from melamine-coated particleboard (MCP) on each side of the assembly, and raise the whole affair above the bench on blocks of wood. Then clamp the assembly with as many clamps as you can muster **(F)**. Before leaving the assembly to dry, be sure to sight the construction to ensure that it's dead flat **(G)**. If necessary, make any adjustments by shimming the work off the bench.

Once the glue has cured, remove the clamps and platens, and if you want, edge the finished shelf with solid wood to conceal the joints. The shelf is now ready to support a heavy load **(H)**.

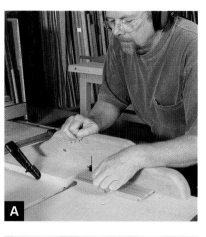

A

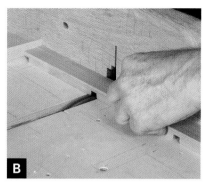

B

C

D

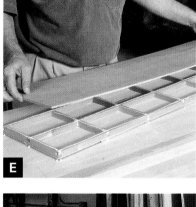

E

F

G

H

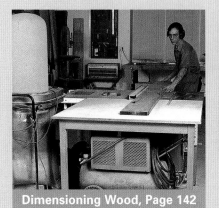

Dimensioning Wood, Page 142

Working Difficult Wood, Page 162

PART FOUR

Cutting Wood

CUTTING PLANKS INTO furniture parts involves not only using the right machines but also understanding your wood well enough to ensure that parts are cut as precisely as possible. This means knowing how to deal with wood's inherent quirks when performing basic operations such as jointing, planing, ripping, and crosscutting. You need to know how to best deal with knots, cracks, severe warp, and other defects. Learning to cope with these imperfections is part of the challenge of cutting wood and can help you turn scrap lumber into prized treasure. This part of the book describes how to approach these processes so that your milled parts are strong, beautiful, and cut to the exact shapes and sizes you need.

Dimensioning Wood

Milling Solid Wood

Sizing Plywood

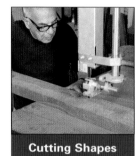

Cutting Shapes

Cutting Veneer

I N THIS SECTION we'll look at the milling process, which involves turning rough planks into finished parts ready for joinery or assembly. In order to size stock accurately, it helps to understand how your woodworking machines work. It's equally important to become familiar with how your material reacts under different machining processes. Following the correct milling procedure allows you to take control of dimensioning boards so you get the parts you need. Dealing with large stock, such as oversize boards or full sheets of plywood, is another challenge you can successfully tackle if you approach it in a sensible manner and with a few helpful aids. And producing complex shapes, such as the flowing curve of a chair leg, requires the right tools and knowing how to use them correctly.

Milling Raw Stock

Dimensioning stock involves milling the material so that it is straight, flat, of a consistent thickness, and has square edges. Properly done, the process flattens any warped surfaces and yields pieces that are smooth enough for layout work and joinery. The milling sequence can be outlined in a general way by tracing the route of the lumber from machine to machine:

A small engineer's square is accurate for reading the edge of a board to check whether it's perpendicular to an adjacent surface.

producing wood that is warped or rough. Making your stock truly flat and square is a job worth doing yourself.

When milling wood, you'll need to be able to set up machines to make square cuts, such as when setting a table saw blade square to the table. You'll also need to be able to accurately check the resulting cuts, so invest in quality squares, and use the appropriate size for the surface you're reading.

During the milling process, ear and eye protection are needed to combat the roar of machinery and the flow of dust and chips. Blade guards are a must. If, like most of us, you find your stock table-saw guard clumsy, fit your table saw with one of the excellent aftermarket versions. To save fingers and place pressure against tables and fences, make sure to use push sticks, push blocks, and hold-downs when appropriate.

An often overlooked piece of safety equipment is the table-saw splitter, or riving

Blade guards and push sticks save fingers. This tall push stick clears the guard and is made from plywood so its heel won't split or break during use.

1) At the jointer, begin by flattening one face of the board.
2) At the thickness planer, dress the board to its final thickness.
3) Back at the jointer, straighten and square one edge.
4) At the table saw, rip the board to final width.
5) At the miter saw or table saw, crosscut the board to final length.

Milling lumber in the proper sequence is necessary to ensure stock that's ready for furniture. If you try to save time by buying premilled stock, one of the above steps may have been overlooked or performed poorly,

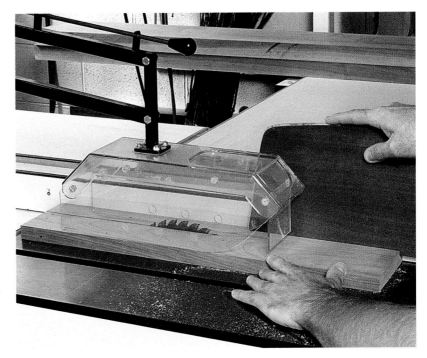

HOW WOOD PINCHES A SAW BLADE

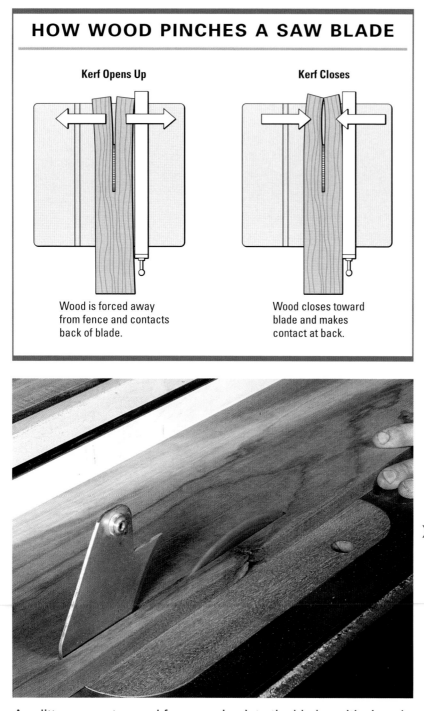

Kerf Opens Up

Wood is forced away from fence and contacts back of blade.

Kerf Closes

Wood closes toward blade and makes contact at back.

A splitter prevents wood from moving into the blade as it's ripped, eliminating the chance of kickback. This aftermarket "snap-in" Biesemeyer splitter is easily removed and replaced without the use of tools.

knife. This little piece of metal can be a lifesaver by preventing kickback, which is caused by the blade lifting the workpiece and hurling it towards you with great force. Kickback most commonly happens when you're ripping a board. Sawing can release internal tensions inside the board, allowing the two separated parts to warp and press against the rising rear teeth of the blade, which then lift and throw the board (see the drawing at left). A splitter doesn't allow the wood to press against the blade. Unfortunately, most stock splitters are troublesome to install and use. The answer is to buy an aftermarket splitter that can be installed or removed without tools.

Milling stock correctly also involves removing knots, splits, and other defects. Learn to carefully inspect a board after it has been cleaned up in the thickness planer but before cutting to final dimension. Most cracks and other blemishes show up easily at this stage. If a knot isn't a visual problem, you can leave it in, but be sure to tap it to make sure it's sound and won't fall out later.

▶ See *"Filling Knots with Epoxy"* on p. 173.

One of the trickiest parts of checking for sound stock is inspecting for end checks—those cracks at the ends of boards that result from the drying process. Hairline checks can be hard to see, so it's best to cut slices off the end of the board, and then check the slices for cracks. First crosscut an inch or two from the rough end, then cut off a slice about $1/8$ in. thick. Check the slice for cracks by gently bowing it with your hands. If it

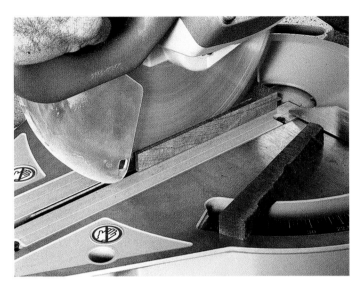

To check for hairline end checks, first crosscut a thin slice from the end of a board.

Bend the sample slice by hand. If it contains checks, it will snap easily.

bends a fair amount without breaking, the end of your board is sound. However, if it snaps easily, you'll have to keep cutting further into the board until your test slice doesn't break.

Cutting to Final Length

You can crosscut to final length using a miter saw or table saw. Final cuts sometimes involve removing just a whisker from the end of a board. Unfortunately, the hard end grain can cause blades and other cutters to deflect, misaligning the cut when you try to remove just a hair from the end of a piece. One trick to reduce this deflection is to make the cut very slowly. However, this doesn't always work, and you may need to try another approach.

A nice trick for removing just a smidgen of wood off the end of a piece is to use the side of your miter saw blade. Lower the blade, and butt the end of the workpiece against the plate (not the teeth). Gently lift the

You can remove about 1/64 in. by pushing the stock into the blade's plate and then lifting up the saw and cutting.

Clamp or hold the work against the trimmer's fence, and start to lever the blade across the wood.

The miter trimmer lets you remove very thin shavings for a perfect fit, and the finished cut is glassy smooth (inset).

Shaving the end of a piece with a low-angle plane offers more precision than any other method.

stopped blade while holding the work firmly, and then make a cut. You'll remove about ¹⁄₆₄ in., or the amount of set on the blade.

One way to shave miters is to use a knife-cutting machine called a miter trimmer. After a miter has been rough-cut on a miter saw, the workpiece is clamped into the

machine with the fence angled at 45 degrees. The tool has a massive, fixed knife that levers its way across the wood, leaving a shaved surface that's super-smooth and at a true 45-degree angle.

For super-precise cuts, try setting a low-angle plane for a very light cut and shaving the end of a piece. A handplane can take shavings so thin that they fall from the cut as dust. The nice thing about using a plane to trim work is being able to remove such an exacting amount of wood that it allows you to sneak up on a perfect fit.

Flattening on a Jointer

All rough wood has some degree of warp, and the best tool to use to begin straightening your stock is the jointer. As woodworker Paul Anthony demonstrates here, start by sighting along the plank to determine its curves so that you can place the cupped or bowed side down on the jointer table **(A)**.

▶ See *"Types of Warp"* on p. 8.

Make sure to joint with the grain to avoid tearout. One way to inspect a rough board's grain orientation is to take a few swipes on the edge of the plank on the jointer **(B)** to reveal the grain lines in the wood **(C)**.

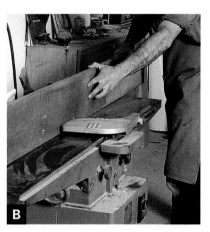

Once you've noted the direction of the grain, set the infeed table for a medium cut (about $\frac{1}{32}$ in. to $\frac{1}{16}$ in.), and place the bowed side down on the table. Long planks can be maneuvered without strain if you stand away from the infeed end of the table and gently bow the board so it flexes, placing pressure on the infeed table **(D)**. Continue walking up to the jointer behind the board, keeping one hand over the infeed table while the other hand lifts the trailing end of the board slightly to make the leading end press down onto the outfeed table **(E)**.

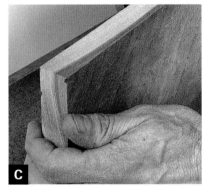

As your hands approach the cutterhead, keep the board moving with one hand while you reach for a push block with the other **(F)**. Use the push block to place pressure over the outfeed table near the knives, and use a second push block with a heel at its end to grab the end of the board so your hands are safe while above the cutterhead **(G)**. As the board nears the end of the cut and starts to hang off the outfeed table, use your upper body weight over the push blocks to keep the stock from tipping **(H)**.

(Continued on p. 148.)

After the first cut, check the face to see how much stock you've removed. You're looking for a cut that continues uninterrupted for the length of the board. Here, a few more passes are needed (I).

Boards with a bow in the middle will be flattened as material is gradually removed from each end, until the center is lying against the jointer tables. It's more efficient in this case to take several passes at a time from each end of the board, rather than running it full length each pass. When flattening the trailing end, you can swing the guard away from the fence and pull the board halfway back to take another pass (J). Then simply place it onto the tables and make another pass (K).

Once the freshly cut surface runs uninterrupted along the board's length, stop to eyeball the plank for straightness (L). If you notice any significant curvature, take another pass. When you're done, the board should be flat over the majority of its surface, although it can still contain some uncut areas (M).

Planing to Thickness

After jointing one face, you're ready to bring the board to the desired thickness using the thickness planer. Start by measuring the thickest part of the board **(A)** and adjusting the depth of cut on the planer to that dimension **(B)**.

Note the grain orientation, and be sure to feed the plank into the planer in the correct direction to avoid tearout. Make the first pass with the jointed side down on the bed, standing at the end of the board **(C)**.

[TIP] To minimize planer snipe, lift the board slightly as it enters the planer, and again as it exits.

Stay on the infeed side of the planer as you guide the stock through the machine to support the overhanging end **(D)**. Once the board is centered in the planer and well supported, move to the outfeed side and support the opposite end to keep it from tipping up and into the cutterhead **(E)**.

(Continued on p. 150.)

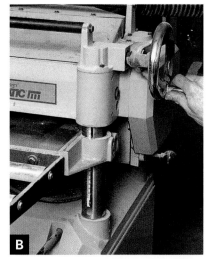

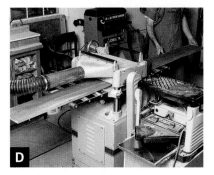

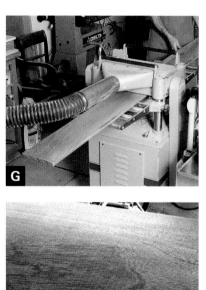

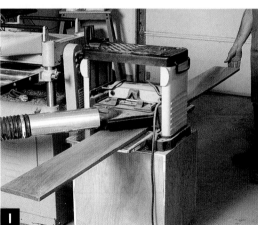

Once you've established a continuously cut surface on the first planed face, flip the board end for end and onto its opposite face **(F)** before sending it through the planer again **(G)**. This reorientation keeps the grain in the correct direction and ensures that you take equal amounts from each side to minimize warp.

> ⚠ **WARNING** **Removing material from only one side of a plank will usually cause it to distort due to uneven stresses inside the wood. Be sure to cut both sides equally to keep the plank flat.**

A large planer with an induction motor is a great machine for taking aggressive cuts when you're milling rough stock, although it may produce a rough, washboardlike surface. Unfortunately, when you're taking a very light cut, the serrated-metal feed rollers may leave a series of fine-line impressions in the board **(H)**. For a better final cut, some woodworkers finish up by taking a light pass with a benchtop planer, which has a higher-speed universal motor that provides more cuts per inch. These machines also have smooth rubber feed rollers that won't leave marks in the board **(I)**.

Ripping a Wide Plank on the Table Saw

After jointing and planing your stock flat and to a consistent thickness, you're ready to saw it to width on the table saw. But first you'll have to straighten and square one edge on the jointer by standing the stock on edge with one face against the jointer's fence. At this stage, don't try to remove any defects that might be near the jointed edge **(A)**.

After squaring one edge, set up the saw by adjusting the blade height for the thickness of the stock. A good rule of thumb is to raise the blade high enough so the bottom of its gullets are just above the workpiece **(B)**.

Begin by placing the jointed edge against the rip fence. When sawing a long board, stand near its trailing end to begin feeding it into the blade. Place yourself to the left of the blade (as you face it) and concentrate your attention not at the blade but at the fence, to ensure that the stock contacts it fully throughout the cut **(C)**. When you're within reach of the saw table, keep your left hand stationary on the tabletop to apply pressure towards the fence, while your right hand feeds the plank **(D)**.

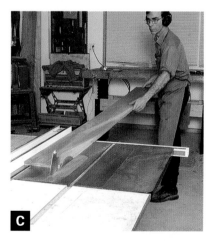

[**VARIATION**] **When ripping thick boards or planks with wild grain, add a short fence to your existing rip fence, with its end aligned with the rear of the blade. Make the fence 1 in. thick so it's easier to set up cuts using your fence's cursor. Ripping in this manner is perfectly safe and creates space for the wood to spread apart towards the fence without binding on the blade.**

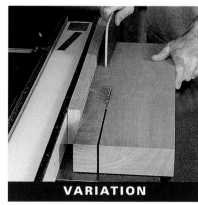

VARIATION

(Continued on p. 152.)

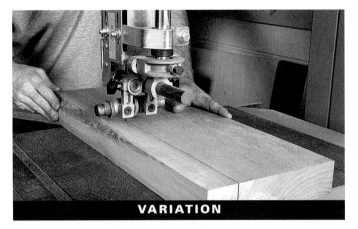

VARIATION

[**VARIATION**] When you deal with thick, heavy, hard-to-handle stock, it can help to first reduce the size and weight of the piece on the bandsaw. Thanks to its downward cutting action, the bandsaw has no potential for kickback. You can set up a fence, or simply gauge the width with a pencil, and then saw to the line freehand. After bandsawing, move back to the table saw and make a trim cut to clean up the bandsawn edge.

As you near the end of the cut, move your left hand out of the way and push the board past the blade. For safety, ride one finger along the fence to ensure that your hand stays away from the blade (**E**). At the end of the cut, the board is likely to tip over the end of the saw table due to its overhanging weight. The safest approach is to have an outfeed table behind the saw to support the work. Also, apply downward pressure to the board as you feed it past the blade (**F**).

If there were any defects near the original jointed edge, orient the sawn edge against the rip fence and adjust the fence to the desired width of cut, taking note of the defects so you remove them in this final pass (**G**).

E

F

G

Ripping Narrow Boards from a Wide Plank

Due to internal stresses in almost all boards, ripping multiple narrow sections from a wide board requires the right approach to ensure that your sawn stock remains straight. Begin by setting the rip fence for a cut about ⅛ in. wider than your desired finished width. With the jointed edge against the fence, feed the work smoothly past the blade with your left hand keeping pressure against the fence **(A)**.

Whenever you're ripping stock that's less than about 4 in. wide, use a push stick as the end of the board nears the blade **(B)**. As the board separates, guide the dimensioned piece with the push stick while your left hand pushes the freed section past the blade **(C)**.

Without resetting the fence, continue ripping the remainder of the board into separate, slightly oversized pieces. To illustrate how wood moves after ripping, group the individual boards back together in the order that they were sawn. Chances are, you'll notice gaps between them, which reveals bowed edges from the sawing process **(D)**. To re-straighten the edges, take each board back to the jointer and re-joint one edge **(E)**. With such narrow stock, you can use the same push stick you used on the table saw to keep your hands clear of the knives **(F)**.

After jointing each board, orient its jointed edge against the rip fence and trim the opposite edge to finished width **(G)**. Remember to use a push stick for the last portion of the board **(H)**.

[**TIP**] **For optimal cutting, keep your blade clean. Spray the blade with a citrus-based cleaner, and then use a nylon abrasive pad or a brass brush to scrub the gunk from the blade.**

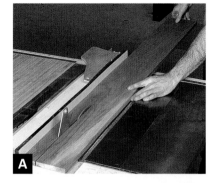

Crosscutting Using the Miter Gauge

The miter gauge lets you make excellent cross-cuts on the table saw, but you'll only use it for small work, as it can't safely support long or very wide stock. With the power off, position the stock at your cutline, holding it firmly against the gauge's fence with your left hand (**A**). Push the stock and gauge in an even, controlled movement, using your right hand on the gauge's knob to feed the work past the blade (**B**).

Once the cut is made, use your left hand to slide the workpiece slightly away from the blade (**C**) before pulling the work and gauge back to you (**D**). This prevents you from splintering the sawn edge as you retract the workpiece.

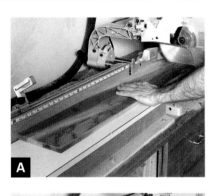

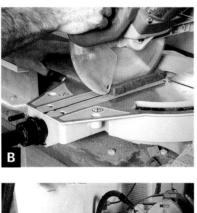

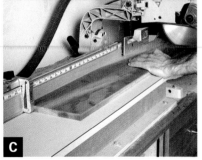

Cutting to Length with a Miter Saw

A better option for crosscutting, particularly with long or heavy stock, is to use a power miter saw, also called a chopsaw. The first step is to cross-cut one end of the workpiece perfectly square by holding the stock firmly and accurately against the saw's fence. For the best results, build a crosscutting station to house your saw so you'll have longer work tables and a longer fence against which to register the stock (**A**). Be sure to remove enough stock from a rough end so the sawn edge is free of end checks and other defects (**B**).

Next, flip the stock end for end, registering the previously cut end against a stop block as you cut the opposite end to finished length (**C**). If your stock is longer than the working fence of your sawing station, you can make an extension that allows you to accurately register longer boards (**D**).

Crosscutting with a Table-Saw Sled

Wide panels, such as case parts, are best crosscut on the table saw. If a panel is short enough, it's a simple matter to set the rip fence and guide the work past the blade. But do this only if the edge that bears against the fence is long enough to keep the panel from veering away from the fence during travel **(A)**.

To crosscut long and wide stock, you can build and use a shop-made sled. Runners attached to the bottom of the sled ride in your saw's miter-gauge grooves, and a stout fence at the front of the sled registers the stock square to the blade for square cuts every time. The workpiece can be carried primarily to the left of the blade **(B)** or to the right, depending on how your table saw is set up **(C)**. Either way, be sure to support the overhanging end of a long workpiece with a spacer of the same thickness as your sled's base at the far end of your saw.

For repetitive cuts in parts that are longer than your sled's fence, you can clamp an extension to the fence and then clamp a stop block to the extension **(D)**. The block will accurately register multiple parts and ensure that your final cuts are all to the same length **(E)**.

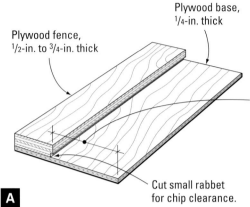

Plywood base,
¼-in. thick

Plywood fence,
½-in. to ¾-in. thick

Make base ½ in. or so
wider than distance from
circular saw's base and
attach to fence. The first
time jig is used, the sawn
edge becomes the
reference cutting edge.

Cut small rabbet
for chip clearance.

A

B

C

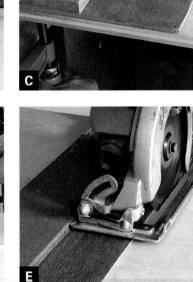

D

E

Cutting Sheet Parts with a Circular Saw

Because of its size, a full-sized sheet of plywood can be cumbersome to handle in the workshop. If it's too much of a struggle to cut the sheet on your table saw, try pre-cutting it into smaller, slightly oversized pieces first, using a portable circular saw and a shop-made saw guide. The pieces can then be easily trimmed to final size on the table saw.

The jig is very simple to make, and consists of a plywood base onto which you glue or nail a plywood fence to guide your saw (**A**). To set up the cut and prevent tearout, lay out what will be the width of your saw kerf, and then score both sides of the kerf line with a sharp knife (**B**). Clamp the jig so its base aligns perfectly with the appropriate line (**C**).

With the panel supported on both sides of the cut, simply push your saw along the jig's base, making sure the edge of the saw rides along the fence during the entire cut (**D**). You'll minimize tearout if you use a crosscutting saw blade and position the best side of your panel facing down, since the blade's cutting action lifts fibers up (**E**).

Sawing Large Sheets on the Table Saw

To cut a full sheet you'll need an outfeed table. It helps if you have infeed support in front, such as a table that's the same height or slightly lower than your table saw's height. Lay one end of the sheet on the infeed table, with the opposite end on the saw table, and one edge against the fence but away from the blade, and turn on the saw. Walk back to the end of the panel, stand at the far corner of the sheet to triangulate your feed pressure, and move the panel into the blade by pushing diagonally towards the rip fence **(A)**.

To keep the sheet against the fence at the start of the cut, try lifting the end of the panel slightly so it bows a bit. This will increase pressure on the fence as you push the sheet into the blade **(B)**.

Walk with the panel as you push it forward, staying on the far side to maintain pressure against the fence **(C)**. As the sheet nears the end of the cut, move to the back of the panel and guide each divided section with one hand, again keeping your eyes on the fence **(D)**. As the parts separate, lean over the saw to place downward pressure over each piece, then push the keeper piece past the blade while holding the offcut stationary **(E)**.

Once you've separated the parts from the sheet, be sure to place the sawn edge of each piece against the rip fence and trim the opposite factory edge, which is typically not very straight nor particularly smooth **(F)**.

A

Bandsawing Complex Shapes

Sawing curved parts is best accomplished on the bandsaw, where there's no kickback to contend with due to the downward force of the blade. To prepare a leg blank for subsequent pattern-shaping, furniture maker Sam Maloof first uses a template to outline the part onto a plank of walnut. Using a template in this manner allows you to pick the best parts of a board and avoid defects **(A)**.

B

For really large boards, it pays to have a helper. To begin the cut, assistant Mike Johnson supports the trailing end of the blank while Maloof steers it at the blade **(B)**. Once the majority of the wood is on the table, it's a one-person affair to maneuver the stock while pushing it forward to follow the outline **(C)**.

C

Straddle the stock on either side of the blade, using your rear hand to push the work while your forward hand does the steering **(D)**. If the stock is too heavy and you don't have a helper to support the outfeed side, you can walk around the back of the table and pull it through **(E)**.

D

E

When enough wood has been trimmed away, steering long stock through the blade is possible without help **(F)**.

One trick is to push the work lightly into one side of the blade on its rear edge (away from the teeth), and then gently rotate the work as it bears against the blade to cut the curve. This technique allows you to make minute changes without overcutting past your line **(G)**. To crosscut a long piece, use your left hand to guide the cut while your right hand supports the overhanging stock **(H)**. Using these techniques, you can saw very precise curves in any kind of stock **(I)**.

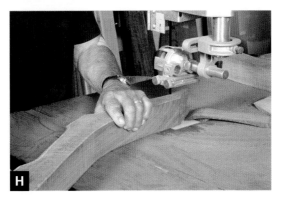

Cutting and Joining Veneer

Cutting and dimensioning veneer can be tricky because this material is so thin that a standard cutting approach with conventional tools will result in broken or shattered wood. The first step is to saw the veneer by hand to rough length. Using a veneer saw, lay your material underneath a piece of MDF that has a straight edge, and use the edge to guide the saw **(A)**. Don't try to make the cut in one pass or you'll tear the veneer. Instead, make several scoring cuts, pulling the saw towards you until the blade passes through the work and into the scrap wood below.

To join these two pieces of maple veneer edge-to-edge **(B)**, furniture maker Frank Pollaro first saws each edge straight and square using the same technique as in crosscutting, but this time sawing along the grain. Again, light scoring passes work better than heavy cuts **(C)**.

Once the parts are cut, you'll need to tape them together in preparation for gluing onto a substrate. While holding the two sheets together, run a piece of moistened veneer tape across the joint at one end. Make sure to tape what will be the show face of the veneer **(D)**. Immediately after sticking the tape to the wood, use a roller to set the tape tightly to the veneer **(E)**. Continue working your way along the joint, sticking tape across the joint line every few inches **(F)**.

Finish up by laying a long strip of tape along the joint line **(G)**. On a long piece like this, it's best to immediately press the moistened tape onto the veneer by hand before it loses its tackiness, then follow up with the roller **(H)**.

The finished piece is ready to glue to a substrate **(I)**. On the back side, which will contact the substrate, the seam is tight and the surface is smooth, ensuring that there won't be any gaps or bumps on the show side **(J)**.

➤ See *"Gluing Veneers"* on p. 248.

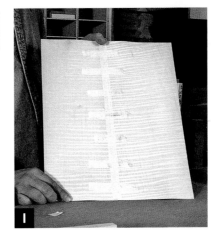

Working Difficult Wood

Getting Clean Cuts

Making Repairs

Flattening Veneer

MANY SPECIES of woods are difficult to work, particularly some of the denser tropical varieties such as purpleheart, bubinga, or teak. Very hard woods blunt cutting edges, which can then scorch the wood fibers. Even milder woods can be troublesome, especially when the grain pattern is uneven or highly figured. For example, quilted bigleaf maple or bird's-eye maple both have a tendency to tear, leaving small pockets of ragged fibers that spoil the surface. Several species have interlocked or reversing grain that rises in opposite directions side by side, making smoothing surfaces a serious challenge. Brittle woods and delicate veneers both have a tendency to chip when sawn. And highly figured veneer is often so buckled that it resembles a mogul slope at a ski resort, making it difficult to press onto to a substrate.

Other vexing problems are splits and cracks, unsightly knots, and small chunks that break off from surrounding wood. You'll also come across woods with resins that can accelerate burning. Some woods contain deposits, like the abrasive silica found in teak, which can dull cutting edges quickly. And certain woods are known to pose serious health risks when worked. Fortunately, there are a number of approaches you can take to overcome these difficulties, as I'll discuss in this section.

Preventing Tearout

Tearout is a common problem, especially when you're working with figured woods. The problem is often prevented by sharp cutters and a slower feed speed—the rate at which the work is fed past the cutter or the cutter past the work. Unfortunately, even super-sharp knives and a slower pace may not overcome the tendency for fibers to chip below the surface of exceptionally tear-prone woods, such as bird's-eye maple.

Most woods prone to tearing will do so during thickness-planing. One way to minimize this is to take a super-light cut on the last one or two passes. Another approach is to wet the stock with water to soften the fibers just before taking a light final cut. Wait a few minutes for the water to be absorbed by the wood before planing. Don't worry: Moisture won't soak in very deep. After planing, any residual moisture should dry up after 30 minutes or so.

If you have a planing session scheduled for a large amount of difficult wood, try adding a 15-degree back-bevel to your planer knives and perhaps your jointer knives as well (see the drawing on p. 164). Beveling the back of your knives effectively increases the cutting angle from the standard 50 or 60 degrees to 65 or 75 degrees. The result is a steeper angle of attack and a cutting edge that's less likely to dig below the surface, lifting up fibers or chips. You can grind the bevel yourself, although a sharpening service is more likely to do a consistent job on knife sets. The downside is that the knives (and the machine) will have to work harder to make the cut, so deep cuts won't be possible. And the planed surface won't have the customary sheen you're used to, but a somewhat duller appearance and slightly rougher feel. For practical reasons, it's best to keep a spare set of knives ground with back-bevels to use

To minimize tearout on figured wood, soften the surface fibers by using a sponge to saturate the wood with water before surface planing.

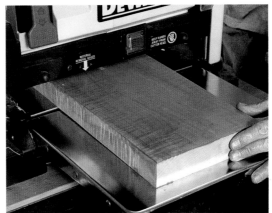

Adjust the planer for a super-light cut, wait a minute or two for the surface fibers to become saturated, and then make a last pass through the planer.

Tilt the scraper forward when pushing the tool or backward for a pull cut. Bowing the scraper along its length helps the middle bite to take thicker shavings.

only when you're machining really cantankerous woods, and then switch back to your stock knives for normal milling.

The last resort for dealing with tearout is to use a hand scraper. This simple, easy-to-use tool can save the day when all your machines and fancy setups have failed to provide clean cuts. While a scraper leaves a somewhat rough surface, it removes fibers without tearing them, making it a great choice for smoothing really wild wood or surfaces that suffered tearout from a previous machining operation.

► See *"Using a Hand Scraper"* on p. 227.

Crosscutting can also cause chipping, especially in brittle, open-pored woods like wenge, most of the oaks, and many of the denser ring-porous species. Even worse are plywood and other sheet goods such as MCP (melamine-coated particleboard), which are notorious for chipping and splintering due to their brittle composition and ultrathin surface coatings and veneers. Although some chipping can occur on the top side of boards and panels cut on the table saw, it's most noticeable on the bottom. To minimize this, use a high-quality crosscut blade with 60 or more teeth (for a 10-in. blade). For even cleaner and safer cuts, make or buy zero-clearance throat plates and install them on your crosscutting machines. These inserts support the wood fibers adjacent to the saw kerf as the blade exits on the underside of the workpiece, greatly reducing tearout. A zero-clearance throat plate also prevents small offcuts from jamming in the throat-plate opening and possibly exploding.

BACK-BEVELING YOUR KNIVES

Standard Cutting Angle

Planer or jointer knife

Rotation

Typical cutting angle of 50° - 60°

Wood

New Angle with Back-Bevel

1/16 in.

15°

Higher cutting angle of 65° - 75°

Grind bevel on back of blade.

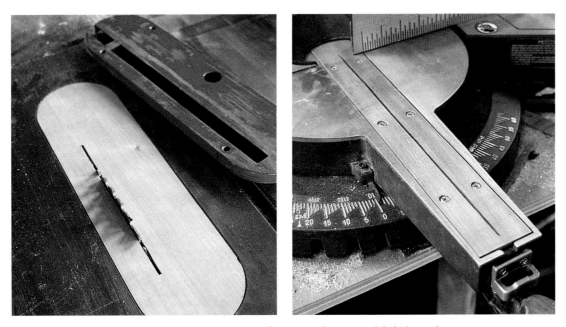

To minimize exit tearout on a table saw (left) or a miter saw (right), replace your factory throat plate with a commercial or shopmade zero-clearance version.

To virtually eliminate tearout in plywood or MCP, you can use a sharp knife to score through the veneer fibers or surface coating on both sides of the cutline before sawing. After incising two parallel lines, lay the scored side down on the table saw for cross-cutting, and set the fence. The technique requires careful fence positioning to ensure that the blade lines up precisely in the middle of your marks. But the clean results are worth the extra effort.

If you want an absolutely perfect surface on only the top side of your work, and the underside doesn't matter because it won't be seen, you can virtually eliminate top-side splintering by raising the table-saw blade as high as possible. This creates less forward rotation as the teeth enter the material, a major cause of topside chipping. Be sure you make this cut carefully and deliberately, since the blade will be much more exposed than during normal cutting.

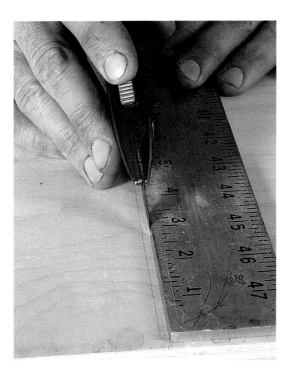

To eliminate tearout in plywood, score the cutline by guiding the knife with a long, heavy straightedge, making two scoring cuts alongside the kerf you'll be cutting.

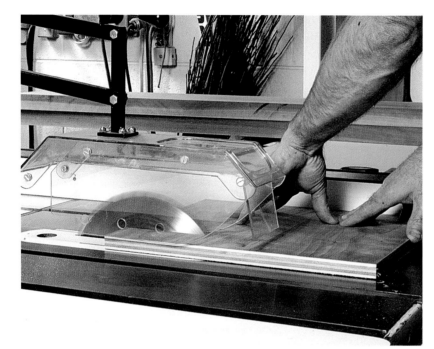

To avoid chipping on the top side of a panel, use a good-quality crosscut blade, raising it as high as it will go.

You'll experience less tearout and burning by moving the work with constant momentum at the appropriate speed, with the grain oriented so that it slopes away from the cut.

When routing, you can utilize many of the same approaches you use for clean cuts on the table saw. Whether you're using a handheld router or a router table, rout with the slope of the grain whenever possible. And keep the work or tool moving at a constant and appropriate feed speed.

A special technique applicable only to routers and shapers is to feed your stock or the router backwards, a process known as *climb cutting*. Instead of lifting and tearing unpredictably, a climb cut removes only tiny slices of wood with each cut, dramatically reducing tearout (see the drawing on facing page). However, because you're feeding the work or bit in the direction of the cutter's rotation, the bit will want to throw a handheld router away from the workpiece. If you're using a router table, the bit rotation will try to pull the workpiece out of your grip.

Using a power feeder on a router table is the safest method for climb cutting. But handfeeding is possible if you take some precautions. To reduce the pull, remove as much excess material as possible before routing. For example, you may trim your parts on the table saw first, move the router fence into the bit, or raise or lower the cutter, depending on the cut you're making. The idea is to leave 1/8 in. or less of material for the climb cut. Alternatively, you can rout most of the stock in the conventional forward direction, then readjust the bit or fence and make a light climb cut. However, because a climb cut wants to move the bit away from the work, it's always best to take a final "insurance pass" cutting in the standard direction, which pulls the bit into the work to ensure a fully cut profile.

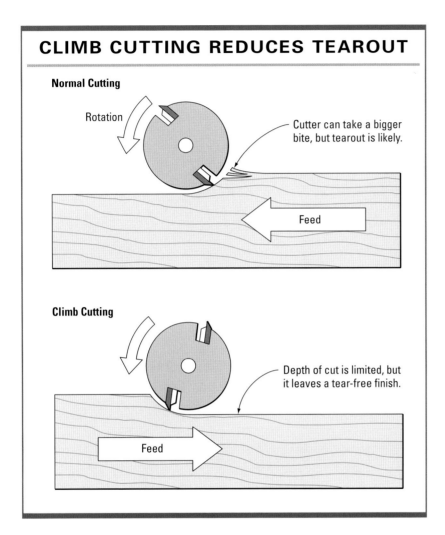

CLIMB CUTTING REDUCES TEAROUT

Normal Cutting

Rotation

Cutter can take a bigger bite, but tearout is likely.

Feed

Climb Cutting

Depth of cut is limited, but it leaves a tear-free finish.

Feed

Avoiding Burning

Burning or scorching stock is quite common. When ripping or routing, a cutting tool generates enough friction to create intense heat. Dense species are particularly susceptible, but so are many softer resinous woods, like cherry. Burning wood should be avoided whenever possible because it produces a black smear that's difficult to remove. The biggest causes of burning are slow feed speeds and sudden stops, both of which serve to increase friction and usually result in black marks. So why not just send that board through lickety-split and be done

with the dark stuff? Well, faster feeding may reduce burning, but the trade-offs are torn fibers and cutters that deflect or bog down. The idea is to seek a comfortable balance, since different woods and different machine setups require different feed speeds. You'll have to experiment to find the right feed speed. Just remember to keep the work or the tool moving during the cut to avoid burns, and keep your blades and cutters free of pitch and other resins by scrubbing them with a blade/bit cleaner on a regular basis.

When you rip into the middle of stock, or make a closed cut, sometimes the stock

Closed cuts can contribute to burning. To fix the problem, you can rip burn-prone woods slightly oversized and then saw them to final size by taking a light trim cut.

Pulling up the tape on this sample of black cherry reveals how much the surrounding area has darkened after only a few hours in sunlight.

burns no matter what you do. For most closed cuts, it makes sense to rip twice instead of just once. Make the first cut about $^1/_{32}$ in. oversize, and then reset the fence and take a second skimming pass to remove any burn marks from the first pass while trimming the part to the desired size. Alternatively, you could remove the last $^1/_{32}$ in. on the jointer, but be careful: It can be tricky to get a parallel cut on this machine.

Keeping an Eye on Color

The hue and tone of all woods eventually change as time goes by. Most woods react slowly, as exposure to light and other environmental conditions affects the pigments and chemicals in the wood. This color-altering process is eagerly anticipated by woodworkers, since most woods develop a richer patina as they age. However, some woods change color in short order, which can cause havoc during the building process. One of the best examples of this is black cherry, a photosensitive wood that darkens

after only a few hours' exposure to sunlight and air.

While ultimately color change is a good thing, wood that darkens during the building phase can result in mismatched parts when it's time to assemble or apply a finish. The best prevention is to cover light-sensitive woods with a sheet when you're not working them. Also, avoid stacking odd-shaped parts together, so that any exposure to light occurs evenly.

Making Repairs

Most of us have suffered wood chipping or cracking at an inopportune time. A typical scenario might be a small piece splintering off the edge of a board while you're profiling the edge, leaving an irregular or torn surface. In fact, many of the boards we work with already contain blemishes, such as knots,

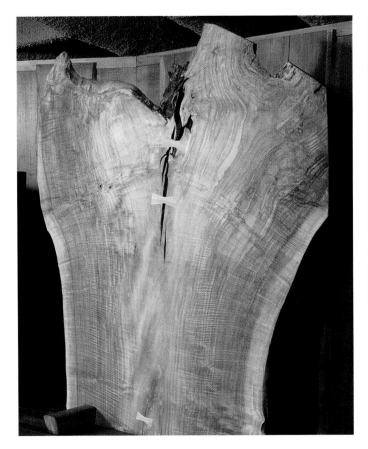

This stunning but potentially flawed panel of oak will make an extraordinary tabletop thanks to the butterfly inlays that span and stabilize large cracks in the end of the plank.

splits, or cracks. Rather than throwing all this stuff on the firewood pile, we owe it to ourselves to get into the habit of routinely repairing cracks, replacing missing chunks, and inlaying new wood into blemished or damaged areas. This approach ensures that our work is sound and free of unsightly imperfections. To that end, the photo essays in this section provide plenty of approaches.

One repair approach that takes a slightly different tack involves highlighting a damaged area rather than hiding it. For example, long cracks in the middle or ends of boards can be bridged with an inlay of decorative wood, which adds visual interest while it stiffens the area and prevents any splits from worsening.

Working Hazardous Woods

Many species of wood can cause mild or even severe physical reactions when they're worked. Typical examples are some of the tropical woods, such as cocobolo and imbuya, both of which can bring on respiratory problems and harsh skin reactions. But more common woods, such as some of the oaks or pines, are also known to affect certain people. Most of these reactions occur from inhaling the tiny dust particles we generate as the wood is worked. In some cases, chemicals in the wood can mix with sweat and enter the bloodstream through the skin, causing some unlucky woodworkers to fall ill from simply touching the wood.

An air-supplied helmet encloses your entire face and draws in fresh, filtered air for cleaner breathing.

Defend yourself from aggravating woods by wearing safety goggles and a respirator and by donning long-sleeved clothing.

Some woods can also be hazardous to plants and animals. While most woodworkers find black walnut perfectly safe to work, its shavings can be harmful to plants and deadly to horses and other hoofed animals if used as bedding. Unfortunately, there is no standard for gauging toxic woods because different woods affect people differently, if at all. However, a few general safety precautions are in order.

Safety Gear

If you're working a new or suspect wood, your best line of defense is to wear extra protection. This includes donning gloves and full-length clothing to cover exposed skin, and using goggles to protect eyes and a cartridge-type respirator to protect your lungs. A respirator filters out particles much better than most paper dust masks. For better face and lung protection, you can wear a helmet that seals off your entire head from dusty air while supplying fresh air via a filter mechanism.

One thing to keep in mind with potentially unsafe woods is that repetitive or long-term exposure can sensitize you to a specific wood. This means that once you've developed a reaction to a particular species, your next exposure to that wood can cause a much more severe reaction. When this occurs, the safest approach is to avoid that particular wood altogether.

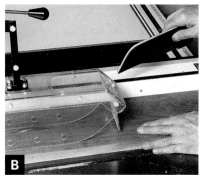

Ripping Without Burning

Ripping long stock on the table saw without hesitating or stopping is the best way to eliminate burning, but the technique requires some choreographed handwork. Start by placing a push stick nearby, carefully oriented so you can grab it easily. Begin to feed the board with your right hand as your left presses the stock down on the table and sideways against the fence **(A)**.

When it's time to grab the push stick, maintain forward momentum by switching, and feeding the board with your left hand while your right picks up the stick **(B)**. Complete the cut by removing your left hand once the stock is separated and pushing the keeper piece past the blade with a push stick **(C)**.

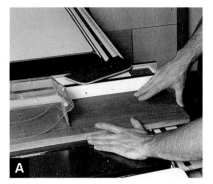

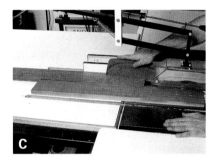

Routing in the Correct Sequence

When routing around two or more edges where end-grain cuts are inevitable and badly sloped long grain is probable, such for as a four-sided panel, begin by routing the end grain first, which will most likely tear at the back of the cut. It certainly will with cherry, a somewhat brittle wood **(A)**.

Make the next pass on the adjacent long-grain edge **(B)**. The beginning of this second cut removes the end-grain tearout from the first pass **(C)**. Continue cutting in this sequence for any remaining edges.

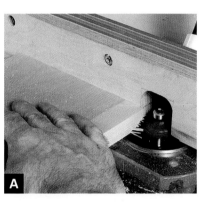

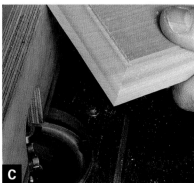

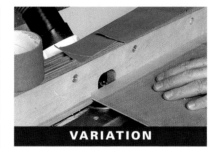

Taking Light Cuts

To reduce tearout, take multiple cuts instead of one heavy pass. Adjust the bit height or depth so that the first cut removes a fair amount of wood, but not so much that it taxes the bit (you'll hear it complain) or makes the stock hard to push **(A)**.

Between passes, adjust the bit to cut about ⅛ in. more, depending on the bit profile **(B)**. On the final one or two passes, take a light, skimming cut **(C)**. These light cuts generate wispy chips and fine dust, completing the profile without tearing fibers.

[**VARIATION**] **Instead of altering the fence setting to take lighter cuts, use tape as shim material. Set the fence for the final pass, and then add a few layers of masking tape to its face. Take successive cuts with the stock against the tape, removing a layer or two after each pass (far left). Then remove the tape altogether and make a last, final pass with the stock against the fence (left).**

Wetting Before Routing

If you soften the fibers of wood with water before routing, you'll reduce the chances of tearout. The technique can be used throughout the routing process, but is usually only necessary on the last few passes. Soak a sponge with clean water and liberally wet the surfaces to be routed, and then wait a minute or two for the fibers to relax **(A)**.

Lubricate the fence with paste wax to help overcome some of the friction caused by the damp stock, and set the bit or fence for a light cut. Then rout as you normally would **(B)**. Routing removes most of the moisture and leaves a tearout-free edge.

Filling Knots with Epoxy

Two-part, slow-set epoxy is great for filling small gaps on the surface of work because it doesn't shrink, and the slower setting time allows any trapped air bubbles to rise to the surface and escape before the adhesive hardens.

First clean out any loose stuff, and then dribble the epoxy into the cavity. If the crack travels through the board, cover the back side with plastic wrap or waxed paper. Try to mound the epoxy over the blemish. This may require a couple of applications because of the adhesive's high viscosity and its willingness to run everywhere but up (A).

Once the epoxy has cured hard, use a sander or scraper to level the mound and smooth the surrounding area (B). Because most knots and inclusions are dark, and because dried epoxy is clear, the repair blends into the surrounding area and is barely noticeable (C).

Filling Gapped Joints with Wood

Gaps or cracks in assembled joints are not uncommon, particularly with dovetail joints (A). Luckily, the gap can be patched with a little slip of wood, which blends better than filling the area with epoxy.

To make the gap a consistent width for patching, use a fine saw to cut a straight kerf and clean out any dried glue at the same time. Make sure not to cut past the baseline of the joint (B).

To make the patch, select a piece of stock from the same project, and rip it to thickness until it just fits into the gap. Then force some glue into the crack and onto the repair piece, and tap it home with a small hammer (C). Once the glue has dried, plane and sand the repair flush with the surrounding joint.

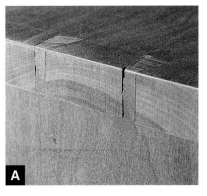

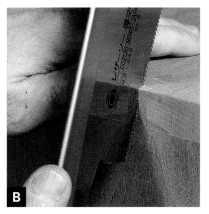

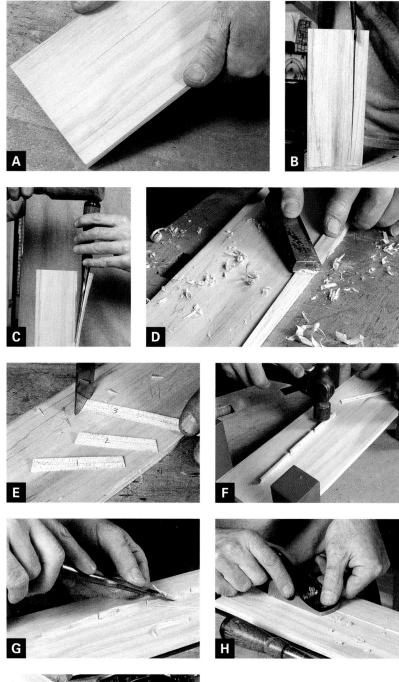

Filling Cracks with Wood

Filling cracks with wood is more involved than using epoxy, but it's a better disguise and worth the effort when you're faced with long splits, particularly in lighter-colored woods **(A)**.

For the most effective camouflage, make your filler piece from the same stock as the wood you're repairing. Start by splitting a section of the stock with a chisel **(B)**. Then use the chisel again to sever a thin strip from the board, orienting the flat back of the chisel towards the strip in order to slice it to even thickness **(C)**. This riving approach creates a flexible strip that's more durable for tapping into the crack.

Bevel the strip on both sides with a chisel **(D)** or by running it over an upturned block plane until the edge is as sharp as a knife's. Then chop the strip into shorter sections for easier installation. Number the strips so you can glue them in sequence for a continuous grain pattern **(E)**.

Spread glue on the edge of each strip and tap it carefully into the crack. Clamps on either side of the crack help prevent further splitting **(F)**. Once the glue has cured, pare away most of the projecting material with a chisel **(G)**. Finish up by leveling the strips and smoothing the surface with a small plane **(H)**. The completed repair is hard to detect, even with a trained woodworker's eye **(I)**!

Replacing Lost Chips

If you chip a piece of wood from a part you're working on, stop what you're doing and hunt for the piece—even if you have to get down on your hands and knees with a magnifying glass. Although it's possible to mend a damaged part using a piece of similar wood, the repair will be more noticeable. The reason your lost chip is so important is that it precisely matches the color, texture, grain pattern, and grain direction of your board—not to mention that its shape is a dead-on match **(A)**.

When you've found the lost chip, gently push it into its cavity to make sure it fits well. You may need to remove a few torn fibers to get the separated part to mate perfectly **(B)**.

Remove the chip, spread some white or yellow glue into the recess and onto the chip itself, and then use masking tape to clamp it back in place. Stretch the tape as you wrap it around the repair to provide sufficient pressure for a good bond **(C)**. Be sure to use as much tape as needed to pull the chip tight without gaps **(D)**.

Wait for the glue to set, and then carefully remove the tape and sand the area to level it and remove any excess glue. The repair should be practically impossible to detect **(E)**.

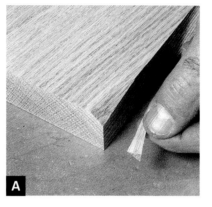

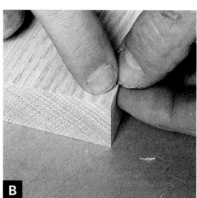

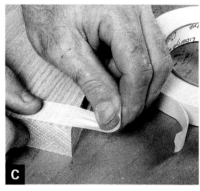

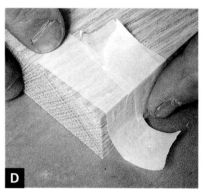

Gluing Down Slivers

If you find a raised split or sliver that's still partially intact, you can glue it back without too much fuss. First prepare a toothpick by rounding over one of its ends with some sandpaper. Then begin the repair by using a slim knife or other thin prying tool to lever the crack open as much as you can without breaking it. Force some white or yellow glue under the sliver with a finger **(A)**.

[TIP] A craft knife, such as X-Acto®
brand, makes an excellent tool for cutting
and prying into small parts. You'll find
them at art-supply stores.

With the knife still holding up the split, use the sharp end of the toothpick to add a dot of cyano-acrylate (CA) glue on top of the white glue **(B)**. Immediately remove the toothpick and use the opposite rounded end to push the sliver into the adhesive and hold it there while the CA glue bonds, which occurs almost instantly **(C)**. The water in white or yellow glue will activate CA glue in seconds, so you can remove your toothpick "clamp" and allow the CA glue to hold while the stronger white or yellow glue dries. When all the glue has thoroughly dried, smooth and level the repair with some fine sandpaper wrapped around a sanding block.

Inlaying a Wood Patch

Letting in a wood patch into large cracks or dings is a good way to hide blemishes while repairing structural weaknesses. Start by outlining the defect on the board in pencil, and then cutting a patch slightly larger than the outline. Use the same type of wood for the repair, and select and orient the grain so that it matches the workpiece as well as possible. Be sure to mark the work and the patch to note its proper orientation **(A)**.

Use a small plane to cut a slight back-bevel all around the patch **(B)**. Then position the patch over the blemish with the larger surface facing up, and mark around its narrower base with a knife **(C)**.

Next, set up a plunge router with a ¼-in.-dia. straight bit (a spiral upcut bit works best for this) and set the bit so it projects about ⅛ in. less than the thickness of the patch **(D)**. Plunge the spinning bit into the repair area, guiding the router freehand and staying ¹⁄₁₆ in. to ⅛ in. inside your knife lines **(E)**. Chisel out the remaining waste by registering the tip of a chisel into the knife lines and chopping straight down **(F)**.

(Continued on p. 178.)

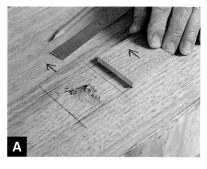

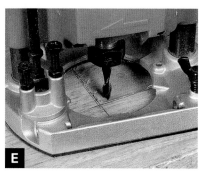

G

H

I

J

K

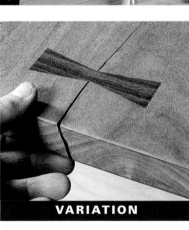

VARIATION

Before gluing the patch into place, plane a small chamfer around its bottom edge to ease installation **(G)**. Spread glue into the recess and onto the edges of the patch, and then push the patch into the recess by hand, making sure to orient the grain in the order that it was marked **(H)**. Place a scrap block over the patch and drive it all the way home with a few sound taps from a hammer. You should see glue squeeze out along the entire joint **(I)**.

Once the glue has dried, plane and sand the patch flush with the surface **(J)**. The completed repair will fool most passersby **(K)**.

[**VARIATION**] **Instead of trying to conceal a blemish such as a large crack, you can call attention to it instead by inlaying a wooden butterfly across the grain for visual impact as well as strength.**

Filling Knotholes

Knotholes can have visual appeal but generally require some repair work to make them sound enough for furniture. This cherry knot is typical fare, with soft punky wood that should be removed in its center, surrounded by beautiful swirling grain at the perimeter **(A)**.

Chuck a straight bit into a plunge router and set it for a ⅜-in. depth of cut. Then, staying away from the outer walls, guide the router freehand to remove most of the knot's center and create a flat bottom **(B)**. Use a small gouge to clean up to the walls and to pick away any loose bark or other debris, until the walls of the hole are sound **(C)**. Finish prepping the knothole with some fine sandpaper by easing over the sharp upper edges of the wall and whisking away remaining loose fibers **(D)**. Give the hole a blast of compressed air to ensure that it's clean.

Lay some waxed paper under the knothole, and then mix a batch of two-part, fast-setting epoxy (five-minute epoxy works well). Dribble it into the center of the hole, being careful not to drip any on the walls **(E)**. This initial round of adhesive stiffens any loose parts and lays the groundwork for subsequent filling.

Once the epoxy has set to the touch, add another layer, but this time use a slow-setting epoxy. If you like, you can get creative by adding Japan colors or colored metal flakes to your new batch **(F)**. As before, dribble the liquid into the center of the hole without splashing the sides. A toothpick gives a more precise, pinpoint aim at this stage **(G)**. You can add enough epoxy to level the hole if you wish, but leaving a depression adds a unique touch. In the latter case, continue adding the epoxy until the hole is only half filled and a portion of the walls remains visible. A coat of finish over the repair and the surrounding wood makes this knothole pop **(H)**.

A

B

C

D

Flattening Veneer

Most veneers are flat enough to glue to a substrate, but wildly figured woods and burls are normally heavily buckled and often quite brittle and fragile. This type of wood must be flattened before it's glued to a core, or it will break apart when pressed.

Flattening can be a two-part process, depending on your work schedule and the type of veneer glue you use. The first stage is to flatten the sheet by softening the fibers. Start by spritzing the veneer with clean water, first spraying one side **(A)**, which will cause the sheet to curl to the opposite side, and then spraying an equal amount of water on the curled side **(B)**. Wait a minute or two for the moisture to soak in and the fibers to relax, during which time the sheet will level out somewhat. When the veneer has softened, lay a sheet of newspaper on your bench, place the veneer on top, cover the veneer with another sheet of paper, add some stiff plywood or MDF over the paper, and add weight on top **(C)**. In a few minutes the sheet will be flat enough for the next step.

If you're going to store your flattened veneer, you'll need to monitor it at this stage by removing the damp newspaper and replacing it with fresh stock daily until the newspaper does not show any more signs of moisture, which can take about a week **(D)**. If you try to stash it while the fibers are still moist, you'll invite mold to take up residence, which will destroy your prized wood. Once the veneer is thoroughly dry, store it on a flat shelf between sheets of plywood or MDF with weight on top. It will be ready for veneering when you are.

If you're going to veneer within the week using hide glue, you can move to the next stage once the veneer is flat, even if it is still damp. This step prepares the sheet for gluing and stiffens it so it's easier to handle. Start by brushing hot hide glue onto both sides of the sheet (**E**). While the glue is still warm, lay an old sheet of newspaper onto what will be the show face. (Avoid newspaper with fresh ink, or the dyes may transfer onto the wood.) Adhere the paper to the wood by gently rubbing it with a soft brush (**F**).

Now flip the assembly over, lay some plastic wrap or waxed paper over the glued, core side of the veneer, and then place a piece of plywood or MDF over the stack (**G**). Immediately clamp the assembly to the work surface (**H**).

Once the glue has cooled, peel off the waxed paper and you're ready to apply the veneer. The newspaper side faces up, while the substrate side already has a coat of glue ready to be warmed up and pressed to the substrate with a household iron and the hammer-veneering technique (**I**).

▶ See *"Hammer Veneering"* on p. 249.

Bending Wood, Page 184

PART FIVE

Bending Wood

THERE IS SOMETHING deeply satisfying—and curiously magical—about bending a piece of stiff, straight wood. We feel like the alchemists of old, altering our material in a way that normally can't be done. To bend wood, we must rely on its inherent plastic nature when it is treated in the right manner. As we've seen, wood is quite flexible in its natural green state, and it's possible to introduce curves simply by working it while it's still wet. But there are other, more controllable methods for bending wood, including kerfing it, sawing it into thin strips, or introducing steam and heat until the material softens enough to force it into a curve. In this part of the book, you'll find plenty of methods for conjuring up the curves of your dreams.

Bending Wood

Green Bending

➤ Bending a Simple Slat (p. 197)

Kerf-Bending

➤ Bending a Kerfed Board (p. 198)

➤ Filling Kerfs with Laminates (p. 200)

Bent Lamination

➤ Laminating with a Two-Part Form (p. 202)

➤ Veneering Curves in a Vacuum (p. 203)

➤ Laminating Free-Form in a Vacuum (p. 204)

Steam-Bending

➤ Steam-Bending a Simple Curve (p. 206)

➤ Steam-Bending a Severe Curve (p. 207)

➤ Steam-Bending a Complex Curve (p. 209)

MANY WOODWORKERS consider bending wood a mysterious art. However, there's no magic to it. Although it does involve skill and a particular understanding of your material, bending wood is fundamentally a science with its own basic rules. Thanks to wood's somewhat pliable nature, it's possible to make almost any degree or type of curve you can dream up. The simplest approach involves using green wood, which is more supple than dried stock. More complex strategies include kerfing, laminating, and steaming. Kerfing involves cutting kerfs in a piece of wood to thin its cross section, thus allowing it to bend more easily. Laminating means building up a curve by gluing together multiple thin strips of wood. Steaming wood plasticizes it, making it flexible enough to bend into a curve. In this section I'll discuss all these bending strategies so you can select the ones that work best for you and your project, or try your hand at all of them.

Choosing Good Benders

Some woods bend quite easily. Others won't bend without breaking no matter what you do. Experience with a particular species or even a specific log is your best guide, and even then, parts can break. Selecting good bending stock is part of the challenge of bending wood. Certain species are known to

Good bending stock includes (from left to right) green hickory, air-dried soft maple, air-dried Northern ash, green white oak, and air-dried cherry. Three butt sections of cherry and walnut (background) will make excellent benders.

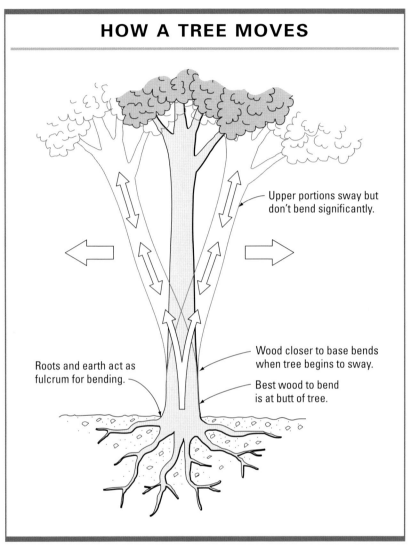

HOW A TREE MOVES

Upper portions sway but don't bend significantly.

Roots and earth act as fulcrum for bending.

Wood closer to base bends when tree begins to sway.

Best wood to bend is at butt of tree.

bend quite well, especially those with long, tubular fibers, such as the oaks, hickories, and ashes. Other popular woods for bending include soft maple, cherry, sweet gum, and yew. However, it's possible to bend even dense or brittle woods such as hard maple or rosewood if you follow a few guidelines.

Due to a tree's natural sway, the butt area of the trunk generally produces wood that's more pliable (see the drawing above right). But you need to know how to detect that section in a board. For example, let's say you need to select a 4-ft.-long bending section from an 8-ft.-long board. Take your bending section from the end that has more widely

spaced growth rings, which indicate the butt end of the tree. In addition to the lower half of the tree, fast-grown wood, which usually displays a whiter color or more sapwood, is generally easier to bend.

If you're steam-bending, green wood is best, and the fresher the better. Air-dried wood is a good second choice and is easier to bend than kiln-dried stock. But for general bending, it is most important that the wood has minimal grain runout along its edges.

Straight grain that runs the full length of the piece will make it much less susceptible to breaking along the grain lines.

The best way to get straight wood is to rive it. But you can also use straight-grained sawn stock—cutting the straight-grained areas from wider boards if necessary.

➤ See *"Using Rived Wood"* on p. 124.

How Wood Bends

Essentially, bending wood involves deforming its fibers by either stretching or compressing them. During a stretched bend, longitudinal fibers are pulled and elongated. The opposite happens during compression, when individual fibers are shortened in the same way an accordion works, while also sliding past each other as the piece shrinks along its length. Most bends consist of both stretched fibers (along the outer curve) and

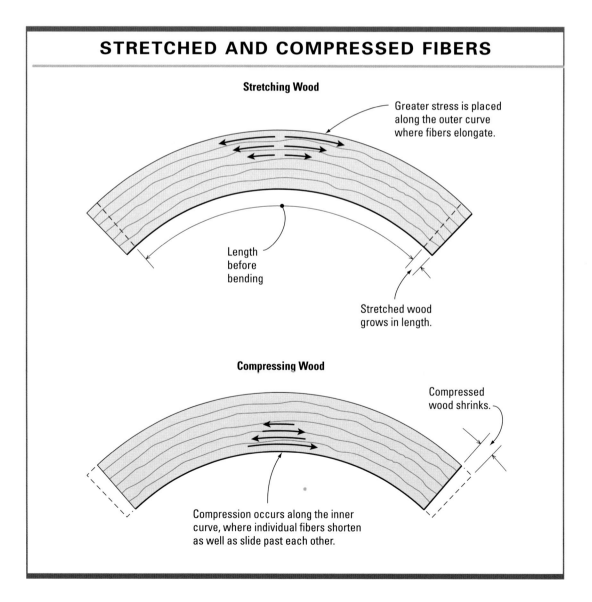

STRETCHED AND COMPRESSED FIBERS

Stretching Wood

Greater stress is placed along the outer curve where fibers elongate.

Length before bending

Stretched wood grows in length.

Compressing Wood

Compressed wood shrinks.

Compression occurs along the inner curve, where individual fibers shorten as well as slide past each other.

The steam-bent cherry at left cracked at the outside of the curve due to tension from stretching. The fibers of the steam-bent hickory at right separated along the inner curve due to compression.

Compression wrinkles across the grain of this steam-bent walnut leg don't go very deep, and can usually be eliminated afterwards by planing or scraping.

compressed fibers (along the inner curve). But when wood is kept from stretching by the use of end blocks on a bending strap, for example, the entire piece can come under compression. How much the wood deforms and what type of tension the fibers experience depends on the bending approach you take and the severity of the bend itself. For example, a 3-ft. length of wood can easily "grow" more than 1 in. when stretched and can shrink by the same amount when compressed. That's a lot of fiber movement!

Because of this stress to the fibers, there's always the risk that your wood will deform too much during a bend. The result will either be tension or compression failure, or sometimes both in the same piece. If your stock is oversized enough, you may be able to cut away the blemished areas after bending. Small creases and bumps commonly caused by compression can often be cleaned up with a few swipes from a plane or scraper.

Keep in mind that almost all bent wood, especially bent-laminated and steam-bent stock, experiences two reactions, known as springback and spring-in. Springback is the tendency for the curve to spring outward toward a larger radius after the bending process. Springback typically happens when wood is stretched but also will take place during mild compression bends. Spring-in, which occurs when wood is

You can readily bend thin, green stock by utilizing a form, such as your knee.

Bending Green Wood

The simplest way to bend wood is to work with green stock, using relatively thin pieces, which are flexible enough to bend quite easily by hand. Once bent, green wood must be restrained in that shape until it dries, typically by holding it in a shop-made form. Unfortunately, you can't significantly curve wide green stock because the bending force required is too great and the fibers will most likely separate. But for narrow parts or shallow curves, it's an easy, low-tech way to go.

Kerf-Bending

Sawing a series of kerfs in wood effectively reduces its thickness, making it pliable enough to bend. This approach is quite predictable and works well with dried wood because you don't have to worry about warpage after the cuts are made and the wood starts to shrink. Once you've created the curve, you'll need to glue or nail the part to a curved framework or other structure to maintain the bend, or fill the kerfs with epoxy. Also, you'll need to conceal exposed kerfs either with veneer or with frame pieces cut to the finished curve.

The trick with kerf-bending is to figure out how thick to leave the uncut face area. You'll need to experiment, but you'll probably find that an uncut thickness of $1/8$ in. or so works for most woods. Brittle or extra-dense woods will require thinner sections. Also, the farther apart the kerfs are spaced, the more rigid the material will be. For example, if you saw a $1/8$-in.-wide kerf deep enough to leave $1/8$ in. of wood beyond the kerf, and locate a kerf every $1/8$ in. to $1/4$ in., you can get a board to bend to a radius of 20 in. or less, depending on the wood. For

heavily compressed, is the opposite of springback, and results in the radius tightening after the initial bend. Different woods will have different spring tendencies, and the amount of movement is usually slight. For example, a 20-in. radius might spring in or out $1/8$ in. to $1/4$ in. Thicker wood and more dramatic curves result in greater amounts of movement. The only way to deal with these traits is to compensate by over- or under-bending your stock. Unfortunately, there are no firm guidelines for this. Experience and the type of wood are your best guides.

One rule stands above all else: The more severe the curvature and the thicker the wood, the harder it will be to bend, and the higher the risk that the fibers will fail. To get started, it's a good idea to begin with thin stock and try to bend mild curves. Once you get a feel for the techniques involved and the bending properties of different woods, you can graduate to more complex curves.

Laminates are generally pliable enough when cut to a thickness of ⅛ in. or less. But as you add multiple laminates, you'll encounter greater resistance. This means that thicker assemblies require thinner laminates than do thinner assemblies. You can test the thickness of the laminates you'll need by bending a sample piece around your form. You should be able to bend the piece easily to the shape of the curve with only light hand pressure.

Once you know the correct thickness, saw the laminates to rough size on the bandsaw, resawing them from a thick block that's been cut slightly oversized in width and a few inches oversized in length. Unless your blade leaves an exceptionally smooth surface, it's usually best to follow up each cut by planing or jointing the sawn face of the block before

By using the table saw to cut a series of regularly-spaced kerfs into the underside of a plank, you can easily curve a thick, wide board.

consistent curves, it's very important that you space your kerfs evenly and cut them to a consistent depth. Otherwise, you'll introduce flat or kinked areas in the show surface.

Laminating Wood

Lamination-bending involves making pieces from strips of dry wood (the laminates) that are thin and pliable enough to bend. You spread glue on their surfaces and clamp them in layers over a curved form. The cured glue between each layer is what holds the curve, and the multiple gluelines make the assembly very strong, rigid, and stable.

Check the laminate thickness by bending a test piece around your desired curve.

The bandsaw is the best tool for resawing laminates to thickness as long as you use a fence that's 90° to the table, or at least parallel to the blade.

Clean up the bandsaw marks by sticking the laminates to a flat melamine and running them through the planer.

resawing the next laminate from it. After slicing all the laminates, smooth the sawn sides by securing the pieces to a smooth, flat panel with double-sided tape, and passing them through the thickness planer until they're the desired thickness for bending.

Most laminate-bending requires the use of a multiple-part form—typically made of two parts. You position the stacked and glued laminates over the bottom form, which is shaped to the desired inner curve of the work. A mating form (or a series of shaped blocks) on top helps distribute clamping pressure (see the drawing on facing page). To generate the desired curve, start with a drawing and then transfer the outline of the curve to the form with a series of pin-pricks from an awl. Draw the full curve by inserting nails into your awl marks and then positioning a flexible ruler against the nails.

A simpler approach is to use a vacuum-bag setup, which requires only one form over which to place the laminates. The bag, under vacuum, then places the necessary pressure

MAKING A BENDING FORM

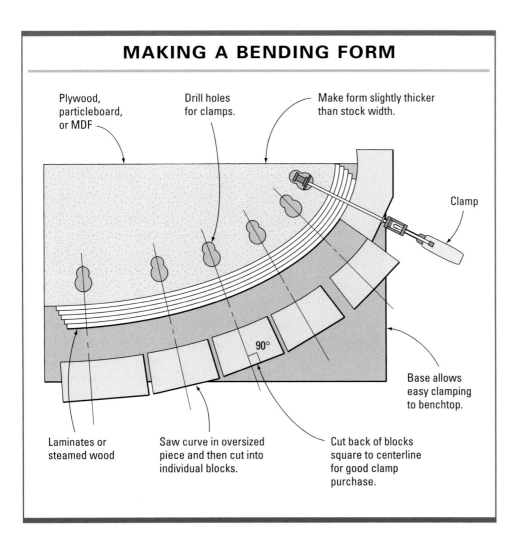

Plywood, particleboard, or MDF

Drill holes for clamps.

Make form slightly thicker than stock width.

Clamp

Laminates or steamed wood

Saw curve in oversized piece and then cut into individual blocks.

90°

Cut back of blocks square to centerline for good clamp purchase.

Base allows easy clamping to benchtop.

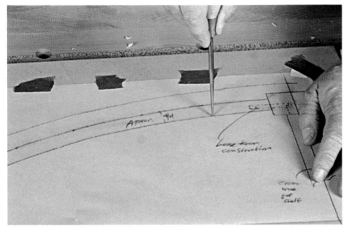

Draw your desired curve on paper, and then use an awl to transfer the curve as a series of pricks to the first layer of the form.

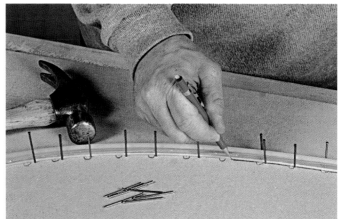

Connect the dots by inserting nails in the awl marks and scribing along a flexible ruler held against the nails.

CONSTRUCTING A FORM FOR VACUUM-BAG CLAMPING

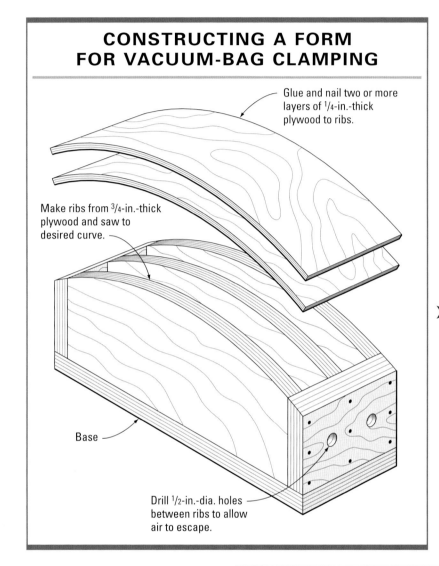

Glue and nail two or more layers of 1/4-in.-thick plywood to ribs.

Make ribs from 3/4-in.-thick plywood and saw to desired curve.

Base

Drill 1/2-in.-dia. holes between ribs to allow air to escape.

over the top of the laminates to press them together as the glue cures.

Because the bent laminates are always in tension, it's best to use a glue that dries hard and rigid, such as plastic resin or epoxy. Softer adhesives, such as white or yellow glue, do a decent job of maintaining the curves but have a tendency to creep over time, often leaving telltale bumps of glue along the gluelines or slightly shifted laminates.

I get great results using Unibond 800, a plastic-resin glue that consists of a resin you mix with a powder.

▶ See *"Choosing and Using Glue"* on p. 237.

With bent laminations, keep in mind that the joint faces won't look like solid wood, especially if you use a lot of thin laminates. To conceal the multiple gluelines as best you can, glue the laminates together in the same sequence in which they were sawn from the block. This approach keeps the grain pattern as continuous as possible.

To avoid shifting of the cured glue or small movement of the laminates, use an adhesive that cures super-hard, such as the resin/powder variety of plastic-resin glue shown here.

Steaming Wood

Introducing moist heat into the pores of wood via steam is an age-old approach to bending wood. When you heat the fibers as well as the lignin that helps bind them together, solid chunks of wood—as much as 2 in. or more in cross section—can be bent into severe curves without noticeable damage to the fibers. Once the wood cools and dries, the curve sets.

The best wood for steam-bending is green stock. Air-dried and kiln-dried stock are second and third choices, respectively. Failure rates are likely to rise when you're using dry wood, since the lignin has already been set, particularly with kiln-dried wood. Also, it takes longer to moisten and thus heat the inside of dry stock, whereas the abundant moisture already inside green stock helps conduct heat quickly so the steaming process is more effective. However, regardless of the moisture content, you can increase your odds of bending success by paying attention to your stock's grain orientation. For most woods, such as the oaks and hickories, your best bet is to bend the tangential face, and not the radial surface. Certain woods, such as ash, prefer a mix of radial and tangential grain and respond best when the grain runs diagonally through its cross section.

To heat and soften wood, you'll need to produce steam inside a container where the temperature is least 200°F, which you can do by building a steam box (see the drawing on p. 194). Your steam box can be simple or elaborate, but the essential idea is to create a sealed box with an access door for the wood, a temperature gauge, a drain to liberate excess water, and a few small holes to release

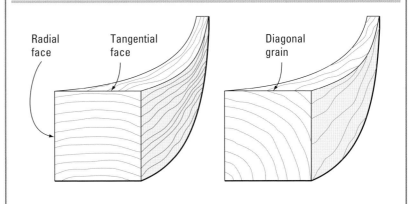

GRAIN ORIENTATION FOR BENDING

Radial face

Tangential face

Diagonal grain

Most woods respond best when you bend the tangential face, and sometimes a face made from diagonal grain. Avoid bending wood on the radial face when possible.

This simple steam box is made from exterior-grade plywood sheathing, with steam piped into the box via an electric kettle.

BUILDING A STEAM BOX

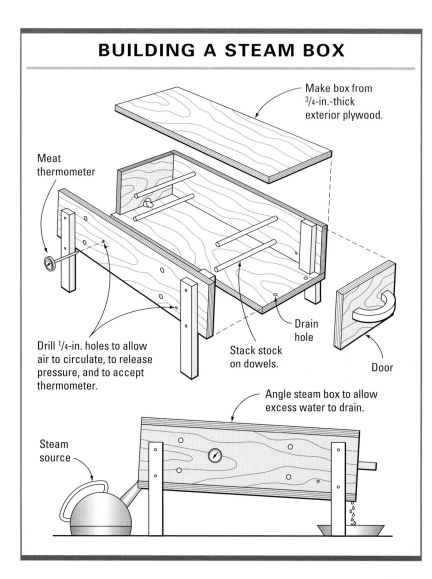

Make box from 3/4-in.-thick exterior plywood.

Meat thermometer

Drill 1/4-in. holes to allow air to circulate, to release pressure, and to accept thermometer.

Stack stock on dowels.

Drain hole

Door

Angle steam box to allow excess water to drain.

Steam source

pressure. Your steam generator can be as simple as a kettle of water boiling on a portable stovetop with the steam piped into the box. Or you can set up a more involved system, perhaps hooking a propane supply to a pressure cooker or even an enclosed heating element.

Steaming times will vary depending on the wood and your particular setup, but a good rule of thumb is one hour per inch of thickness, and perhaps a few minutes more.

Be careful, though: Over-steaming will soften the wood to the point where it will lose its strength and become brittle and difficult to work. Again, as with most wood bending, experimentation is the key to success.

Once the wood is ready to bend, you'll need to work quickly and deliberately, pulling it from the steam box and placing it onto a curved form for bending. Be sure to wear heavy gloves and to practice the sequence ahead of time. The wood will be very hot for quite a while, but it loses elasticity much more quickly, so smooth steps in the actual bending process really count.

As with laminate-bending, you'll need to make bending forms. However, steam-bending forms are generally much simpler to make because there's no need to distribute clamping pressure over the entire surface. One-part forms that support the inner curvature will suffice for most simple curves, as long as you devise a method for holding the ends in place, such as with clamps or wedges. For shallow curves, you can force the wood against the form by hand. Dramatic bends require extra hands or help from rigged-up ropes and pulleys or any scheme that employs leverage to help bend the wood to the form. Two-part or multiple-part forms are great for more complex curves, where you might have a compound bend such as an S curve. Here, you may need to secure long wood or metal poles to the upper form to gain leverage and help the wood deform to its new shape.

For really severe bends, a bending strap or two placed over one or both faces can do a lot to prevent failures by limiting stretching. Fixed or adjustable end blocks attached to the strap butt against the ends of the stock

A steel bending strap with steel end blocks wraps around the outside curve to contain the wood fibers and prevent them from splitting.

This multiple-part form includes bending straps above and below the workpiece for greater control during a severe compound bend.

and help control the bend. Commercial straps are available, or you can make your own from thin steel. It's best to use galvanized or stainless steel so the metal won't react with wood tannins and turn the stock black. For simple bends, you can load the hot wood between end blocks and onto a single strap, placing the strap on the outside of the work. This one-strap approach usually results in slight stretching along the outer curve and mild to medium compression on its inner surface.

For challenging, complex shapes where you introduce two or more significant curves in really thick stock, it's best to use two straps, one outside and one inside the curve. A two-strap approach usually results in heavy compression along both the outer and inner curves because the straps and end blocks restrict fibers that would normally stretch.

Once you've bent the wood to your form, let it set. This can take a few minutes to a

half hour, depending on the wood and the degree of curvature. If you have more parts to bend, it makes sense to free up the form by removing the bent part and placing it in a cooling form, which is essentially a one-part bending form shaped to the inner, finished curve. (Remember that your bending form may be over- or under-curved to allow for

Once the curve has set for a few minutes, transfer the blank to a cooling form so you can continue bending other blanks.

spring.) A cooling form can be as simple as a piece of rope tied off at the ends to hold the curve. A more involved form might be made from stacked plywood or MDF shaped to the finished curve and drilled with holes for clamp purchase. If you have a lot of identical parts to make, you can bend them all in one session if you have several cooling forms to move the bent parts to.

For bent green stock, you'll need to allow the wood to dry before further tooling, just as you would with any green wood. With dry air- or kiln-dried wood, keeping parts in the cooling forms for a day or two is usually sufficient for the moisture content to return to normal. Green stock can take a month or more, depending on the thickness, species, and working environment. Luckily, cooling forms also make excellent drying forms, and leaving your bent wood in them for a month or more ensures that it will dry evenly without significant warpage.

Bending a Simple Slat

With fresh, green wood that's not too thick, you can make a shallow bend over a simple form by hand. Start by centering the stock over the form **(A)** and then using your upper body weight to press the wood to the curve **(B)**. Avoid sudden force, or the wood might crack. Instead, keep constant pressure over the part until you feel it wants to bend.

[VARIATION] To help with a simple bend, fashion a metal strap from thin steel sized a little longer than your stock, with wood handles bolted to the ends. Use the strap over the part to gain better control and to apply more consistent pressure over the entire piece.

As soon as the wood is bent, transfer it to a drying form, which can be as simple as a straight piece of wood with two end blocks, one of which is adjustable **(C)**. Adjust the space between the blocks as necessary, and then rebend the stock so it's captured between them. This second bending requires very little force once the initial bend has been made **(D)**.

Because you're working with green wood, you'll need to let the part dry to the correct moisture content, which can take weeks or even months. The easiest way to do this is to leave the part in the drying form and hang it out of the way in an area where air can freely circulate **(E)**.

A

B

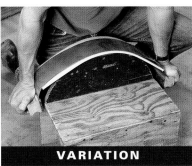

VARIATION

C

D

E

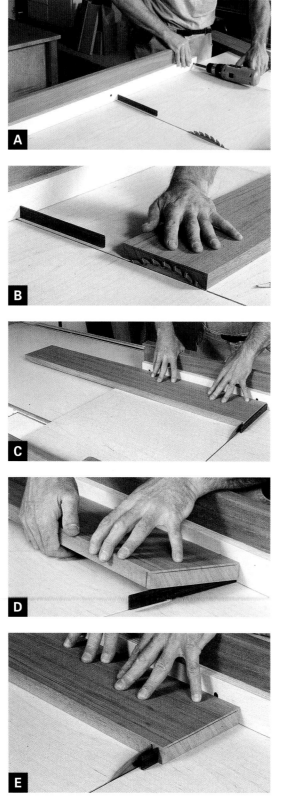

Bending a Kerfed Board

Sawing a series of regularly spaced saw-blade slots, or kerfs, across the grain of a plank will effectively thin it enough that the remaining intact stock can be bent, even in a relatively wide board. To regulate the spacing, it's best to use an indexing stick attached to an auxiliary fence that's fastened to a crosscut sled or your saw's miter gauge.

Make the index stick from dense hardwood, and install it in a saw kerf that you've sawn into the auxiliary fence. The kerf should be equal to the thickness of the sawteeth and slightly shallower than the depth of the kerfs you'll cut into the stock. Then fix this fence to the sled so the index stick is positioned to the left of the blade at a distance equal to the desired spacing between the kerfs, in this case, about ¼ in. **(A)**. Make the stick slightly longer than the width of your stock to ease the positioning and removal of the workpiece. Raise the blade to within ⅛ in. of the top surface of the stock, which should also be slightly above the top edge of the index stick **(B)**.

For the first cut, butt the stock against the stick, turn on the saw, and push the sled and stock past the blade **(C)**. After cutting the first kerf, slip it over the index stick, making sure the board fully contacts the fence and sled surface **(D)**. Then saw the second kerf by once again pushing the stock and sled past the blade **(E)**.

Continue in this fashion to slot the entire board, cutting each kerf and then slipping it over the index stick to make the next cut **(F)**. As you reach the end of the board, place a support panel under its overhanging end to support the stock and keep it from flexing **(G)**.

Once you've sawn all the kerfs, sight down the edge of the board to check that they're all the same depth **(H)**. Gentle hand pressure should be enough to bow the board to the desired curve **(I)**.

A

C

E

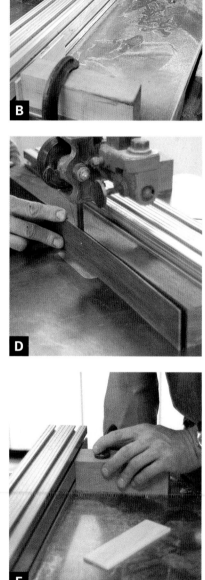

B

D

F

Filling Kerfs with Laminates

If you saw a series of kerfs parallel to the grain of a long blank, and then glue veneer into the kerfs, you can bend the sawn stock to a gentle bow and the glue will hold the curve. The method involves both kerf-bending and laminate-bending techniques.

Start by calculating the number of regularly spaced kerfs you'll saw in your blank and the number and thickness of your filler laminates. After milling the blank to width, place it between the blade and the bandsaw fence and lock the fence into that position. Then clamp a block behind and butted against the fence at each end **(A)**.

To set up for cutting equally spaced kerfs, mill two shims, each of which is equal in thickness to the width of one saw kerf plus the thickness of one filler laminate. Release the fence, insert the shims between the blocks and the fence, and then relock the fence to the table **(B)**.

As a design accent, you can use contrasting wood for the laminates and angle them where they'll stop in the stock. To do this, draw an angled line on the top face of the blank **(C)**. Make the first kerf cut by guiding the stock against the fence, stopping when the blade touches the line you drew **(D)**.

To cut the second kerf, unclamp the fence blocks, remove the shim **(E)**, and reclamp the block up against the locked fence **(F)**.

Then unlock and move the fence (**G**), reinstall the shims, and tighten the fence again (**H**). Saw your second kerf as before, stopping when the blade reaches the marked line (**I**).

Continue in this manner, sawing a series of kerfs by resetting the fence, blocks, and shims after each cut. As you saw, keep pressure against the flexible strips just in front of the blade so the stock bears fully against the fence (**J**). You'll cut the last kerf with the blade one laminate-thickness away from the fence (**K**).

Once you've sawn all the kerfs in the blank, adjust the fence to the thickness of a kerf cut and saw all the laminates from another blank equal in height to your working blank. If you choose a contrasting wood, your laminates will stand out in the finished piece (**L**).

Using stock at least as thick as your working blank, make a two-part gluing form, drawing the inner and outer curves to match the desired curvature, then sawing them out on the bandsaw. If your sawcuts are rough or if the curve is not precisely fair, insert a piece of thin, smooth wood between each form and the working blank to even out the curve during glue-up. Then spread glue on all the laminates, press them into the kerfs, and begin clamping up the blank, working outward from its unkerfed end (**M**).

As you continue to add clamps, the form will begin to close over the blank, drawing the laminates together (**N**). Use enough clamps to ensure that all the joints pull tight without gaps (**O**). Once the glue has cured, you can clean up the two kerfed faces by sweeping one face over the jointer and then planing the opposite face smooth in the thickness planer.

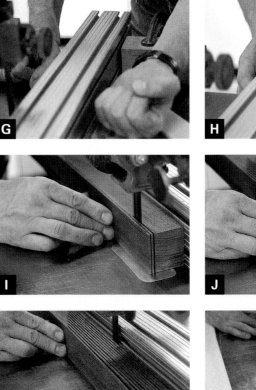

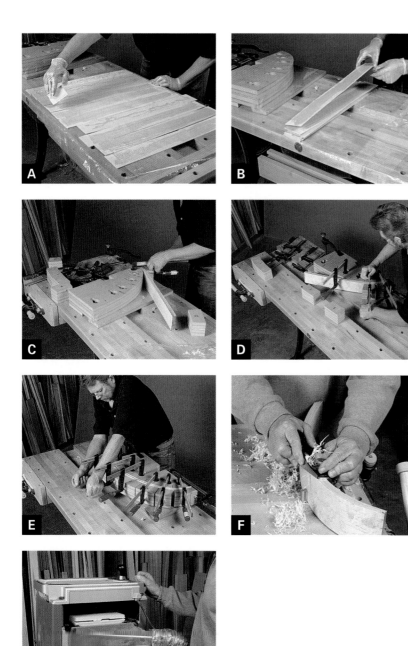

Laminating with a Two-Part Form

You can create a beautiful, strong curved part by gluing multiple strips of wood together around a curved form. Start by laying out your laminates in the same sequence that they were cut in from the block. Apply glue to both sides of each laminate, except for the two outside surfaces. A layer of plastic wrap beneath the work protects your work surface from adhesive, and a credit card is handy for spreading glue evenly **(A)**. Stack all the laminates together, making sure the two uncoated surfaces face outside **(B)**. Adjust the stack until all the edges are reasonably flush.

Position the stack in the form, and clamp an outer block at one end of the form, again checking that the edges of the laminates are as flush as possible **(C)**. Working along the form in sequence, clamp the next block adjacent to the first one. A slightly loose clamp ahead of the sequence helps get the bend started **(D)**. Once you've added the last clamp, go back and check that all the clamps are tight **(E)**.

When the glue has cured, straighten the edges by first cleaning up one edge with a plane, removing dried glue and leveling the laminates with each other **(F)**. With one edge reasonably flat, place this edge down and plane the opposite edge in the thickness planer **(G)**. Once the second edge is clean, turn the stock over and plane the opposite edge to make the piece consistent in thickness. Then continue planing alternating edges until you reach your desired final width.

Veneering Curves in a Vacuum

A vacuum-bag setup makes a great tool for gluing curved parts together, especially veneer work. Laying veneer over a curved substrate, or core, lets you utilize some of the world's finest woods while building curved panels that appear to be solid wood. You'll need to build a curved, one-piece form, and then use this to create the core by stacking multiple laminates, or sheets, of thin, bendable plywood onto the form and gluing them together in the vacuum bag. Once you've made the core and trimmed it to rough size, you're ready to add the veneer facing. Cabinetmaker Peter Breitfeller starts by masking the contact surfaces of the form with clear packing tape to prevent excess adhesive from gluing the veneer to the form **(A)**.

Spread or roll glue onto one face of the core. (Never apply glue to veneer, or it will curl uncontrollably.) Lay the veneer onto that side, then flip the assembly over and apply glue to the opposite side of the form **(B)**. Position the second sheet of veneer onto the second side of the form, and then tape the assembly to the form to prevent it from shifting once it goes into the bag **(C)**.

Carefully slide the assembly into the bag **(D)**. Then seal the bag closed **(E)** and turn on the vacuum pump. As air is being evacuated, smooth out the bag over the assembly to ensure that there aren't any significant wrinkles where it contacts the veneer **(F)**. Once the glue has set, remove the work from the bag and let the glue cure for a day before working the curved part any further.

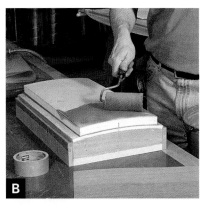

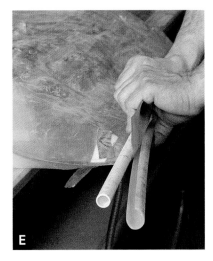

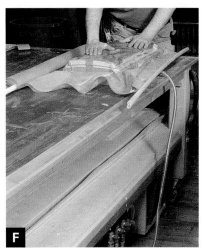

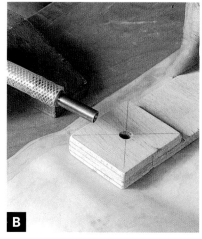

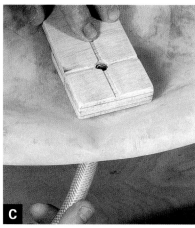

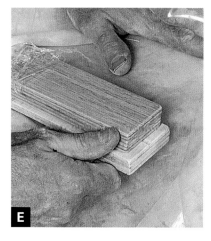

Laminating Free-Form in a Vacuum

All sorts of wild laminate bends are possible with a vacuum bag, forgoing any type of form at all and simply pushing the work into a bend while the vacuum takes effect. To do this, you'll need to make a pliable platen slightly larger than your laminates. The laminates will rest against the platen, which provides a way for air to escape during evacuation. Using bending plywood (a commercially available ⅜-in.-thick plywood that bends easily in one direction), cut a series of ⅛-in. grooves in the surface to provide channels so air can escape **(A)**. At one end and on the ungrooved side of the platen, glue on a block of plywood and then drill a hole through the center of the block and through the platen for the pump's air nipple, centering the hole in one or more grooves cut on the opposite side **(B)**. Place the platen inside the bag, and then install the nipple through the bag and partway into the platen **(C)**.

Apply glue to all the laminates and stack them together. Tape the middle of the stack, and then wrap all but the leading edge of the stack with plastic wrap to prevent glue from oozing into the bag **(D)**. Slide the stack into the bag and over the platen, making sure that the unwrapped portion rests over the hole in the platen to prevent plastic from impeding suction **(E)**.

[**VARIATION**] Instead of using a pliable plywood platen, you can buy a commercial plastic mat called EvacuNet, which you cut to fit under your laminates to evacuate the air. The material can be bent in any direction, facilitating compound curves. Make sure the end of the mat falls over the air exit hole, and keep the work back a few inches from the hole.

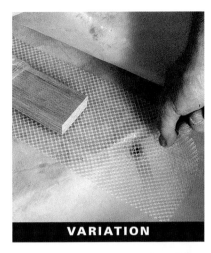

VARIATION

Seal the bag and turn on the pump. As soon as the bag starts to draw over the work, shut off the pump **(F)**. Before the full vacuum is drawn, you can form the curve you desire. Using a clamp as a stop block, place one end of the bag and workpiece against the stop and lift the opposite end to curve the work **(G)**. Once you have the curve you like, turn the pump on again and let it draw a full vacuum. At this point, the bag will hold the curve without further assistance from you **(H)**. Once the glue has set (preferably overnight), remove the work from the bag and check the joints, which will be rough with glue and have slightly shifted laminates but should reveal no gaps **(I)**. After the adhesive has fully cured, smooth one edge on the jointer, place that edge against your table saw's rip fence, and trim the second edge smooth and parallel to the first.

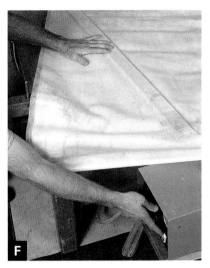

F

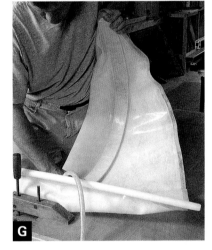

G

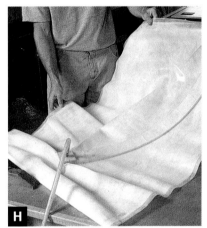

H

I

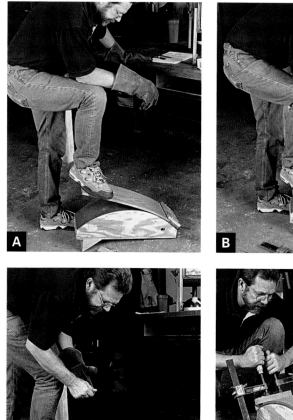

Steam-Bending a Simple Curve

A mild bend in medium-thick stock can be accomplished very simply with a curved form and pressure from your feet to coax the bend. Woodworker Lon Schleining starts by steaming the wood for the appropriate length of time. Moving quickly, he then pulls the wood from the steam box and immediately hooks one end under a cleat at one end of the form, and places pressure over the opposite end with his foot **(A)**.

Let a portion of your weight rest on the piece to encourage the fibers to stretch and the piece to bend. Avoiding sudden force (which may cause breakage), slowly increase your foot pressure until the piece starts to wrap onto the form **(B)**. Maintain pressure with your foot. When the opposite end reaches the form, get ready to clamp it into place **(C)**.

Once you've made the bend, clamp the free end, using a caul over the wood to distribute pressure. A cleat under the form gives the clamps room for purchase **(D)**. Let the wood cool and dry in the form for 24 hours.

Steam-Bending a Severe Curve

Dramatic bends require more involved strategies, such as the use of a bending strap and a powerful system for pulling the curve once the wood has been steamed. Chairmaker Don Weber prepares for the bending process by storing the strap atop the steamer as the wood cooks. This heats up the strap, which will help keep the stock hot during the bending process **(A)**. He begins by pulling a thick blank of green, rived white oak from the steamer, immediately placing it between end blocks and onto a bending strap **(B)**.

A shopmade bending form with a windlass-type mechanism provides the necessary force to bend thick chunks of wood. Moving deliberately and quickly, wedge the assembly against a dowel and the center of the form. Then attach a cable to each end of the bending strap, and begin to crank the windlass to draw the assembly to the form **(C)**. Moving slowly but without stopping, keep turning the windlass as the piece begins to conform to the form **(D)**.

With the windlass cranked all the way in, the stock is almost fully engaged with the form **(E)**.

(Continued on p. 208.)

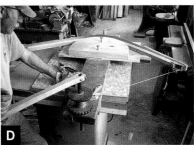
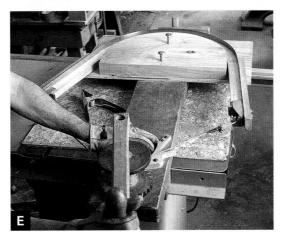

To coax the last bit inward at the ends, clamp across the form and the assembly to help draw the ends closer to the curve **(F)**. At this point, use a block of wood and a hammer to tap the stock down so it makes good contact with the form's backing surface, ensuring that the stock will be flat **(G)**. Then go back and fully clamp the assembly to the form until the ends are tight against it **(H)**.

At this point, the stock needs to cool. Being green wood, it must also dry thoroughly before being put to use. Rather than tying up the bending form for a month or more while waiting for the part to dry, wrap a length of string around the ends of the stock while it's still in the form, and then remove the assembly from the form and let it dry in a well-ventilated area of your shop **(I)**.

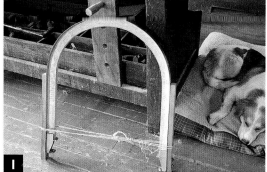

Steam-Bending a Complex Curve

Bending multiple curves in the same piece requires building a multiple-part form that helps shape the piece to the desired curves. If your stock is really thick, such as a 2-in.-square blank, you're better off using bending straps on both sides of the stock and devising some sort of leverage to help power the bend once the piece goes into the form.

Monitor the heat and the time while you steam the workpiece, and when it's time to pull it from the steam box, be sure to wear heavy gloves. Here, chairmaker Brian Boggs selects a piece of green, sawn hickory from a stack of steaming wood **(A)**.

[TIP] **To speed up the steaming process, turn off the steam every half hour or so to cool the steam box, but not below 150°F. This creates a vacuum, which draws more moisture into the wood.**

To make an S bend, place the hot wood on top of the lower bending strap and insert it into the bottom form **(B)**. Use a wrench to crank an adjustable end stop into the end of the blank, squeezing the fibers somewhat and ensuring that the part is well-seated in the form **(C)**.

Using all your body weight and a long wooden bar to increase leverage, slowly and steadily lower the first half of the top form and the attached upper bending strap onto the bottom form, making the first bend at one end of the blank **(D)**. Place a metal pin through a plywood bracket to hold the position.

Next, using a second bar, lower the second half of the top form onto the bottom form to make an opposite bend at the opposite end of the blank **(E)**. Tie off this second form by wrapping some rope around the second and first bars **(F)**.

Once the wood has sat long enough for the curve to take a set, remove it from the bending form and transfer it to a cooling form, placing one end against a stop and under a block-and-bolt clamping system **(G)**. The wood will spring back slightly once it's out of the bending form, but it's supple enough at this point to rebend to the major curves of the cooling form by arm power alone **(H)**.

Once you've bent the stock as far as it will go by hand, pin it in place on the form by sliding a bolt through plywood braces secured to the sides of the form **(I)**.

If necessary, use a clamp to squeeze the stock further to the form's surface **(J)**, or use wedges in strategic locations **(K)**. At the opposite end, draw the clamping block and the work tight to the form by snugging up the nuts over the block. An impact driver fitted with a socket head makes clamping quick, but a regular wrench will just as well, only more slowly **(L)**.

[**VARIATION**] **For convenient and faster clamping to a cooling form, you can devise a block-and-bolt clamping system and use an impact wrench to quickly clamp the workpiece to the form. This removable system can be placed almost anywhere along the curve to ensure that the work is drawn up tight.**

Once the stock is secure on the form, store the part on the form until it's fully dry, especially if you're working with green stock **(M)**.

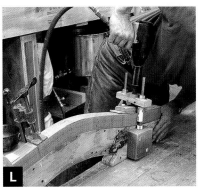

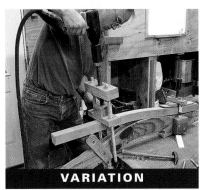

Smoothing and Preparing Wood,
Page 214

Gluing and Clamping Wood,
Page 236

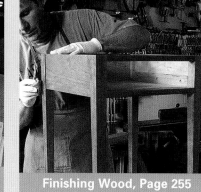
Finishing Wood, Page 255

PART SIX

Smoothing, Gluing, and Finishing

IT MIGHT BE ARGUED that the bulk of your work is done once your joints have been cut and all the parts dimensioned. The truth is, when it comes to the visual impact of the stuff we make, the most important work has yet to begin. Smoothing surfaces, gluing parts together into a unified whole, and applying a stunning finish all combine to create the final effect. Most finishes magnify any blemishes, which makes smoothing and refining your wood such a vital phase. Selecting the right glue and gluing up in an ordered manner can take the pain out of assembly, ensuring that all your joinery comes together without misalignment. Once you're ready for finishing, you'll want to choose the best finish for your wood and apply it like a pro. These final sections will help you complete your masterpiece in a way that makes all your hard work pay off—and that leaves you with fantastic-looking furniture.

Smoothing and Preparing Wood

Planing and Scraping

➤ Smoothing with a Plane (p. 225)

➤ Using a Hand Scraper (p. 227)

Sanding Wood

➤ Flattening with a Belt Sander (p. 228)

➤ Using a Drum Sander (p. 229)

➤ Using a Random-Orbit Sander (p. 231)

➤ Sanding a Small Table by Hand (p. 232)

➤ Hand-Sanding Contours (p. 233)

Making Repairs

➤ Steaming Out Dents (p. 234)

➤ Filling Small Cracks (p. 234)

Preparing for a Finish

➤ Raising the Grain (p. 235)

WOOD THAT HAS BEEN sawn or otherwise cut requires one final task before finishing to make it as attractive as possible. This last step is to smooth its surface, removing the marks from our tools and cleaning up any other small blemishes. Smoothing can be accomplished in several ways. Of course, we're all familiar with sanding wood, but there are alternatives that are often more effective and less tedious or dusty, such as scraping and planing. This section details how to approach the smoothing process, including knowing when to smooth your parts and what tools are most effective at the task.

What is Smooth Wood?

After you've cut all your joints and dimensioned your stock, many of your wooden parts will have saw marks from the bandsaw, miter saw, circular saw, or table saw. Most will display *machine marks* or *mill marks*, terms used to describe a series of regularly spaced scallops on the surface produced by the router, jointer, or thickness planer. You'll also come across a depression on the ends of

HOW MACHINE MARKS ARE MADE

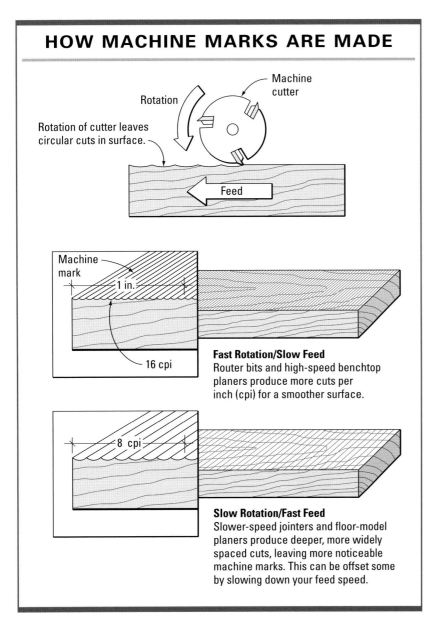

Rotation

Machine cutter

Rotation of cutter leaves circular cuts in surface.

Feed

Machine mark

1 in.

16 cpi

Fast Rotation/Slow Feed
Router bits and high-speed benchtop planers produce more cuts per inch (cpi) for a smoother surface.

8 cpi

Slow Rotation/Fast Feed
Slower-speed jointers and floor-model planers produce deeper, more widely spaced cuts, leaving more noticeable machine marks. This can be offset some by slowing down your feed speed.

The line running across the face of this oak board shows the extent of snipe—the thinner area at the end of the board created during thickness planing. The series of regularly spaced lines along the edge indicate machine marks created by jointer knives.

boards known as *snipe*, a common flaw that occurs when wood is passed through a thickness planer and sometimes when pushed across a misaligned jointer.

Generally, saw marks are readily apparent and can be removed with a swipe of a plane or a quick sanding. But the more subtle machine marks left by rotating router, jointer, or planer cutters can be harder to detect.

Some of us mistake these surface marks for figure markings in the wood. The lines left by router bits and high-speed benchtop planers are faint and easily fool the eye. Jointers and heavy-duty planers, with their slower induction motors, create more widely spaced, deep marks that are easily detected and leave a rougher surface (see the drawing above). Increasing the rotational speed of the cutter and slowing down the feed speed can reduce these marks and make the surface smoother, but they'll still be there.

Even subtle machine marks will be accentuated after you apply a finish, so it's important to hunt for them diligently and remove them during the smoothing process. To help you see machine marks, set up an incandescent task light immediately behind and almost level with the workpiece surface. Then stand in front of the piece and sight across its surface. You'll quickly see these marks left by your machines. Just be sure to remove them completely before starting the finishing process.

Scrape the surface of legs before assembly so you don't have to smooth up against inside corners later.

When Should You Smooth Parts?

You often have the option of smoothing parts before cutting joints or gluing pieces together. Sometimes this is the best approach because you can easily lay boards flat on your bench. However, this can compromise your joinery or make it impractical to glue parts together. While ultimately there is no one easy answer, it's generally best to smooth parts after the joinery work is done, but before assembly. For example, in a complex assembly such as a three-way miter joint, it makes sense to smooth the individual parts because you can easily access areas such as inside corners that will become hard to reach after assembly. As long as you stay away from the joints themselves, your joinery won't be compromised.

➤ See *"Choosing Joints"* on p. 104.

When preparing boards for gluing together into a panel, you can save effort by first jointing the edges, and then sanding or handplaning the surfaces of individual boards. After smoothing, glue the boards together and then use a sander or a scraper to level just the areas at the joints, so you don't have to work the entire panel.

The flip side is that some work is far easier to smooth after assembly. Parts joined cross-grain to each other are the best examples. In a top with breadboard ends, for instance, it's best to scrape or sand adjoining parts after putting them together, leaving you with one smooth, level surface.

Smoothing individual boards before glue-up is a lot easier than tackling a long, wide panel.

After glue-up, a quick swipe with a scraper takes care of any small misalignments along the joint line.

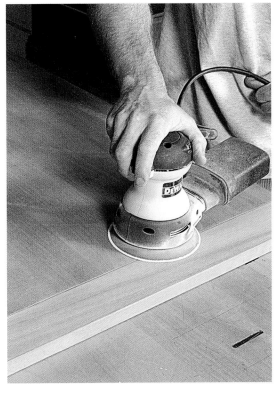

Sanding cross-grain surfaces, such as this breadboard end, after assembly is more reliable than trying to smooth and level them beforehand.

Power-Sanding Versus Handplaning

Sanding your work with a power sander is sometimes the only way to dependably smooth parts without breaking a major sweat and risking tearout. But don't overlook the lowly handplane as a viable alternative. It produces less noise, less dust, is often faster, and will typically leave a flatter surface in experienced hands. While it's worth investigating the types of sanders and sanding techniques available, I encourage you to take the time to master the plane so you can use it in situations where sanding would be less desirable or inappropriate.

When it comes to fine sanding of very large, flat surfaces, a random-orbit sander is easier on your arms than scrapers or planes. However, power sanders are available in a variety of forms to suit almost any purpose. For example, a sanding disk that mounts to your table-saw arbor provides a fast way to sand convex curves or small, flat pieces. The

Fine-sanding large surfaces such as tabletops is easily done with 220-grit sandpaper attached to a random-orbit sander.

You can mount a disk sander on the table saw for smoothing and truing up outside curves. Press lightly to avoid burns.

trick is to use a gentle touch, holding the work lightly against the spinning disk to prevent burning.

For effective smoothing of concave surfaces such as a chair's crest rail, inflatable drum sanders are available in various diameters. More affordable for the small shop is a benchtop oscillating-spindle sander, which can be fitted with large or small spindles, depending on the sweep or diameter of the curve you need to sand.

Keep in mind that you should sand in the direction of the grain whenever possible. When you're sanding flat work, the direction is usually obvious. However, when sanding curved work, such as the concave curve of a rail, you'll want to sand "downhill" (see the drawing on facing page). Sanding in this manner is more effective because it reduces the chances of pulling out fibers or burning the stock. It also leaves a finer scratch pattern and a smoother surface.

Another critical aspect of the sanding process is moving through a succession of sandpaper grits, as shown in the chart below. Each grit size leaves a specific scratch depth and pattern on wood. Thus, the idea is to leave the finest scratch pattern possible by moving through successively finer grits, since

Common Grits in Sandpaper

GRIT #	DESCRIPTION
40, 60 & 80	Very coarse
100 & 120	Coarse
150 & 180	Medium
220 & 320	Fine
400	Very Fine

An inflatable drum sander makes quick work of smoothing and refining inside curves, such as those on a crest rail.

A benchtop oscillating-spindle sander is slower-going but leaves a smoother surface, thanks to the up-and-down action of the rotating spindle.

each successive grit is necessary to remove the scratches left by the previous coarser grit. For general furniture making, this usually means starting your sanding process with 100-grit or 120-grit paper (for fairly coarse sanding), resanding the entire surface using 150 grit or 180 grit, and then finishing with 220 grit, again sanding the entire surface. Some woodworkers follow this with 320 grit, but this is overkill for most woods and usually only makes sense for sanding finishes.

➤ See *"Finishing Wood"* on p. 255.

If you decide to skip a grit instead of following this regimen of moving through the grits, you risk leaving the odd deep scratch here and there in your work.

The downside of sanding is that it typically doesn't create perfectly level, flat, or square surfaces, especially when you're working near an edge or balancing a big sander

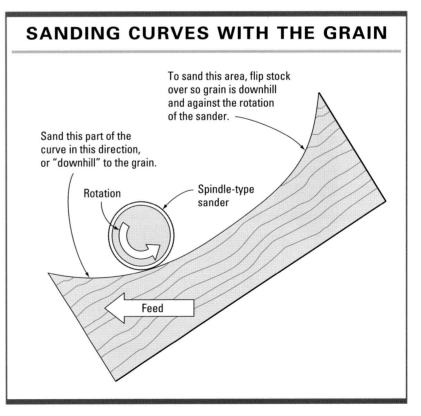

SANDING CURVES WITH THE GRAIN

To sand this area, flip stock over so grain is downhill and against the rotation of the sander.

Sand this part of the curve in this direction, or "downhill" to the grain.

Rotation

Spindle-type sander

Feed

A sharp plane set for a very fine cut can shave a joint level while keeping the surrounding surfaces flat.

Leveling the harder end-grain pins with the softer long-grain side of a dovetailed drawer is best done with a plane to ensure that the drawer sides stay flat.

on a small surface. This is where the hand-plane excels. When you're faced with an assembly that needs minor leveling, such as the joints in a door frame, a handplane will quickly flush up parts without the risk of rounding over or dishing the surface. If you set the plane for a very light cut, cross-grain tearout will be minimal and can be cleaned up easily with some light sanding by hand.

One of the great things about a sharp plane is that it can accurately flatten a surface that consists of both end grain and long grain. For example, when smoothing the sides of a dovetailed drawer, you're faced with smoothing both the long-grain face of the drawer side and the end grain of the pins on the drawer front. Sanding tends to abrade softer face grain more than end grain, leaving an out-of-flat surface. A plane will produce more consistent results, leaving you with flat drawer sides that slide smoothly in and out of a case.

For me, the most compelling aspect of using a plane is the speed and accuracy with which I can get my work done. When all is said and done, it's simply faster to plane than to sand. Add to this the benefits of no rounded surfaces, no dust, no vibration, and no harsh noise—just an enjoyable swishing sound and a pile of gleaming shavings at your feet. So why not plane your wood when you can?

Sanding by Hand

Whether your work is smoothed with a power sander, a plane, or a scraper, it will probably require a final sanding before it's ready for a finish. This final fine sanding will even out any inconsistencies in the surface that might otherwise show as a patchwork of light and dark areas when a finish is applied, such as the glossy surface left by a handplane next to a duller, power-sanded area. In addition, all power sanders leave some sort of definable scratch pattern in your work that needs to be removed to prevent a dull or lackluster look after finishing. Therefore, the best way to do this final sanding is by hand.

Although you'll want to do much of your sanding by simply backing the paper with your hand, everyone's sanding-tool arsenal should include a sanding block or two. Wrapping sandpaper around a block does two things: First, sandpaper backed by a block is more effective at sanding and lasts longer. And second, it ensures that you won't accidentally dish a surface or round it over. Felt blocks, corked-backed wood blocks, plain wood blocks, or even flat chunks of marble all have their place when it comes to hand sanding. Felt and cork provide the necessary cushion for most block-sanding tasks, but harder materials such as stone or hardwood also have their advantages.

Sanding blocks make sanding more effective and ensure that your work stays flat. You can make them or buy them, but make sure that they're sized to fit your hand comfortably.

➤ FOLDING AND HOLDING SANDPAPER

You'll get better sanding results and more life out of your sandpaper if you learn to cut, fold, and hold it in the correct manner. With this folding technique, the grit side of one quarter always touches an adjacent paper-only side, keeping your paper fresh and ready for action. This approach works best for fine sandpaper, such as 220-grit and up.

1. Starting with one-third of a sheet, fold it in half, making a sharp crease at the fold line. **2**. Open up the folded paper and fold one half side into a quarter. **3**. Fold the first half side onto itself and over to the second half, creating four quarters. **4**. With your paper folded for action, the correct grip is to grasp the paper with three fingers and a thumb, while slipping your pinkie under the working side to maintain your grip. **5**. When the first two sides become worn, open them up. **6**. Fold the used quarters onto themselves while opening up the remaining two unused sides. **7**. Finish by wrapping the two fresh quarters around the worn quarters, leaving you with two new sides ready for sanding.

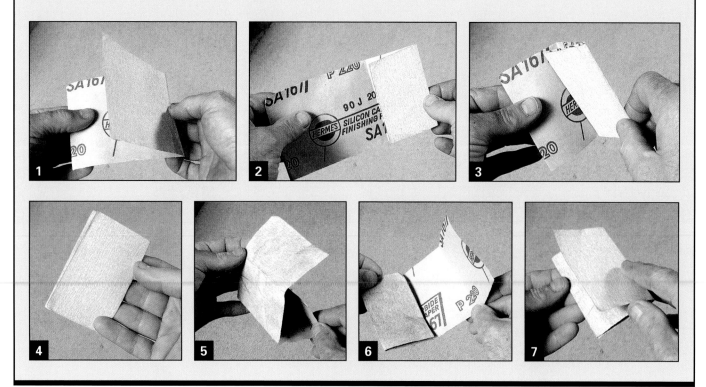

Holding your work between bench dogs allows you to sand an entire surface without having to stop and reclamp. Use lots of downward pressure, and keep the block moving in the direction of the grain.

The basic approach when sanding by hand is to sand with the grain whenever possible, using a soft-faced felt- or cork-covered block for large, flat surfaces. Be sure to keep the paper free of debris by regularly tapping it with the palm of your hand. And change paper when the grit is worn. I'll repeat this one: Don't be cheap. Throw away worn paper, and grab a fresh sheet. Over-using a sheet only serves to burnish the surface and will not smooth it consistently.

While a cushioned sanding block will take care of most of your hand-sanding chores, a harder block is very effective for light shaping of wood, such as gently rounding over a surface. For example, you should ease any sharp edges on your parts. A hardwood block wrapped with 220-grit sandpaper is excellent for this job and will help to ensure a consistent radius.

A hardwood block wrapped with 220-grit paper will accurately round over the edges of a tabletop as well as its corners.

During hand-sanding, torn areas on the surface are revealed by sanding dust that packs into the cavities (left). Before sanding further, smooth the blemished area with a scraper (below).

There are two primary reasons for rounding over any sharp corners in your work. First, wood is a hard material, and any area that hasn't been eased over will feel uncomfortable. Equally important is that sharp wood invites chipping or splintering. Rounding these areas with even as small a radius as $^1/_{32}$ in. makes your furniture inviting to the touch and ensures that it will fare much better over the years.

One of the benefits of sanding by hand is that it often reveals areas that have been inadequately machined before smoothing. For example, sanding dust will quickly fill any torn areas in the surface, indicating that more serious smoothing is necessary before final sanding. When you see these dust-packed cavities, scrape the area to remove the tearout before continuing your sanding regimen.

Smoothing with a Plane

Planing wood to remove machine marks is faster than sanding and leaves a more reliably flat surface. With a sharp blade set for a light cut, start by noting the direction of the fibers so that you can plane with the grain of the wood **(A)**. Instead of clamping a board to the bench for planing, it's best to use a bench with bench dogs, which grasp each end of a board without impeding plane travel. Be sure to push or tap the board flat to the benchtop as you snug up the dogs **(B)**.

Starting at one end of the board, place the front, or toe, of the plane on the work, applying lots of downward pressure at the toe to prevent tipping **(C)**. As the entire plane body engages the surface, equalize your downward pressure by using both hands to push the tool onto the surface as you propel it forward **(D)**. At the end of the board, apply downward pressure at the rear, or heel, to prevent the plane from diving onto the bench as it exits the wood **(E)**. Each pass along the board should be done in one swift movement.

(Continued on p. 226.)

Make all subsequent passes by overlapping the previous cut, moving in a sideways pattern across the board **(F)**. Be sure to stop now and then to clear any debris from the board that may stick to the plane's sole, impeding the cut **(G)**. As you progress, keep an eye on the flatness of the surface by regularly checking it with a straight-edge **(H)**. To correct any out-of-flat areas, simply plane a little more in the high spots.

Be aware that any snipe at the ends of a board probably won't be removed by the first few passes of the plane. The depressed area of the snipe will be revealed by its duller reflection **(I)**. You'll probably plane the entire surface several times before the iron reaches to the depth of the sniped areas.

On the last few passes, retract the iron slightly for an even lighter cut, which produces an even smoother surface. At this point, the plane should begin to take a continuous shaving from one end to the other **(J)**. You're done when each pass across the stock produces a full-length and full-width shaving **(K)**.

Using a Hand Scraper

There are many times that a handplane will tear the wood, no matter how carefully you set up the plane and sharpen its iron. This typically occurs when working highly figured woods, such as this walnut board with its swirling grain. Slight tearout shows up as duller, lighter-colored areas and requires smoothing before a finish is applied **(A)**. Instead of sanding, it's much faster and more effective to scrape the area with a hand scraper, also called a card scraper.

While a scraper can generally cut in any direction without tearing, it's best to scrape with the grain when possible for the smoothest surface. You can push the scraper, tilting it forward and bending it slightly with your thumbs until it starts to bite into the wood. Push the tool in sweeping, fluid movements to avoid overscraping in one area, which can leave a hollow **(B)**. Sometimes it's easier to pull the scraper, again tilting it in the direction of the cut and placing your fingers at the back of the tool in the center to guide the cut **(C)**. Like a plane, a properly sharpened scraper makes shavings, not dust, although the shavings are much finer than those you typically get from a plane **(D)**. (The scraper shaving is shown at the left in the photo.)

One of the great things about card scrapers is that they will cut cross-grain wood without significant tearing **(E)**. In addition to card scrapers, you can use large or small scraper planes, which work in a manner similar to handplanes. Large scraper planes excel at working large surfaces, while small scraper planes are great for smoothing highly figured edges without dishing them or scraping them out of square **(F)**.

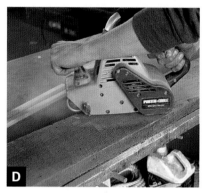

Flattening with a Belt Sander

Belt sanders remove wood in a hurry and therefore are best used for rough work only. However, they come in handy for leveling twisted boards, especially on old or salvaged wood that might contain metal fasteners, such as this reclaimed plank of chestnut (**A**). Hitting a hidden nail in this kind of wood with a handplane or fine sander could do serious damage to the tool, while a belt sander fitted with a coarse belt will grind it flush without complaint.

Start by clamping the board to a bench, shimming it underneath where necessary for support. Then use a pair of winding sticks (two shopmade sticks with parallel edges) to read the surface for twist, noting the high spots (**B**). Begin sanding the high spots by holding the tool at a 45-degree angle to the board, which makes for a more aggressive cut (**C**). Once you've leveled the high spots, continue sanding the entire board at the same diagonal angle (**D**). After sanding the surface in one direction, switch to the opposite diagonal by holding the sander in the opposite direction. Be sure to stop now and then to recheck the surface for flat with your winding sticks (**E**).

Once the surface is flat, finish by sanding with the grain, moving the sander in an even pattern across the board to avoid digging into one area (**F**).

VARIATION

[VARIATION] A belt sander makes a great tool for smoothing small parts if you turn it upside down and clamp it securely in a bench vise. Instead of taking the tool to the work, lightly press the work onto the flat area of the belt to smooth and refine its surface.

Using a Drum Sander

A drum sander can be a lifesaver when you're faced with a board that's too wide or gnarly for your thickness planer **(A)**. Keep in mind that you should begin with a relatively straight plank because, like a thickness planer, a drum sander will not flatten a board; it will only smooth it and bring it to a consistent thickness.

Start by setting the sander's cutting depth to the thickest part of the board, and begin sanding by placing the cupped side of the board down onto the bed of the machine. You'll know the cupped side is down when sanding marks appear on the top side in the middle of the plank **(B)**. As the board exits the machine, be sure to support its weight at the outfeed end **(C)**.

Reset the cutting height, but no more than about ⅟₃₂ in., and even less on really wide stock or dense hardwoods. Take another pass on the same side **(D)**. Drum sanding is a much slower process than thickness planing, and only very light cuts should be made. The third or fourth pass reveals that only about half of the first side of the plank has been sanded **(E)**.

(Continued on p. 230.)

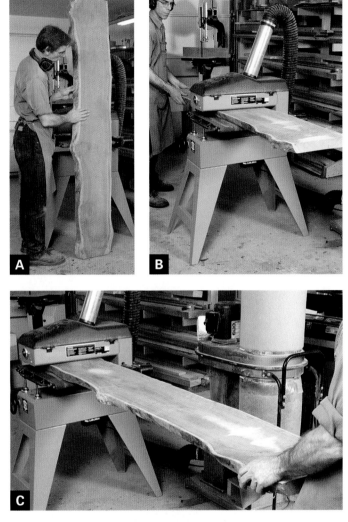

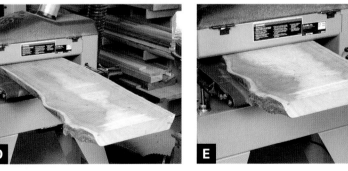

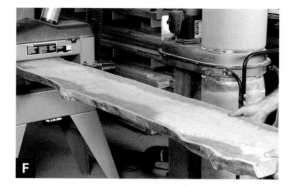

When most of the surface has been sanded **(F)**, flip the stock over, adjust the depth of cut, and begin to sand the opposite side. Since this was the cupped side, the first few passes will abrade only the outer edges of the plank **(G)**. Continue sanding this face, adjusting the depth of cut with each pass until most of the surface has been smoothed **(H)**.

At this point, you can flip the board over with each pass, adjusting the depth of cut until all the rough areas are removed on each face. On the last two passes on each face, send the board through without adjusting the depth of cut. This two-pass approach produces the smoothest surface and a plank that's ready for finer sanding with an orbital sander and eventually by hand **(I)**.

Using a Random-Orbit Sander

Random-orbit sanders leave a finer scratch pattern than regular orbital sanders and have become the finish sander of choice in most shops. They work well on small parts but really shine when sanding large areas because they remove large amounts of wood relatively quickly. The key to using the sander correctly is to move it in the general direction of the grain of the wood and to let the weight of the sander itself do the work, without pressure from your hand **(A)**.

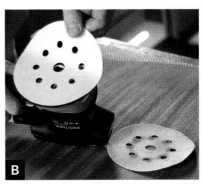

It's important to change sanding disks when they become worn. Many sanders have a hook-and-loop pad that allows you to attach fresh hook-and-loop disks by simply peeling off the old one and pressing a new one into position. Holes in the disks allow dust to be sucked through the pad and into a shop vacuum hooked up to the tool, keeping the work and the work area relatively free of dust **(B)**. To get the most life out of a disk, regularly wipe or blow the work surface free of debris, and clean the disk by giving it a few taps with the palm of your hand **(C)**. Failure to keep the work or the disk clean results in a buildup of sanding nibs on the disk **(D)** that then leave heavy scratch marks on your work.

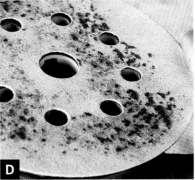

For most woods, it's best to begin sanding with 150-grit or 180-grit paper. Once the surface is smooth, switch to 220 grit and sand the entire area again to remove the scratch pattern left by the previous grit. Since random-orbit sanders leave a fine but detectable scratch pattern, always follow up by sanding with the grain by hand, using the last grit you used on the sander **(E)**.

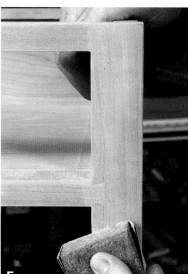

Sanding a Small Table by Hand

All wood should be sanded by hand before finishing to make it as smooth as possible and leave as fine a scratch pattern as is practical. This small table is a good example of how to approach the technique, and the methods used here can be applied to all your sanding jobs.

Always sand with the direction of the grain. Whenever possible, use a sanding block to back up your paper. On broad surfaces, such as this top, use a cork or felt block **(A)**. As most of these surfaces were first smoothed with a hand-plane, it's best to start with a quick sanding with 150-grit or 180-grit sandpaper, followed by a rigorous sanding using 220-grit paper. An exception to this method is when you're sanding end grain, which scores deeply when sanded by too coarse a grit. Here, after planing, use the same cork or felt pad and sand along the edge with 220-grit paper **(B)**.

When you're faced with inside corners, such as where a leg stands proud of a rail, position your paper flush with the end of your sanding block and sand in short jabs towards the leg **(C)**. As you sand, check to see that you've sanded evenly by looking for an even, dull sheen over the entire piece.

When faced with cross-grain parts, always sand the enclosed or trapped part first, moving in the direction of the free part and overlapping it slightly, such as on this rail where it meets the leg **(D)**. Then follow by sanding the free area to smooth it while removing the cross-grain sanding marks left by the previous sanding **(E)**.

Sanding without a block is always a part of the sanding process, and you'll generally tackle work this way when reaching into areas where a block would limit your access. Remember that you're refining the surface just before applying a finish, so take care not to introduce new scratches in the work you've just smoothed. After smoothing one surface, such as the top of this table, place a clean piece of carpet or other soft material under the top to protect it while you smooth the rest of the piece **(F)**.

Hand-Sanding Contours

Refining and final-sanding the curves in your work can be problematic without the right tools. For large, sweeping surfaces such as curved door panels, you can use a sponge-type sanding pad (available at most automotive-supply stores) that accepts stick-on sanding disks. The pad has enough give to conform to large-radii concave and convex surfaces **(A)**.

For large or tight curves, try making your own sanding blocks in different radii from scrap hardwood **(B)**. Then pick the block that matches as closely as possible the curve you need to sand, and wrap sandpaper around it to smooth the surface.

Commercial sanding pads can be used to smooth really tight contours and fillets. Made from a firm, rubbery material, they're available in a variety of profiles to match just about any sanding job you're likely to encounter **(C)**. These pads work best with fine sandpaper, as coarser-grit papers tend to break or deform when pushed into deep profiles.

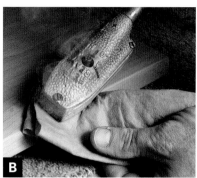

Steaming Out Dents

Dings and dents are bound to happen, but thanks to the elastic nature of wood fibers, small dents are a snap to fix, as long as the fibers aren't torn **(A)**. To raise the crushed fibers back to the surface, start by setting a household iron or edgebanding iron to its hottest temperature, and thoroughly soak a clean paper towel with water. Hold the wet towel directly onto the blemish, and then press the hot iron onto the towel **(B)**. The iron will produce steam (without burning or scorching the wood), which softens the fibers and allows them to rise to the surface.

Typically, the dinged area is now a small bump on the surface. Once the wood had dried, sand the area level with fine sandpaper and the ding disappears **(C)**.

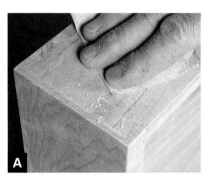

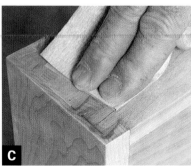

Filling Small Cracks

Sometimes small blemishes surface during your final, prefinish inspection. A good case in point are hairline gaps at joint lines, such as in this dovetail joint. To remedy the situation, start by sanding the area with fine sandpaper, producing dust and pushing it into the cracks **(A)**.

Next, use a thin solution of shellac (a 1-lb. to 3-lb. cut) and the tip of a toothpick to drop some finish into the cracks **(B)**. Before the shellac dries (which takes only minutes), sand the area with fine sandpaper **(C)**. You may need to repeat the procedure a few times until the gaps are filled with the dust/shellac mixture and are level with the surface. Don't worry about the darker appearance of the repaired area; the first few coats of finish you apply will blend it into the surrounding surface.

Raising the Grain

If you plan to use water-based finishing products on your project, it's wise to pre-raise the grain after finish-sanding your piece and before beginning the finishing process. This is because the first coat of a water-based stain or finish tends to raise wood fibers, especially on softer woods. Although you can sand away the raised fibers after the first coat dries, this can remove irregular amounts of stain or finish in the process, creating unsightly splotches that are difficult to fix. Grain doesn't need to be pre-raised on very dense woods or when you're using oil or solvent-based finishes.

Using filtered or distilled water, soak a clean rag and thoroughly wet the surface of your work **(A)**. Don't overlook any end-grain areas, which aren't subject to the same amount of fiber raising but nevertheless will feel rough to the touch if left unattended **(B)**.

> ⚠ **WARNING Avoid tap water when pre-raising grain. It often contains iron salts that can react with tannin-rich woods, producing gray spots.**

Once the wood has dried, which may take only 10 minutes or so, sand the surface with your finest grit **(C)**. Don't sand aggressively, or you'll cut through the wetted layer and expose fresh fibers that will rise once more. Sweep your hands over the surface when you think you're done; it should feel as smooth as silk, which tells you you're ready for finishing **(D)**.

Gluing and Clamping Wood

Gluing Oily Wood

➤ Gluing Oily Wood (p. 243)

Clamping Up

➤ Clamping Moldings with Tape (p. 244)

➤ Pulling Miters Tight (p. 245)

➤ Clamping Panels Flat (p. 246)

➤ Using Vacuum as a Clamp (p. 247)

Gluing Veneers

➤ Veneering with Platens and Cauls (p. 248)

➤ Hammer Veneering (p. 249)

➤ Hammer Inlay (p. 251)

Removing Glue

➤ Removing Excess Glue (p. 254)

GLUING UP TABLETOPS, doors, cabinets, and other complex assemblies can be tricky business, as can be laying up veneer. If you screw up, all your hard work may be down the drain. That's why it pays to glue up and clamp in an orderly and efficient manner. Woven into the fabric of this sticky scenario is the glue you choose. Some adhesives are easier to use, and it's worth getting to know those

that can expand your woodworking horizons. And while most of us will never have enough clamps for every need, there are some great alternatives you can employ when clamps are few or when they simply can't reach where you need to go. In this section, I'll discuss glues and clamping, and how to make your glue-ups successful even in the most challenging situations.

Different glues for different jobs (from left to right): Glue pot for heating glue and hide-glue granules; modern white and yellow glues; Unibond 800, a powder/resin type of plastic-resin glue; and two-part epoxy with easy-to-use pumps.

Choosing and Using Glue

There are many types of glue for the woodworker, and you can pick and choose the type you use depending on the particular project you're gluing up. One of the best—and often most overlooked—is hide glue. Woodworking's oldest glue, hide glue is a natural adhesive made from the bones and tissue of animals. Hot hide glue must be heated in a pot and applied while warm. The glue is easy to work with and is reversible, which is possibly its best feature. This means you can reactivate it with heat and water—even hundreds of years in the future, letting you (or your descendants) repair your furniture without having to remove old glue or retool the joints as you would with modern synthetic glues. In addition, hide glue has greater shear, peel, and cleavage strength

than modern glues, all important attributes for our woodworking joints. It's a glue worth getting to know.

Many of us exclusively use common water-based white and yellow glues because these modern synthetic adhesives are so convenient. While yellow glue is slightly stronger than white glue, both are plenty strong enough for bonding wood. In fact, like hide glue, they are much stronger than the internal bonds of the wood fibers. Yellow glue is thicker than white glue, which some find advantageous. However, thinner glues are easier to apply and spread and offer a longer open time, giving you more time to get the clamps on. The good news is that you can dilute yellow or white water-based glues as long as you don't add more than about 10 percent water.

Mixing a few drops of water into water-based glue will improve its viscosity without damaging its bond strength. Add water until the mixture flows like heavy cream (inset).

It's a good idea to keep some specialty glues in the shop, too. Water-resistant and water-proof glues come in handy for outdoor projects that will be subject to a lot of moisture and extreme wet/dry cycles. Polyurethane glue and plastic-resin glue—both water-resistant—and waterproof two-part epoxy are all good candidates here. You can also use the newer water-resistant yellow and white glues, which hold up well under moisture.

In addition to water resistance, epoxy and the powder/resin variety of plastic resin glue have other advantages. They both cure to a rigid, hard film, which makes them less prone to creep, the tendency for the dried glue to rise slightly above the surface or shift between a joint line, sometimes misaligning a joint long after a finish has been applied.

Plus, the two adhesives don't contain moisture. These attributes make epoxy and plastic resin excellent candidates for joints that are under a lot of stress, such as bent laminations.

▶ See *"Laminating Wood"* on p. 189.

They're also great glues to use when you don't want to introduce moisture during glue-up, such as while veneering in a vacuum.

▶ See *"Veneering Curves in a Vacuum"* on p. 203.

Except for hide glue, which accepts stains and finishes, you must be careful not to leave any glue on the surface of wood before applying a finish. If you do, the glue invariably shows up as a dull or glassy spot. To avoid this, it pays to learn how to apply your glue properly so you don't make a mess in the first place. You should also know how to clean up any excess that squeezes from your joints.

Some furniture makers like to prefinish parts of their projects before final assembly, which can make the finishing process go more smoothly later. If you do this, be very careful not to get any finishing material on areas that will be glued. To prevent problems, mask off any areas that will be subsequently glued, or work up to joint shoulders carefully without getting finish on the joints themselves. Otherwise, the finish may clog the pores of the wood, inviting joint failure.

Undetected glue left on the surface of wood will show up as an ugly smear once you apply the first coat of finish.

Prefinishing parts before final assembly lets you work comfortably on a flat surface and apply finish to areas that would be difficult to access after gluing up.

Don't get any finish in your mortises, on tenon faces, or anyplace where glue must bond to bare wood.

Narrow and wide acid brushes let you put glue where you need it. Pouring glue into a small, non-tipping tin makes it easy to get the precise amount on the brush.

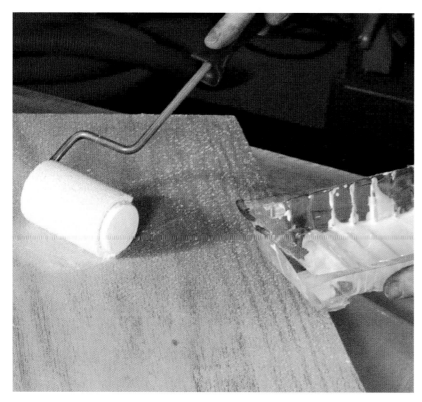

A 3-in. foam roller, sliced on the bandsaw from a 12-in.-long tube, makes an efficient applicator for covering big surfaces.

Applying Glue

It's common for beginners to use too much glue when gluing up. Usually this isn't a problem, except that it wastes glue and makes a mess of your glue-up table. But overgluing your joints can also lead to wayward glue getting into the pores of your show surfaces, only to reveal itself later as an unsightly smear under your finish. On the other hand, applying too little glue can starve a joint as the glue is forced into the pores from the clamping process, leaving little to hold the joint at the joint line. To get a better handle on applying glue, there are a few tools and techniques you can employ.

For complex assemblies, it's best to pour your glue into a small can, such as a cat food tin, and then use small brushes to apply the glue. When gluing wide surfaces, use a 3-in. foam roller instead of a brush. The foam holds a lot of glue without dripping, and lets you apply it evenly.

▶ KEEP YOUR GLUE FRESH

Dry hide glue lasts nearly forever and can be stored indefinitely if kept away from moisture. Not so with modern white and yellow glues, which typically have a shelf life of about a year. To ensure that your white or yellow glues are fresh, date them when you buy them, and throw out anything that's been sitting on your shelves for more than a year. If you're in doubt about a specific glue's worthiness, glue up a sample joint and then break it apart. If the break occurs on the glueline, your glue is suspect and should be replaced. To help preserve glue, keep it from freezing. If white or yellow glue gets too cold, you'll notice that it pours from the bottle in stringy clumps. If this happens, throw it away and use fresh glue. You'll sleep better knowing that your joints are well bonded.

Most glues aren't date-stamped at the factory. If you label them with a permanent marker when you buy them, you'll always know when your glue is fresh.

So how much glue is enough? The idea is to wet the fibers of the wood you're about to bond. An even, thin film is sufficient as long as both parts are wet. On closed joints such as a mortise and tenon, where you can't easily place pressure over the joint, you should wet both the tenon and the mortise. On open joints that can be manipulated, such as an edge joint, you need only apply glue to one surface. This works because you can either rub the parts together by hand to wet the

With closed joints such as mortises and tenons, brush glue both in the mortise and on the tenon to ensure a good bond.

On open joints, such as an edge joint, you can run one fat bead down the center of one edge.

Rubbing the parts of the joint together, or simply clamping it, distributes glue to the unglued face. Squeeze-out is a good sign that the fibers are well-coated with adhesive.

Taking apart a properly wetted edge joint reveals healthy amounts of glue on both sides of the joint, but not so much that excess glue makes a mess once the clamps go on.

mating edge, or let clamp pressure do the job. Either way, look for beads of excess glue escaping the joint line once the joint is clamped. The trick is to apply enough glue to produce a thin film that coats both sides, without having so much that glue oozes all over the place once the clamps are applied.

Gluing Oily Wood

Many tropical woods—particularly rosewoods—contain oils and resins that can impede glue and prevent a good bond. To ensure that your glue-up is successful, it's best to clean the joint before applying adhesive. If possible, joint the surface just before assembly **(A)** or carefully sand the area that will receive glue, using a hard block to avoid rounding over the edges **(B)**.

If your joints have been sitting for a while, rub them with a rag dampened with naphtha, a quickly evaporating solvent that will carry off excess oils **(C)**. Once the surface looks dry to the touch, glue it up immediately **(D)**. Don't dawdle or the oils can rise back to the surface of the joint, and you'll have to repeat the cleaning procedure.

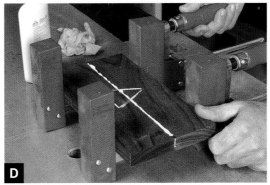

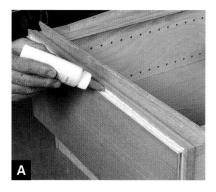
A

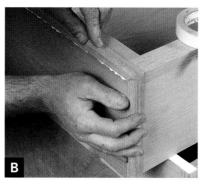
B

C

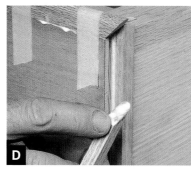
D

E

F

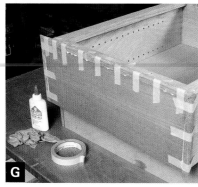
G

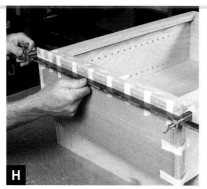
H

Clamping Moldings with Tape

Ordinary masking tape makes a great clamp for areas where ordinary clamps can't easily reach, such as when you're gluing moldings or other delicate parts, or when you don't need the strong pressure that regular clamps afford. Plus, using individual strips of tape gives you greater control in positioning parts that have a tendency to slide around when coated with glue.

[TIP] **Buy the cheaper variety of masking tape. It has a weaker adhesive that's less likely to pull or tear off wood fibers when you remove it.**

To glue molding around three sides of a plywood top, begin by applying glue to the front of the case (**A**). Hold a side molding in position, and use it to help align the front molding as you push it into place (**B**). Now attach strips of tape over the front molding and to the case, stretching each piece so that it applies pressure over the joint (**C**).

Attach a side piece next. To prevent a starved joint at the miter, first apply a thin coat of glue to each miter face, and allow these thirstier end-grain areas to absorb glue in the pores (**D**). Then reapply glue to the miters and along the case side, and press the molding tight to the case and the adjoining molding (**E**). Again, stretch pieces of tape over the joint, looking for a healthy amount of squeeze-out along the joint line (**F**). Look for tight joints all along the completed glue-up (**G**). If one area reveals gaps, you can try applying more tape, or use a small clamp to pull the joint home (**H**).

Pulling Miters Tight

Miters can be tricky to glue together because of their angles and the fact that adding glue makes everything want to slide around, misaligning your joints. To help overcome this problem, you can use pairs of biscuits in the miters to reinforce the joint and align it at the same time. Also, adding a few strips of masking tape helps draw the joint closed before the clamps go on.

First, don a glove, grab a handful of biscuits, and then squeeze glue into your palm, mashing the biscuits around in your hand until they're well-coated with glue **(A)**. Moving quickly, install the compressed biscuits in their slots before they have time to swell **(B)**.

Assemble the miters, and then stretch a piece of tape across the center of the joint **(C)**. Apply your clamps so they oppose each other on each corner of the joint, increasing the pressure on each clamp gently and in succession to avoid misaligning the joints **(D)**. Finish by measuring each diagonal, adjusting the clamps if necessary **(E)**. When both diagonals measure the same, the frame is perfectly square.

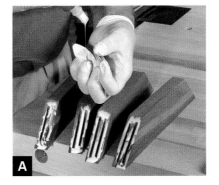

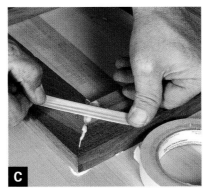

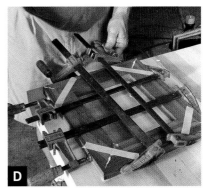

A

B

C

D

E

F

G

Clamping Panels Flat

Creating wide, flat panels from individual boards can be a chore if you don't follow a sensible procedure. The first step is to work on a flat surface, which ensures that your work will be flat. Next, clamp the parts together without glue, and check that there are no gaps along your joint lines. This dry run also ensures that you have all the necessary gear nearby as you start to spread glue **(A)**.

Apply glue to one edge of each board (but not the outermost edges, of course), and then position the boards edge to edge on top of your clamps. Starting at one end of the panel, apply gentle (not full) pressure on the end clamp, at the same time aligning the ends of the boards by twisting them up or down until their surfaces are flush **(B)**. Now move to the adjacent clamp, and repeat the procedure by applying pressure to the clamp while you align the surface in that area **(C)**. Continue to the opposite end of the panel, again applying gentle pressure with the end clamp while aligning the boards with your other hand **(D)**.

Before tightening the clamps further, go over the surface of the joints with a finger to feel for any misalignment **(E)**. When you feel a raised area, place a block of wood over the offending board and give it a sound rap with a mallet to bring the joint flush **(F)**. Once all the joint lines are flush, fully tighten each clamp.

If you wish, wipe off the excess glue now. Then either store the panel flat on your flat bench, or stand it as vertically as possible until the glue has dried **(G)**.

Using Vacuum as a Clamp

A vacuum-clamping system with a vacuum bag provides an efficient method for bonding wood. Work placed in a vacuum experiences about 1,750 lbs. per sq. ft. of pressure—plenty for gluing wood together. The procedure is especially handy with wide work, where regular clamps might not be able to reach into the middle of a panel. You'll need to make a grooved platen to serve as a platform and insert it in the bag. The grooved surface allows air to escape when work is placed upon it **(A)**.

Once your vacuum system is ready to go, roll an even coat of glue onto both surfaces of the boards you're gluing together **(B)**. Place the pieces together, and then tape their edges to prevent the parts from sliding around in the bag. Brown packing tape is a good choice because it's strong, stretches well, and removes easily without tearing the fibers of wood **(C)**. After taping the assembly together, slide it into the bag **(D)**, seal the bag, and then turn on the vacuum pump **(E)**. The pump withdraws air from the bag and should reach 25 in. of mercury, or roughly 1,750 lbs. per sq. ft. As the air is being evacuated, use your hands to smooth out any wrinkles in the bag **(F)**.

It's usually best to leave the work in the bag overnight, or for at least eight hours. Once you remove the piece from the bag, you should see tight seams all along the joint line **(G)**. If you used a water-based glue, remember that the work will still contain moisture, so be sure to store the assembly on a flat surface and allow it to release any dampness for another day or so before putting the part into service.

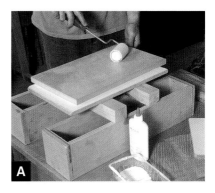

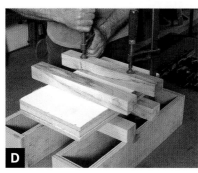

Veneering with Platens and Cauls

If you're not familiar with hammer veneering or don't have access to a large veneer press or a vacuum-clamping system, you can still glue up your veneers by putting together a small-scale press, using clamps and ready supplies you probably already have in your shop.

Using melamine or any other flat, smooth sheet stock, make a platen that's slightly wider and longer than your core material, and place it on top of some thick wood cauls. To allow clamp access, set the platen and cauls atop risers of some sort, like the plywood boxes here. Then position your core material on this setup, and roll glue onto its surface (**A**).

[TIP] Except when hammer veneering, never apply glue directly to veneer, or it will curl uncontrollably.

After applying glue to one face of the core stock, place a sheet of veneer on the platen, position the glued side of the core over it, and glue the opposite face of the core (**B**). Lay the second sheet of veneer onto the core, and then cover it with a second platen (**C**).

Lay cauls across the top platen, making sure they align with the lower cauls. Begin clamping the stack by applying clamp pressure as close to the center as possible (**D**). The idea is to work from the center outward so that the glue is evenly distributed over the veneers. Use as many clamps as you can, spacing them around the stack (**E**). The platens and the cauls above and below them help distribute the necessary clamp pressure so your thin veneers are well-bonded to the core.

Hammer Veneering

Hammer veneering involves using warm hide glue and a veneer hammer, which acts more like a squeegee than a hammer. Start by heating the glue to correct the consistency. At the right temperature, it should flow like heavy cream **(A)**.

Use a brush to apply a liberal amount of the glue to the core material **(B)**. Lay the veneer onto the glue, and then brush more glue on top of the veneer **(C)**. While the glue is still warm, begin to work the hammer back and forth on the veneer. Move generally from the center outward, pushing down hard on the hammer to stick the veneer while working any trapped air or excess glue under the veneer to the perimeter, where it can escape along the edge. At the same time, push any excess glue on top of the veneer off to the sides **(D)**.

[**TIP**] **When the tip of your veneer hammer becomes clogged with cooled glue, lay a scrub sponge in a pan of warm water and rub the tip over the sponge to clean away any excess.**

If you need to cover a core that's wider than your veneer, you can add a second sheet by brushing more glue onto the core, adjacent to the sheet you just laid **(E)**. Lay the second sheet onto the core so one edge overlaps the previous sheet, and as before, brush glue onto its surface **(F)**. Work this sheet with the hammer as you did previously, staying close to, but clear of, the joint line between the two sheets **(G)**.

(Continued on p. 250.)

A

B

C

D

TIP

E

F

G

As you work, check the veneer by tapping it with a fingernail. A hollow sound indicates an area that hasn't stuck to the core **(H)**. To secure an unstuck area, or if the glue cools too much as you're working (it gels as it cools and will cease to grab the veneer), heat up the hammer by placing it in the boiler with the glue pot removed **(I)**. Once the hammer is hot, place its blunt end onto the veneer to warm and reactivate the glue **(J)**, and press again with the hammer.

When both sheets are well adhered and while the glue is still warm, lay a straightedge over the area where the sheets overlap, and use a sharp knife, or preferably a veneer saw, to slice through both sheets **(K)**. Peel up the topmost cutoff strip with a thin blade or artist's palette knife **(L)**, and then lift the remaining edge of the sheet so you can remove the second strip from below **(M)**. Once you've removed the strips, work the joint line, pressing it flat with the hammer **(N)**.

Hammer Inlay

Once you've learned to veneer with hide glue and a veneer hammer, the next step is to try your hand at inlaying a border using similar techniques. Begin by cleaning up the border of your hammer-veneered work by cutting the perimeter to the width of your desired inlay, using a marking gauge. For the cleanest cuts, use a marking gauge fitted with a knife cutter instead of a pin, or guide a sharp knife with a straightedge **(A)**. Heat the glue with the hot head of the hammer **(B)** and remove the excess veneer by peeling it up with a thin knife **(C)**.

Cut your border strips, making them oversized in length. Then, working one side of your panel at a time, spread hot glue along the edges of the veneer and position a strip of inlay along the edge, using the hammer to stick it in place **(D)**. Move to an adjacent side and repeat the process, overlaying a second strip of inlay onto the first **(E)**. At the corner, cut a miter through both pieces by pressing firmly with a sharp knife **(F)**. Remove the two excess pieces **(G)** and rub the inlay at the miter with the hammer. Continue adding and mitering inlay around the entire panel in this manner.

(Continued on p. 252.)

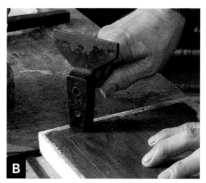

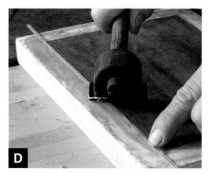

Next, lay a strip of crossbanding (any veneer where the grain direction is 90 degrees to the edge of the work) against the inlay so that it extends past the corner and slightly beyond the edge of the core **(H)**. Follow by laying a second strip of banding at the corner along the adjacent edge **(I)**. As you did with the inlay, cut a miter through both pieces, this time using a 45-degree drafting triangle to guide your knife **(J)**. Peel back the veneer as before and remove the two offcuts **(K)**. Add more glue if necessary, and continue pressing the banding and the miter to the core with the hammer **(L)**. Continue in this fashion to inlay and crossband all four corners.

At this point, excess glue may start to build up on the face of the work. When this happens, use a sponge with a rough surface dipped in warm water to scrub and wipe away any extra glue **(M)**.

To complete the border, brush glue on any remaining areas **(N)** and hammer a new piece in place, letting its ends overlap the previous sections **(O)**. Use a razor knife to slice through overlapping bandings **(P)**, remove the excess, and stick the banding on as before with the hammer.

The veneered panel shows a nice contrast between mahogany veneers in the center, bordered by inlay strips of maple and crossbands of walnut **(Q)**. To complete the project, turn the core over, raise one edge slightly by laying it on a scrap stick, and use a veneer saw to trim away any overhanging veneer on the opposite edge **(R)**.

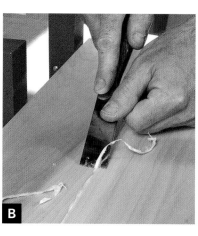

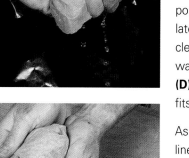

Removing Excess Glue

The best glue-ups result in a bit of excess glue that squeezes from the joint line, indicating that enough glue was used **(A)**. To remove excess white or yellow glue, you have two options. The first is to wait until the glue is in a rubbery state, which usually takes a half hour or so, and then gently cut it away with a sharp chisel **(B)**. Be warned that waiting longer is a recipe for disaster, because fully dried glue has a tendency to rip away wood fibers if chiseled or scraped off at this stage, and sanding the stuff is practically impossible without gumming up your sandpaper.

I think that a better approach is to wipe away excess glue while it's still wet. The challenge is to do this without smearing the glue into the pores of the wood, where it's bound to show up later. Start by thoroughly wetting a clean rag with clean water **(C)**, and then wringing out all excess water until the rag is damp, like the nose of a dog **(D)**. Fold the rag into a comfortable shape that fits your hand.

As soon as you've clamped a joint, wipe the joint line with a swipe from your rag **(E)**. Chances are, this first wiping won't remove all the glue and, in fact, sometimes spreads it around a bit. Now take your rag and refold it, exposing a fresh area without glue **(F)**. Repeat your wiping sequence along the joint **(G)**. You'll probably need to repeat the refold-and-wipe cycle multiple times before the joint and its surrounding area are free of any excess glue. And for really messy glue-ups, resoak the rag and squeeze it out several times to clean it, and then repeat the wiping sequence once more.

Finishing Wood

Coloring Wood

➤ Coloring with Chemicals (p. 262)

➤ Fuming Wood (p. 263)

Smoothing Between Coats

➤ Smoothing Between Coats (p. 264)

Applying a Finish

➤ Wiping On a Penetrating Finish (p. 265)

➤ Removing Glue on the Go (p. 267)

➤ Spraying a Lacquer Finish (p. 268)

➤ Finishing Interiors (p. 270)

Smoothing the Finish

➤ Finishing the Finish (p. 271)

THE FINAL STEP to a project almost always involves adding a finish. Not only do finishes beautify wood by deepening its color and accentuating its grain patterns, but they protect wood by slowing down the rate at which moisture transfer takes place. This keeps your finished projects more stable and less likely to warp. Also, a good finish makes cleaning easier, coating the pores of the wood so dust and dirt can't get trapped inside. All the same, you can certainly forgo a finish and simply leave your wood smooth and bare. Many kitchen utensils fare well this way and develop their own "finish" over time through use. But for most of our woodwork, we'll want the best finish we can achieve, which may include coloring the wood. In this final section we'll look at adding color to your wood, picking the right finish, and applying it to make your project look its best.

Coloring Wood

I confess that wood stains don't see a lot of use in my shop. For color, I prefer to select from nature's palette of beautifully colored woods. Having said this, of course I do use stains now and then, and so will you. And when you do, you have several options to choose from, including pigment stains, dye stains, and chemical stains.

Pigment and Dye Stains

Pigment stains and dye stains consist of colored particles in a liquid that acts as a carrier. When applied to wood, the particles lodge in the pores, imparting their color to the surface. The particles in pigment stains are much larger than the particles in dye stains. Therefore, they tend to primarily lodge in large pores, like those in ring-porous woods such as oak and ash, resulting in excessively dark rings and an unnatural appearance on those woods. Pigment stains don't do a very good job of coloring dense, close-pored woods like maple because the pores are too small to offer a home to the pigment particles. Although pigment stains are convenient and reliable, they tend to obscure and cloud wood's natural character.

For a staining effect that comes closest to wood's natural look, dye stains can't be beat. With these stains (sometimes called aniline dyes), the particles are much smaller and tend to disperse more evenly on the surface.

To prevent splotching, brush on a wet coat of wood conditioner before staining. Let it soak into the pores for a few minutes, then remove any excess with a clean cloth.

They do a much better job than pigment stains, particularly at coloring dense woods, and are available in practically any color and hue, including intense, brilliant colors.

When stained, some woods are subject to blotching, a tendency for the wood to accept the stain unevenly. This can result in unattractive patches of darker or lighter areas that can spoil the look of a project. Woods prone to blotching include softwoods like pine and fir, as well as hardwoods like alder, aspen, soft maple, and birch. Highly figured woods such as curly cherry can also be a problem.

One way to overcome this trait is to use gel stains, which are absorbed by the wood more evenly, although not as deeply as ordinary pigment or dye stains. Another approach is to prime the surface with wood conditioner, which fills the pores slightly while allowing subsequent application of stains and finishes.

Chemical Stains

Another way to "stain" wood is to use chemicals to transform its natural color. The nice thing about chemicals is that they change the color of the fibers themselves, without adding anything to disrupt the wood's natural grain pattern. The effect can mimic the look of the same wood years later, after it has mellowed with age and developed a beautiful patina.

As shown in the chart on the facing page, there are many chemicals that work well to color wood. However, there are two—potassium dichromate and potassium permanganate—that consistently darken wood in deeper shades of brown, which is the natural tone that wood achieves over time as it oxidizes and reacts to light.

Chemicals that Color Wood

CHEMICAL, MIXED IN WATER TO 15% SOLUTION	COLORING EFFECT	WOODS THAT REACT WELL
Alum	Reds and purples	Most hardwoods
Ammonia	Yellow-browns and browns	Oak, especially white oak
Calcium oxide	Deepens natural colors	Walnut, cherry, mahogany
Copper sulfate	Greens and grays	Most hardwoods
Ferrous sulfate	Grays and blacks	Most hardwoods
Potassium bitartrate (cream of tartar)	Gray-browns	Most hardwoods
Potassium dichromate	Browns, with orange highlights	Walnut, cherry, mahogany
Potassium permanganate	Browns, with orange and purple hues	Mahogany

Potassium dichromate's orange hue reacts favorably with walnut, darkening its natural color and adding brown hues to provide an "aged" look in minutes. It also works well on cherry, although it tends to add brown tones that aren't typically found in the natural-aged wood. Potassium permanganate, which has an intense purple tint, does a great job on mahogany by slightly darkening it, adding a brown shade while highlighting its natural orange undertones. In fact, most hardwoods will respond favorably to these brews, but be aware that results can vary, even within the same species and the same cut of wood. It's always best to first experiment on the specific wood you'll be coloring.

> **⚠ WARNING** Mix potassium permanganate and potassium dichromate in glass containers only. Don't use metal, which may react to the chemicals.

► See *"Coloring with Chemicals"* on p. 262.

Mixed with water to form a solution, each chemical is available in crystal form. (Look for a supplier under "Laboratory Equipment and Supplies" in the yellow pages.) Both potassium dichromate and potassium permanganate are applied in an identical manner.

The method is simple: Stir one or two tablespoons of the chemical into a quart of

► See *"Raising the Grain"* on p. 235.

clean, lukewarm water. Apply the solution with a rag or sponge, liberally soaking the wood and letting it stand for 15 minutes or more before wiping off the excess. Let the wood dry, which may take a few hours, then cut back the raised fibers with fine sandpaper.

Then apply your finish of choice.

Another way to chemically color your wood is to fume it using ammonia, which reacts with natural tannins in the wood, creating a darker shade of brown. The tech-

▶ WORKING SAFELY WITH CHEMICALS

When staining with chemicals, treat them with caution to avoid exposure, which can cause severe reactions and even death. (Potassium dichromate is the worst offender here. Ingesting even a small amount can be fatal.) When fuming, wear a cartridge-type respirator rated for ammonia fumes, and use chemical cartridges rated for the chemicals you'll be using. Work in a well-ventilated area, wearing heavy chemical-resistant gloves, as well as goggles to protect your eyes from accidental splashes or fumes. (Swimming goggles work well.) When handling or storing these potions, don't let any of this stuff touch your skin. And of course it's very important to keep containers out of the reach of children.

nique works best on tannin-rich woods, of which white oak is the best contender.

▶ See *"Fuming Wood"* on p. 263.

However, many other woods also react well with this technique, especially if you precoat them with a solution of tannic acid. It's worth experimenting with different species to see the results. You'll need industrial-strength ammonia with an aqueous solution that contains between 26 percent to 30 per-

cent ammonium hydroxide. (Household ammonia has less than 5 percent.) Most blueprint-supply or business-supply stores carry gallon containers. As with the chemicals mentioned earlier, fuming alters the surface color of the wood itself without filling the pores or disturbing the grain pattern, resulting in a very natural look.

Choosing a Finish

Novice woodworkers always ask what the "best" finish is. The truth is, any finish is great as long as it protects the wood and achieves the desired look.

There are two basic types of finishes: film and penetrating. Overall, a film finish is more durable and offers better protection because it more fully seals the surface of the wood, slowing down and limiting the amount of moisture that the wood can take on and give off. But penetrating finishes have a big following because of their ease of application and maintenance and, above all, for their more natural look.

With a film finish such as lacquer, polyurethane, or heavy coats of varnish or shellac, you touch and see the finish itself, which to some degree masks the wood beneath. On the other hand, penetrating finishes like oil, oil/varnish blends, or thinned shellac lie just below the surface, coating the pore walls and saturating the fibers while exposing more of the natural character of the wood and its texture. For me, the project determines which type of finish I'm going to use. While most of my work gets a simple penetrating oil or shellac finish, tabletops and other surfaces that will see hard use will get a few coats of polyurethane or varnish on top of the oil or shellac to protect these more wear-prone surfaces.

FILM FINISHES VERSUS PENETRATING FINISHES

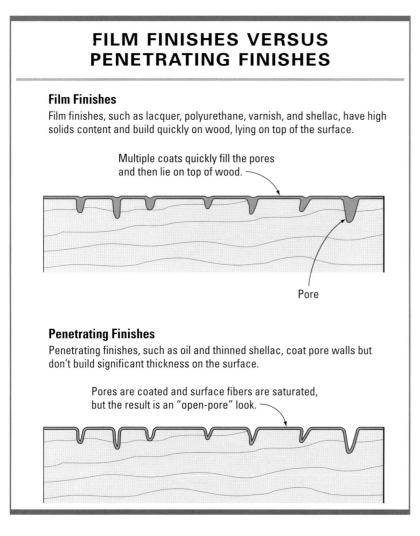

Film Finishes

Film finishes, such as lacquer, polyurethane, varnish, and shellac, have high solids content and build quickly on wood, lying on top of the surface.

Multiple coats quickly fill the pores and then lie on top of wood.

Pore

Penetrating Finishes

Penetrating finishes, such as oil and thinned shellac, coat pore walls but don't build significant thickness on the surface.

Pores are coated and surface fibers are saturated, but the result is an "open-pore" look.

Keep in mind that not all finishes are compatible with each other. For example, you don't want to apply an oil-based mixture over a water-based finish. But for many finishes you can apply a different finish on top of another one as long as you allow sufficient time for the first finish to fully cure, which can take weeks or even months. When in doubt, it's always smart to check with the manufacturer and to make test samples of the finishes you'll be combining.

In addition to choosing a finish for its appearance and durability, you'll want to select it based on its manner of application and maintenance. If you don't have much in the way of finishing facilities or tools, a penetrating finish is probably the way to go. It can usually be applied with a rag and doesn't require a dust-free environment for application. When it wears over time, it can be replenished by simply cleaning and fine-sanding the surface before applying a fresh coat or two. Film finishes, on the other hand, require more in the way of application equipment and facilities. At the very least, you'll need a high-quality brush and a dust-free drying room. For spraying, you'll need a compressor and a spray gun as well as a

▶ ESSENTIAL OIL-FINISH GEAR

Finishing oil has an annoying tendency to dry out quickly, becoming a useless chunk of solidified gunk in the can. To keep it fresh as long as possible, you'll need to limit its exposure to air. To do this, I pour it from its original container into smaller jars, filling each to the brim to crowd out the air.

For wiping cloths, I use regular commercial, lint-free cotton rolls for applying an oil finish. For wiping it off, however, I'm a little more fussy because I want the smoothest lintfree cloth possible, to avoid scratches and cloth residue. The best stuff is pure cotton that's been washed many times. You can buy it from auto-body and finishing-supply stores, but I prefer to make my own from old T-shirts, sheets, and pillowcases. For the greatest absorbency, I use flannel sheets. Whatever cloth you use, make sure it's clean. I cut it into roughly 20-in. squares, which is a good size for one hand when folded. Remove any seams or hemmed areas, but don't tear the sheets to size. Instead, cut them with scissors to avoid creating any loose strands or fuzzy stuff that might get caught in your finish.

Keep your oil in glass jars filled to the brim to prevent the finish from prematurely congealing due to excess air.

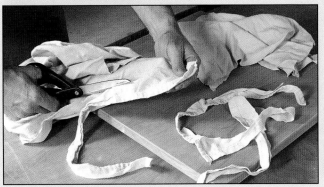

Recycled old, washed flannel sheets make great finishing cloths. Cut them to size with scissors instead of tearing them.

place to spray. A typical film finish doesn't require much maintenance, but it can be difficult to repair when damaged.

Previewing a Finish

It's handy to know how a finish will affect the look of a particular cut of wood. For example, you may be laying out parts for a project and wondering whether the colors of particular boards will match. Or a customer (your significant other?) is impatient and wants a sneak peek at what the finished project will look like. To preview what your finish will look like on your project, you can wipe the raw wood with a sponge soaked in clean water or mineral spirits. (Remember that water will raise the fibers, so you'll have to sand them afterwards.)

To preview what your project will look like under a finish, wet the surface with water, which will mimic the color and hue of the finished wood.

▶ See *"Raising the Grain"* on p. 235.

The wet surface will provide a good indication of the color of the finished piece. Not only will you see the color and tone of the finished wood but also any glue smears you may have missed. And the reflectivity of these clear liquids helps highlight machine marks you might have missed during the smoothing stage.

Cleaning Before Finishing

The last step before applying your first coat of finish is to clean the surface and the pores of your wood, removing any sanding dust or traces of dirt. Leaving this stuff on or in the wood will make your finish coats as well as the wood itself look cloudy. One option is to wipe the surface with a tack rag. You can buy one or make one by impregnating cotton cheesecloth with linseed oil. Gently rub all your surfaces with the cloth, refolding it as necessary to expose a clean surface of the cloth as you pick up dust.

A homemade tack rag of cheesecloth infused with linseed oil does a great job of removing traces of dust before you apply the first coat.

Blow out the pores and give your surfaces a general cleanup by blasting your work with compressed air.

The second approach is to blast your wood with compressed air. A compressor that delivers 90 psi (pounds per square inch) will quickly remove surface dust as well as debris lodged in the pores. Plus, the tip of an air nozzle makes it easy to remove dust trapped in nooks and crannies. Make sure that your air supply is clean and oilfree, and direct the air away from your finishing area to avoid raising dust that may settle back down onto your work.

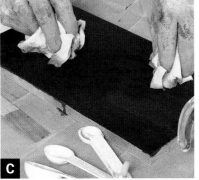

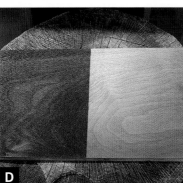

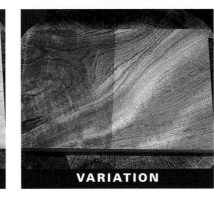

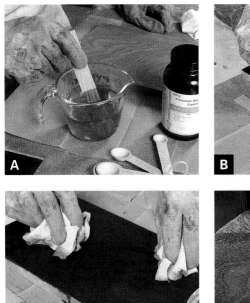

VARIATION

VARIATION

Coloring with Chemicals

To give walnut a warm, aged look, start by mixing 1 or 2 tablespoons of potassium dichromate crystals into a quart of warm, clean water, or ¼ tablespoon to ½ tablespoon into a cup. (The higher concentration of crystals creates a more intense, deeper color.) Stir the solution well until all the crystals dissolve (A).

Use a clean rag to soak the wood, leaving a wet film on the surface (B). The wetting itself darkens the wood immediately, but it takes several minutes before the chemical starts to alter the color of the wood itself. After the wood has sat for 15 minutes or more, use fresh towels to wipe off all the excess (C). After the wood has dried for an hour or more, cut back the raised fibers with a light sanding, using 220-grit paper. Then apply the finish of your choice. This sample board was colored on its entire surface, and then the left side was given three coats of lacquer (D).

[VARIATION] This cherry sample board (far left) was colored with potassium dichromate on its left side only, and then the entire panel was finished with three coats of lacquer.

[VARIATION] Potassium permanganate was used on the left side of this mahogany panel (left), and then the entire surface was given three coats of lacquer. The left side has a deeper, more vibrant tone that approximates the color of aged mahogany.

Fuming Wood

To add color, you can fume wood by exposing it to a strong solution of ammonia. The first order of business is to construct a fuming tent, which can simply be a small, enclosed room or even the inside of a rented van. You can make a fuming tent by building a frame from ¾ in. PVC pipe, connecting long sections with unglued PVC elbows. Cover the frame on five sides with clear window sheeting—the kind of heavy plastic used to insulate windows in cold weather. Tape the sheeting in place over the frame, then use a heat gun or a hair dryer to stretch it tight **(A)**. If you don't glue the frame together, you can reuse it for future projects by adding longer or shorter pipes, depending on the size of the project you want to fume. Before pouring the ammonia, nest your parts together to make sure they'll fit inside the tent.

Use a microwaveable plastic tray or something similar to contain the ammonia **(B)**. For a project the size of this small cabinet, pour the ammonia into the tray to a depth of about ½ in. This is powerful stuff, and a little goes a long way. Place the ammonia tray on the floor next to your parts, and position the tent over the tray and the wood **(C)**. Now let the fumes do their work.

After 24 hours, this white oak cabinet has taken on a lovely, golden brown hue **(D)**. Longer exposure to the fumes—as much as two days—will darken the wood further, and applying a finish will highlight and deepen the color even more.

A

B

C

D

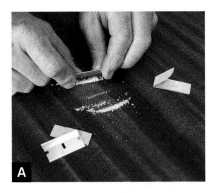

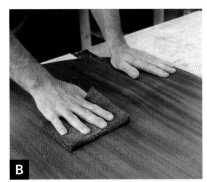

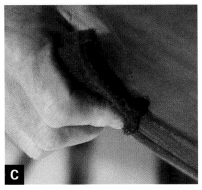

Smoothing Between Coats

The process of smoothing and leveling intermediate layers of finish is known as cutting back, or scuff-sanding. Start by looking for major blemishes such as drips and runs. After the coat has fully dried, use a new, single-edged razor blade to scrape and level any offending areas **(A)**.

With the first two or three coats, my choice of abrasive is a maroon synthetic nylon pad, regardless of the type of finish. Rub the surface vigorously, always moving the pad in the direction of the grain, and doubling up the number of strokes at the edges, which tend to be undersanded **(B)**. For shaped areas, such as routed edges or complex moldings, use the same pad, which will conform to the area you're smoothing **(C)**.

With penetrating finishes, the maroon pad is usually good for smoothing right up to the last coat. For film finishes, I use it to scuff-sand between the first two or three coats. However, after the finish has started to build a film on the surface, I switch to 320-grit sandpaper and use this all the way up to the last coat of finish. Use stearated paper, which has lubricants that help the paper glide over the finish without sticking **(D)**. For more aggressive sanding, try wetting the surface first with water or mineral spirits, and using the same grit paper and sanding block **(E)**. Be careful when wet-sanding like this because you can quickly cut through the finish and into the wood, leaving a bare spot that will need touching up in the finish room.

Between the last few coats on intricate surfaces such as moldings or carvings, use 0000 steel wool instead of the maroon pad, because it leaves a finer scratch pattern and scrunches down better to make more intimate contact with a complex surface **(F)**.

Wiping On a Penetrating Finish

My favorite wipe-on "oil" finish is really a highly thinned varnish. The first step in finishing is to disassemble your project into as many discrete components as you can, which makes the process easier **(A)**. For the first coat, thin the finish with about 10 percent mineral spirits to promote maximum penetration **(B)**. This helps to "pop" the grain and deepen the color of the wood.

Begin the first coat by oiling the most visible area first, such as the top of a table, including its sides **(C)**. Keep an eye on the wood, and if you notice any dry areas, flood a little more oil onto the spot to keep everything wet **(D)**. Let the wet oil sit for at least 10 to 15 minutes, depending on your shop humidity. When the finish starts to feel tacky, rub off all the excess with clean, soft cloths **(E)**. Be diligent about this; leaving wet or damp areas may contribute to an uneven finish.

"As above, so below" is a good bit of finishing Zen. Always apply an equal number of coats to the underside or back of the work, especially on tabletops and other large, unsupported panels, even if you're not going to see them **(F)**. This equalizes moisture transfer in the wood, helping prevent warp.

Let each coat dry overnight, or at least for eight hours. If you finish both sides of a part in one session, place the least visible side down on triangular sticks to minimize contact marks and to allow air to circulate freely around the piece **(G)**.

As you work, it's a good idea to keep your finishing area clean. Once I've applied a coat, I wipe off my work table thoroughly to remove any residual oil **(H)**. This not only keeps the work surface free of drips; over time my finish table has developed quite a nice finish itself.

(Continued on p. 266.)

A

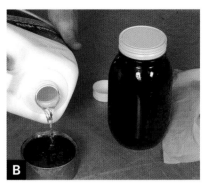

B

C

D

E

F

G

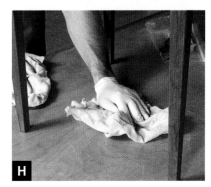

H

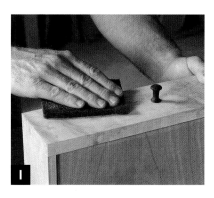

Once the first coat has dried, rub the surface of the wood with a maroon nylon pad to smooth the fibers (**I**). Afterward, apply a second, full-strength coat, this time starting with the least visible surface and moving to the more prominent areas (**J**). On complex areas, such as the base on this table, oil the underside first (**K**) and then turn the project over to oil the top side. Again, let the oil sit for a few minutes to soak into the fibers. As more coats go on, you'll find the finish becomes tackier faster. As before, wipe off all excess finish, making sure to get into any nooks or crevices, such as at joint shoulders (**L**).

Continue in this fashion, smoothing between dried coats and applying new coats until you're satisfied with the look. It usually takes four to five coats before the surface has a nice, even sheen. One way to monitor your progress is to set up a task light behind the work, and then sight across the surface toward the light to look for bare spots or uneven areas (**M**). When the finish is smooth and uniform, you're done.

[**VARIATION**] You can transform a penetrating oil finish into a more durable film-type finish by wiping on as many as six coats of a thicker-bodied wiping varnish, such as Waterlox®. The idea is to lay down a series of thin coats, letting each dry without wiping it off. Using a lint-free cloth dampened (not soaked) with the finish, apply each coat, moving along the grain. Make each layer very thin, applying it in one decisive stroke, slightly overlapping each previous pass. Don't rewipe the passes, or you'll leave streaks. Between coats, store the work in a dust-free environment as it dries, since the surface will be tacky for several hours.

VARIATION

Removing Glue on the Go

One of the great things about an oil finish is that it's forgiving and very easy to work with. For example, even while you're wiping on the first few coats, you can correct a previously unnoticed glue blemish that the finish accentuated **(A)**.

The fix is easy. While the coat is still wet, use a very sharp chisel or a fresh razor blade and carefully scrape the area to remove the bulk of the glue **(B)**. Then rub the area with fine sandpaper to remove any last traces of glue and to smooth and even out the surface. You can use wet-dry sandpaper for large areas, but ordinary finishing paper works fine for touching up small spots **(C)**. Now rub a little extra oil into the sanded area, and continue your finishing routine.

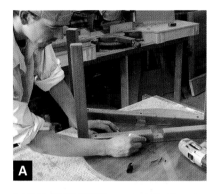

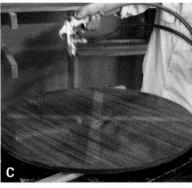

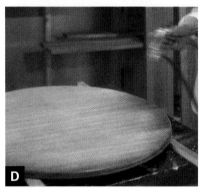

Spraying a Lacquer Finish

Of all the finishes that can be sprayed, one of the most common is nitrocellulose lacquer. It's popular because it is attractive, relatively durable, easy to apply, and quick-drying. Spraying lacquer, however, requires a good spray booth to exhaust fumes and to provide a haven from dust.

Start by disassembling the parts of the project. If necessary, label any pieces that have to go back together in a particular order **(A)**. Plan your spray sequence to move from the least visible surfaces to the most visible. You'll also want to spray all small areas of a part first, then move to larger areas.

When spraying a table like this, for example, begin by laying the top upside-down and spraying the outer edge **(B)**. Then spray the broad surface of the underside with an even, wet coat **(C)**. The idea is to overlap each previous spray stroke, and to move quickly so that the entire surface remains wet (it will look glossy). This gives the lacquer and any ambient cloud of mist time to settle onto the surface and melt into the finish, producing a smooth surface.

Let the underside dry to the touch, which only takes a few minutes, and then flip the top over to spray the top side. Again, start with the narrow edge **(D)**, and then spray the broad surface, remembering to overlap each stroke **(E)**.

Although lacquer dries relatively quickly, you still need to prevent dust from settling into the wet finish. A dedicated drying rack makes a convenient place to store pieces while you're spraying others **(F)**.

Let the first coat dry thoroughly. (Generally, one hour is sufficient, but check the manufacturer's instructions for the specific finish you're using.) Then scuff-sand the surface to level it and to remove any dust nibs. Using a maroon pad, rub firmly and evenly along the grain of the wood, working flat areas such as the top in broad strokes (**G**). Ball up the pad to conform to shaped areas such as a molded edge (**H**).

Wipe or blow away any dust before applying the second coat (**I**). Then spray the bottom edge and side as before. Again, let the work dry to the touch, and then flip it over and spray the top edge and then the top surface (**J**).

Repeat this spraying and scuff-sanding procedure for the second, third, and possibly fourth coats, depending on how many you apply. Once the next-to-last coat has dried, switch from a nylon pad to 320-grit stearated sandpaper to scuff the surface. The paper will leave a finer and less visible scratch pattern (**K**). Afterward, apply the final coat, spraying an even, wet coat on the entire piece (**L**).

When spraying complex parts, such as this U-shaped leg assembly, work from the inside out. Begin by spraying the entire innermost surface of the legs (**M**). Then spray the upward-facing surface (**N**). Let the lacquer dry to the touch, then flip the assembly over and spray the opposite face. Finish by spraying the outermost edge, which will be the most visible surface on the assembled table. On the first few coats, you might want to linger a tad longer on end-grain areas, such as this open-tenon joint, which absorbs the finish more quickly and requires more of it before the pores start to fill (**O**).

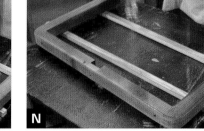

Finishing Interiors

You may want to think twice about applying finishes to enclosed areas like the inside of a cabinet or drawer box. While film finishes such as lacquer and polyurethane are OK, most oil finishes emit an unpleasant odor for years to come when enclosed in an interior. It's also wise to avoid applying a heavy finish to bearing surfaces like the bottom edges or sides of a drawer, because film finishes such as lacquer can stick if used where parts rub together. Therefore, when finishing a drawer, apply your regular finish only to the drawer front **(A)**. Don't use it to finish inside the drawer or on the drawer sides in an attempt to highlight your beautiful half-blind dovetails.

That's not to say that you can't finish interiors. In fact, there are times when it is desirable. For example, a finished drawer interior is easier to clean. In those cases, a diluted form of shellac is the perfect finish. Simply mix a 1-lb. cut of shellac (1 lb. of shellac flakes or granules to 1 gal. of denatured alcohol), and wipe it on the interior surfaces **(B)**. Sand the first coat with 220-grit paper, and apply a second coat if the first looks dry. Once the shellac dries it won't smell.

On bearing surfaces such as drawer sides, use the same thin cut of shellac and rub it on as before **(C)**. The shellac highlights the joinery and brings the color of the wood into line with the rest of the piece. Sand this coat with 220-grit paper and apply another coat if you wish. You can apply one, two, or three coats without fear of building up a surface film that might hinder smooth drawer travel.

Finishing the Finish

I can't remember the last time I didn't wax my final finish to smooth it out. Cabinetmaker Frank Klausz likes to call this final step "finishing the finish." Rubbing out your final coat is a great way to even out any small inconsistencies in the sheen of the finish, and it also makes the final surface as smooth as glass. All it takes is a can of paste wax, some 0000 steel wool, and a little elbow grease.

As finisher John Darrow shows here, start by dipping a ball of 0000 steel wool into the can to load it up with a generous amount of wax **(A)**. (Don't use automotive waxes, which typically contain abrasives.) Beginning at one end of the piece, rub the surface, using moderate pressure while keeping your palm flat to avoid digging into the surface **(B)**. Work in an orderly pattern to avoid missing any spots. And don't hesitate to load up the wool with more wax if the surface starts to look dry or the wool begins to skip as you rub.

When working the end areas, redouble your efforts to ensure that these sections are rubbed as evenly as the middle areas **(C)**. When rubbing the center area of large, flat work, you can ease the chore by using your other hand to help apply pressure **(D)**. Take long, even strokes while keeping a wide stance and rocking into the stroke with your upper body.

Once you've worked the entire piece, check the surface. It should have an even, dull sheen from the wax. At this point, you're ready to buff it and remove all excess wax. Using a soft, clean cloth, start to polish the finish by cutting through the wax, rubbing hard and vigorously **(E)**. You're done when the cloth stops grabbing the surface and glides over it instead **(F)**. The best test is to feel the finish with your fingers; it should be significantly smoother than your best sprayed-on or hand-applied top coat **(G)**. The final result is a finish with an even sheen and tone **(H)**.

Sources

BOOKS, SERVICES, AND ORGANIZATIONS

Carolina Biological
Supply Company
2700 York Road
Burlington, NC 27215
(919) 584-0381

Center for Wood
Anatomy Research
USDA Forest Service
Forest Products Laboratory
1 Gifford Pinchot Drive
Madison, WI 53726

Ethnobotanical
Research Services
Department of Anthropology
Oregon State University
Corvallis, OR 97331
(503) 737-0123

Identifying Wood
Understanding Wood
R. Bruce Hoadley
The Taunton Press

International Wood
Collectors Society
Secretary/Treasurer
International Wood
Collectors Society
2913 Third St.
Trenton, MI 48183

Know Your Woods
Albert J. Constantine Jr.
Macmillan Publishing

Tropical Timber
Identification Center
College of Environmental
Science and Forestry
Syracuse, NY 13210
(315) 473-8788

World Woods in Color
By William A. Lincoln
Linden Publishing

FORESTRY GROUPS

American Forests
Box 2000
Washington, DC 20013
(202) 955-4500
www.americanforests.org

Earth Day Network
1616 P St. NW, Suite 200
Washington, DC 20036
(202) 518-0044
www.earthday.net

European Forest Institute
Torikatu 34
Joensuu, Finland
(358) 13-252-020
www.efi.fi

Forest Engineering Research
Institute of Canada
580 Saint Jean Boulevard
Pointe-Claire, Quebec
Canada H9R 3J9
(514) 694-1140
www.feric.ca

Rainforest Alliance
665 Broadway, Suite 500
New York, NY 10012
(212) 677-1900
www.rainforest-alliance.org

The National
Arbor Day Foundation
100 Arbor Ave.
Nebraska City, NE 68410
(402) 474-5655
www.arborday.org

USDA Forest Service
1400 Independence Ave. SW
Washington, DC 20250
(202) 205-8333
www.fs.fed.us

WOOD MILLS

Granberg International
Chainsaw mills
PO Box 2347
Vallejo, CA 94592
(866) 233-6499
www.granberg.com

Appendix

Hud-Son Forest Equipment
Chainsaw & bandsaw mills
PO Box 345
8187 State Route 12
Barneveld, NY 13304
(800) 765-7297
www.hud-son.com

Log-Master
Bandsaw mills
16576 US Highway 259N
Nacogdoches, TX 75965
(800) 820-9515
www.logmaster.com

Lucas Mill
Circular-saw mills
C/O Bailey's Inc.
PO Box 550
44650 Highway 101
Laytonville, CA 95454
(800) 322-4539
www.baileys-online.com

Mighty-Mite Industries
Circular-saw & bandsaw mills
PO Box 20427
Portland, OR 97220
(503) 288-5923
www.mightymitesawmills.com

Norwood Industries
Bandsaw mills
252 Sonwil Drive
Buffalo, NY 14225
(800) 661-7746
www.norwoodindustries.com

Peterson Portable Sawmills
Circular-saw mills
152 View Road
PO Box 98
Rotorua, New Zealand
(877) 327-1471
www.petersonsawmills.com

Procut Portable Sawmills
Chainsaw & bandsaw mills
9975 Old Summit Lake Road
Prince George, BC Canada
V2K 5T1
(250) 962-0866
www.procutportablesawmills.com

Tilton Equipment Company
Chainsaw & bandsaw mills
P.O. Box 68
Rye, NH 03870
(800) 447-1152
www.tiltonequipment.com

TimberKing
Bandsaw mills
1431 North Topping Ave.
Kansas City, Missouri 64120
(800) 942-4406
www.timberking.com

Wood-Mizer Products
Bandsaw mills
8180 West 10th St.
Indianapolis, IN 46214
(800) 553-0182
www.woodmizer.com

Wood Species

There are some 70,000 different woods known to man. Of these, fewer than 400 are commercially available. And of these, many are used only in their country of origin and aren't exported to other parts of the world. Still, that leaves us plenty of wood choices for our projects. The photos on the following pages show various species from around the world that furniture makers use on a daily basis. More familiar woods are listed first, and similar species are grouped together, such as the oaks, mahoganies, and rosewoods, for easier comparison. I recommend that you get to know these woods and use them as a starting point in understanding the captivating and colorful world of wood.

COMMON FURNITURE WOODS

The 50 woods shown here have earned their reputations as valuable furniture woods. They're listed here with their common name or names, along with their botanical name—a Latin name identifying the genus and (when possible) the species of that genus. Having both names will help you identify lumber at the mill or in a book.

Keep in mind that many geographic designations (e.g., "northern" red oak) aren't necessarily area-specific, due to the ongoing transplanting of species around the world. However, the term does refer to a specific type of tree. In addition, you'll encounter numerous names that differ from the common name. Some of these are commercial terms, often associated with specific areas or locales.

The nomenclature of woods can be confusing. The best approach is to familiarize yourself with as many woods as possible. Thankfully, you'll always have new types of wood to try. The woods shown here are only a sampling of the vast varieties available to us, and importers are constantly bringing in new species.

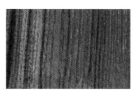

Teak
(Tectona grandis)

Sugar pine
(Pinus lambertiana)

Brazilian rosewood
(Dalbergia nigra)

Hickory *(Carya* spp.)

Eastern white pine
(Pinus strobus)

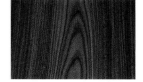

Indian rosewood
(Dalbergia latifolia)

Black cherry
(Prunus serotina)

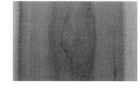

Yellow poplar
(Liriodendron tulipifera)

Cocobolo
(Dalbergia retusa)

Northern red oak
(Quercus rubra)

Black walnut
(Juglans nigra)

Maccassar ebony
(Diospyros celebica)

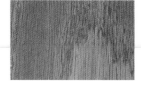

White oak
(Quercus alba)

American mahogany
(Swietenia macrophylla)

Gabon ebony
(Diospyros crassifolora)

Sugar maple
(Acer saccharum)

African mahogany
(Khaya ivorensis)

American white ash
(Fraxinus americana)

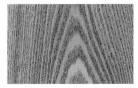

American brown ash
(Fraxinus americana)

Birch (Betula)

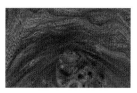

Amboyna
(Narra) (Pterocarpus
indicus)

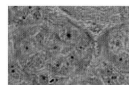

Carpathian elm
(Ulmus procera)

Japanese ash
(Fraxinus mand-
schurica)

Redwood (Sequoia
sempervirens)

Koa (Acacia koa)

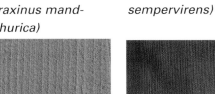

Anegre
(Aningeria)

American beech
(Fagus grandifolia)

Western red cedar
(Thuja plicata)

Jarrah (Eucalyptus
marginata)

American Holly
(Ibex opaca)

Douglas fir
(Pseudotsuga
menziesii)

Yellow cedar
(Chamaecyparis
nootkatensis)

Pear
(Pyrus communis)

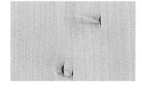

Basswood (Linden)
(Tilia americana)

Alder (Alnus)

Andaman padauk
(Pterocarpus
dalbergiodes)

Sycamore (Platanus
occidentalis)

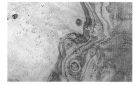

Olive (Olea
hochstetteri)

Butternut
(Juglans cinera)

Bubinga (Guibourtia
demeusei)

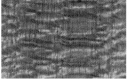

Lacewood (Silky
oak) (Platanus
hybrida)

Gonçalo alves
*(Astronium
fraxinifolium)*

Wenge
(Millettia laurentii)

Zebrawood
*(Microberlinia
brazzavillensis)*

Pau ferro
(Brazilwood)
*(Caesalpinia
echinata)*

Bald cypress
*(Taxodium dis-
tichum)*

Ceylon satinwood
*(Chloroxylon
swietenia)*

Imbuya
(Phoebe porosa)

Pau amarillo
*(Chlorophora
tinctoria)*

Purpleheart
(Amaranth)
(Peltogyne spp.)

Index

Other Books in the Series:

HARDCOVER

The Complete Illustrated Guide to Joinery
Gary Rogowski
ISBN 1-56158-401-0
Product #070535
$39.95

The Complete Illustrated Guide to Furniture and Cabinet Construction
Andy Rae
ISBN 1-56158-402-9
Product #070534
$39.95

The Complete Illustrated Guide to Shaping Wood
Lonnie Bird
ISBN 1-56158-400-2
Product #070533
$39.95

Taunton's Complete Illustrated Guide to Finishing
Jeff Jewitt
ISBN 1-56158-592-0
Product #070712
$39.95

Taunton's Complete Illustrated Guide to Sharpening
Tom Lie-Nielsen
ISBN 1-56158-657-9
Product #70737
$42.00

Taunton's Complete Illustrated Guide to Using Woodworking Tools
Lonnie Bird
ISBN 1-56158-597-1
Product #70729
$42.00

Taunton's Complete Illustrated Guide to Turning
Richard Raffan
ISBN 1-56158-672-2
Product #70757
$39.95

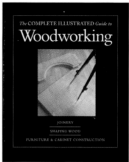

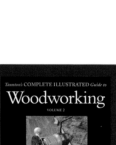

THE COMPLETE ILLUSTRATED GUIDES SLIPCASE SET

The Complete Illustrated Guide to Joinery

The Complete Illustrated Guide to Furniture and Cabinet Construction

The Complete Illustrated Guide to Shaping Wood
ISBN 1-56158-602-1
Product #070665
$120.00

THE COMPLETE ILLUSTRATED GUIDES SLIPCASE SET

Taunton's Complete Illustrated Guide to Using Woodworking Tools

Taunton's Complete Illustrated Guide to Sharpening

Taunton's Complete Illustrated Guide to Finishing
ISBN 1-56158-745-1
Product #070817
$126.00

PAPERBACK

Taunton's Complete Illustrated Guide to Period Furniture Details
Lonnie Bird
ISBN 1-56158-590-4
Product #070708
$27.00

Taunton's Complete Illustrated Guide to Choosing and Installing Hardware
Bob Settich
ISBN 1-56158-561-0
Product #070647
$29.95

Taunton's Complete Illustrated Guide to Box Making
Doug Stowe
ISBN 1-56158-593-9
Product #070721
$24.95